Firm-Level Innovation in Africa

The literature on innovation in Africa is rapidly expanding, and a recurring thread in the emergent literature is the pervasiveness of systemic weaknesses that inhibit the innovation process. Despite these, firms are able to innovate in Africa. It is then logical to ask: how do African firms manage to overcome the prevalent constraints and learn to innovate?

This book directly tackles this question, with a view to improve our understanding of the innovation landscape in Africa. The book brings together some of the latest innovation research from across the African continent, ranging from Tanzania and Ethiopia in the east to Nigeria in the west. The chapters included in the collection adopt different but complementary theoretical and methodological approaches to address a rich mix of interrelated issues. These issues include the factors that enhance or inhibit innovation in African firms, the sources of (knowledge/information for) innovation, policy options for overcoming constraints and facilitating firm-level innovation, the nature and roles of brokers and intermediaries in dealing with innovation constraints and in facilitating the innovation process and the role of interactive learning and acquisition of embodied technology in the innovation process.

This book was originally published as a special issue of *Innovation and Development*.

Abiodun Egbetokun is the Head of the Science Policy and Innovation Studies Department of the National Centre for Technology Management, Ile-Ife, Nigeria. He holds a PhD in the Economics of Innovation from Friedrich Schiller University, Jena, Germany. His research focuses mainly on the microeconomic sources and effects of innovation and entrepreneurship.

Richmond Atta-Ankomah is a Research Fellow at the Institute of Statistical, Social and Economic Research at the University of Ghana, Accra, Ghana. He also holds the position of Visiting Research Fellow with the Development Policy and Practice Unit of The Open University, Milton Keynes, UK. His research focuses on industrial development and firm-level innovation issues.

Oluseye Jegede is a Senior Researcher in the SARChI Industrial Development Unit in the College of Business and Economics at the University of Johannesburg, South Africa. He holds a PhD in Technology Management. His main areas of research are science, technology and innovation policy, and economic development.

Edward Lorenz is a Professor of Economics at the University of Nice Sophia Antipolis, France and a member of the University of Côte d'Azur, France. He also holds the position of Assigned Professor at Aalborg University, Denmark. His work focuses on the comparative analysis of work organization and firm-level competency building in national innovation systems.

Firm-Level Innovation in Africa

Overcoming Limits and Constraints

Edited by
Abiodun Egbetokun, Richmond Atta-Ankomah, Oluseye Jegede, and Edward Lorenz

LONDON AND NEW YORK

First published 2019
by Routledge
2 Park Square, Milton Park, Abingdon, Oxon, OX14 4RN, UK

and by Routledge
52 Vanderbilt Avenue, New York, NY 10017

First issued in paperback 2020

Routledge is an imprint of the Taylor & Francis Group, an informa business

British Library Cataloguing-in-Publication Data
A catalogue record for this book is available from the British Library

ISBN 13: 978-0-367-58704-8 (pbk)
ISBN 13: 978-1-138-60161-1 (hbk)

Typeset in Minion Pro
by codeMantra

Publisher's Note
The publisher accepts responsibility for any inconsistencies that may have arisen during the conversion of this book from journal articles to book chapters, namely the possible inclusion of journal terminology.

Disclaimer
Every effort has been made to contact copyright holders for their permission to reprint material in this book. The publishers would be grateful to hear from any copyright holder who is not here acknowledged and will undertake to rectify any errors or omissions in future editions of this book.

Contents

Citation Information

The chapters in this book were originally published in the journal *Innovation and Development*, volume 6, issue 2 (October 2016). When citing this material, please use the original page numbering for each article, as follows:

Introduction
Firm-level innovation in Africa: overcoming limits and constraints
Abiodun Egbetokun, Richmond Atta-Ankomah, Oluseye Jegede and Edward Lorenz
Innovation and Development, volume 6, issue 2 (October 2016) pp. 161–174

Chapter 1
Bridging gaps in innovation systems for small-scale agricultural activities in sub-Saharan Africa: brokers wanted!
Olawale Oladipo Adejuwon
Innovation and Development, volume 6, issue 2 (October 2016) pp. 175–193

Chapter 2
Technology transfer and agricultural mechanization in Tanzania: institutional adjustments to accommodate emerging economy innovations
Andrew Agyei-Holmes
Innovation and Development, volume 6, issue 2 (October 2016) pp. 195–211

Chapter 3
Absorptive capacity and product innovation: new evidence from Nigeria
M. G. Ukpabio, A. D. Adeyeye and O. B. Oluwatope
Innovation and Development, volume 6, issue 2 (October 2016) pp. 213–233

Chapter 4
Persistence of innovation and knowledge flows in Africa: an empirical investigation
Francesco Lamperti, Roberto Mavilia and Marco Giometti
Innovation and Development, volume 6, issue 2 (October 2016) pp. 235–257

Chapter 5
Effect of knowledge sources on firm-level innovation in Tanzania
Otieno Osoro, Patrick Vermeulen, Joris Knoben and Godius Kahyarara
Innovation and Development, volume 6, issue 2 (October 2016) pp. 259–280

Chapter 6

Embodied technology transfer and learning by exporting in the Ethiopian manufacturing sector

Abdi Yuya Ahmad and Keun Lee

Innovation and Development, volume 6, issue 2 (October 2016) pp. 281–303

For any permission-related enquiries please visit:
http://www.tandfonline.com/page/help/permissions

Notes on Contributors

Olawale Oladipo Adejuwon is a Research Fellow at the African Institute for Science Policy and Innovation, Obafemi Awolowo University, Ile-Ife, Nigeria. He holds a Doctoral and Master's degree in Technology Management and a Master in Business Administration from the same university. His interests are in strategic management of technology/innovation and innovation management/policy.

A. D. Adeyeye is Head of Planning, Programming and Linkages Department, National Centre for Technology Management, Nigeria. He is currently a doctoral student of Science and Technology Studies at CREST, Stellenbosch University, South Africa. His interests are in micro-level innovation and innovation for inclusive development.

Andrew Agyei-Holmes is a Consultant at the World Bank, Washington, DC, USA. He has expertise in international economics, institutional economics and development economics. He was previously a Research Student at The Open University, Milton Keynes, UK.

Abdi Yuya Ahmad is a Lecturer in the School of Social Sciences and Humanities, Adama Science and Technology University, Ethiopia. He earned his PhD in Innovation Economics in 2017 from Aalborg University, Denmark under the Africalics Joint PhD programme. He was the first PhD candidate to be awarded a joint degree with support from the AfricaLics PhD Visiting Fellowship Programme.

Richmond Atta-Ankomah is a Research Fellow at the Institute of Statistical, Social and Economic Research at the University of Ghana, Accra, Ghana. He also holds the position of Visiting Research Fellow with the Development Policy and Practice Unit of The Open University, Milton Keynes, UK. His research focuses on industrial development and firm-level innovation issues.

Abiodun Egbetokun is the Head of the Science Policy and Innovation Studies Department of the National Centre for Technology Management, Ile-Ife, Nigeria. He holds a PhD in the Economics of Innovation from Friedrich Schiller University Jena, Germany. His research focuses mainly on the microeconomic sources and effects of innovation and entrepreneurship.

Marco Giometti is currently undertaking a PhD in Finance at The Wharton School at the University of Pennsylvania, Philadelphia, USA. He focuses on macroeconomics, banking and financial regulation. During his Master's he was a Research Assistant at Bocconi University, Milano, Italy.

Oluseye Jegede is a Senior Researcher in the SARChI Industrial Development Unit in the College of Business and Economics at the University of Johannesburg, South Africa.

He holds a PhD in Technology Management. His main areas of research are science, technology and innovation policy, and economic development.

Godius Kahyarara is a Professor and Senior Lecturer in the Department of Economics at the University of Dar es Salaam, Tanzania. Much of his research focuses on training and education, and forests.

Joris Knoben is a Professor of Business Economics in the Department of Economics and Business Economics at Radboud University, Nijmegen, the Netherlands. His teaching and research activities focus on the influence of a firm's external environment on its behaviour and performance.

Francesco Lamperti is a Junior Researcher at Fondazione Eni Enrico Mattei, Italy and a Research Fellow at the Institute of Economics at the Scuola Superiore Sant'Anna, Pisa, Italy. His research interests are mainly focused on macroeconomics, agent-based and integrated assessment modelling, climate change economics and technological change.

Keun Lee is a Professor of Economics and Director of the Institute of Economic Research at Seoul National University, South Korea. His main research interest is economics of catch-up, including economics of development/transition, economics of innovation and S&T policy, corporate organization and growth and area studies (China, South and North Korea, Japan, Taiwan, India and other developing countries).

Edward Lorenz is a Professor of Economics at the University of Nice Sophia Antipolis, France and a member of the University of Côte d'Azur, France. He also holds the position of Assigned Professor at Aalborg University, Denmark. His work focuses on the comparative analysis of work organization and firm-level competency building in national innovation systems.

Roberto Mavilia is a Professor and Researcher in the Department of Management and Technology at the University of Bocconi, Milano, Italy. He focuses on microeconomics, economics of innovation, international economics, Mediterranean Area economics, knowledge spill over, patent citations and social network analysis.

O. B. Oluwatope is an Assistant Chief Research Officer at the National Centre for Technology Management (NACETEM) (an agency of the Federal Ministry of Science and Technology) at Obafemi Awolowo University, Ile-Ife, Nigeria. She holds a Master's degree in Public Health. Her research focuses on health innovation and gender in Science, Technology and Innovation.

Otieno Osoro is a Lecturer in the Department of Economics at the University of Dar es Salaam, Tanzania. He has expertise in health economics, monetary economics and public economics.

M. G. Ukpabio is a Senior Researcher at the National Centre for Technology Management, Obafemi Awolowo University, Ile-Ife, Nigeria. She holds a PhD in Technology Management. Her research interests span absorptive capacity and firm-level innovation.

Patrick Vermeulen is a Professor of Strategic Management and International Management at Radboud University, Nijmegen, the Netherlands. He is specialised in the strategic behaviour of organisations in their institutional context, organisational change and innovation and innovation in emerging economies.

INTRODUCTION

Firm-level innovation in Africa: overcoming limits and constraints

Abiodun Egbetokun[iD], Richmond Atta-Ankomah, Oluseye Jegede and Edward Lorenz

1. Background and motivation for the special issue

From the perspective of developing countries, innovation is best understood as the process by which firms master and implement the design and production of goods and services which are new to them, irrespective of whether they are new to their competitors (Mytelka 2000). Innovation, then, in a developing country context, should be broadly defined to include processes of adoption and possibly modification of products and technologies that have first been developed elsewhere. The process defined here is not limited to technical functions but also includes organizational and marketing functions (Ernst 2007; UNU-INTECH 2004). These latter aspects are seen as extremely important for African firms (OECD/Eurostat 2005).

The literature on innovation in Africa is rapidly expanding (see, for instance, the special issue of this journal edited by Adebowale et al. 2014), as is the drive towards the measurement of innovation on the continent (AU-NEPAD 2010, 2014). Much of the literature identifies systemic weaknesses and other constraints that inhibit the innovation process on the continent. The characteristics of these constraints as well as concrete interventions to mitigate them are not yet fully understood. Nonetheless, it is interesting to observe that despite all the difficulties, a large share of firms are still able to innovate in the African context. Surprisingly, there are only a few systematic collections of works dedicated to understanding how firms on the continent learn to innovate despite extant limits and constraints. In view of the foregoing, this special issue is dedicated to improving our understanding of the innovation landscape in Africa. Specific issues of interest include:

(1) The factors that enhance or inhibit innovation in African firms
(2) The sources of (knowledge/information for) innovation
(3) Policy options for overcoming constraints and facilitating firm-level innovation
(4) The nature and roles of brokers and intermediaries in dealing with innovation constraints and in facilitating the innovation process
(5) The role of interactive learning and acquisition of embodied technology in the innovation process

This special issue compiles papers from across the African continent, ranging from Tanzania and Ethiopia in the East to Nigeria in the West.[1] The six papers included in the collection adopt different but complementary theoretical and methodological approaches. This introductory article proceeds by highlighting some aspects of the innovation landscape in Africa, with particular emphasis on the prevalence of innovation and the distribution of information sources across countries. It then discusses the most important constraints to innovation in Africa and shows how the articles in this compilation advance the related research agenda. Finally, a number of issues on which knowledge remains limited are raised.

2. An overview of the innovation landscape in Africa

Table 1 presents the results from innovation surveys carried out in 11 African nations showing the share of firms that introduced, during the three years prior to the survey, innovations that are new to the firm but not necessarily new to the market. The data reported in the table are based on the OECD/Eurostat (2005) definition of an innovation as 'the implementation of a new or significantly improved product (good or service), or process, a new marketing method, or a new organization method in business practices, workplace organization or external relations'. The data show that a large proportion of firms in African countries are innovative regardless of the level of development of the country. The rate of innovation in individual countries ranges from 40% in Egypt to 77% in Uganda. This suggests that innovativeness at the micro level may not necessarily depend on the current level of economic growth and that, even within the broad group of developing countries, poorer countries may be more innovative than the relatively richer ones. Underlying this pattern are the varied ways through which firms overcome the various economic and infrastructural constraints to innovation. Some of these ways are discussed in the contributions to this special issue.

The innovation process is affected by a wide range of factors, including firm size and age, research and development (R&D) efforts, the quality or skill level of managers/employees, employee participation and motivation, managerial practices and inter-departmental cooperation and knowledge exchange, factors related to the firms' network and its interactions with outside organizations, and factors specific to the industry. Cohen (2010),

Table 1. Rate of innovation in selected African countries.

Country	Reference period	% firms with an innovation
Egypt	2008–2010	40.1
Gabon	2010–2012	61.5
Ghana	2008–2010	72.5
Kenya	2008–2011	74.1
Lesotho	2010–2012	58.5
Nigeria	2008–2010	65.0
Senegal	2009–2011	63.1
South Africa	2005–2007	65.4
Tanzania	2008–2010	61.3
Uganda	2008–2010	77.0
Zambia	2008–2010	51.0

Source: Adapted from African Innovation Outlook II (AU-NEPAD 2014).
Note: Extensive dissimilarities in the survey methodologies, especially in sampling, across countries disallow statistically valid cross-country comparisons.

De Jong and Vermeulen (2007) and Bhattacharya and Bloch (2004) provide excellent overviews of related studies mostly in the context of developed countries. UNU-INTECH (2004) and Hadjimanolis (2000) provide related reviews for the developing country context. In the literature, one of the most widely acknowledged determinants of innovation is firm-level R&D efforts. Innovation does not necessarily proceed from formal R&D (OECD/Eurostat 2005), especially in the African context where few firms are at the technological frontier of their industry (Mytelka 2000). Yet, internal R&D provides a means to create new knowledge and enhances the firm's capacity to exploit knowledge developed elsewhere (Cohen and Levinthal 1990). It is, therefore, not surprising to observe that in most African countries, many firms that innovate do not engage in formal R&D (AU-NEPAD 2010, 2014).[2] However, this raises questions about the important sources of knowledge for firm-level innovation in Africa. In addition, the capacity of African firms to generate novelty and the ability to exploit externally generated knowledge remain important empirical questions. These issues are taken up in some of the papers in this volume.

Table 2 shows data on the sources of information for innovation across eight countries. The data are derived from the same surveys as Table 1. As in other contexts – for instance, in Europe (Eurostat 2008) – the general indication is that innovation is a connected activity: several sources outside of the firm itself matter for innovation. The most important of these external sources are market-based: customers, suppliers and competitors. Firms in all the countries, with the exception of Kenya, make little use of information from universities or government and private research laboratories. The weak linkages between firms and these knowledge and research institutions is indeed an important constraint to innovation in African countries, especially in the case of science-based sectors.

Table 2. Sources of information for innovation in selected African countries.

		Per cent of innovative firms							
Category	Information sources	Egypt	Kenya	Nigeria	Senegal	South Africa	Tanzania	Uganda	Zambia
Internal sources	Sources within same enterprise group	25.0	95.7	51.7	46.3	41.7	61.9	53.7	5.7
External sources									
Market	Suppliers of equipment	17.3	88.0	39.3	43.9	21.3	32.1	26.1	5.7
	Clients or customers	20.0	89.7	51.7	14.6	41.2	66.7	49	10.9
	Competitors	12.0	80.3	30.0	12.2	11.4	27.4	23	3.3
	Consultants	8.9	53.0	14.6	12.2	4.6	16.7	12.2	0
Institutional	Universities or technical colleges	2.7	33.6	6.8	2.4	2.1	7.1	3.2	2
	Government or private research institutions	3.0	40.2	4.2	2.4	1.5	11.9	5.0	0.5
Other	Conferences	10.3	70.9	11.5	7.3	13.3	16.7	16.4	0
	Scientific journals	8.1	64.1	7.1	4.9	10.1	9.5	8.3	0
	Professional associations	4.8	71.8	20.2	4.9	5.6	20.2	11.3	0

Source: Authors' compilation from African Innovation Outlook II (AU-NEPAD 2014)
Note: Extensive dissimilarities in the survey methodologies, especially in sampling, across countries disallow statistically valid cross-country comparisons.

3. Constraints to innovation in Africa and their implications for policy

Constraints to innovation in a country or continent often appear in the form of characteristics of its domestic innovation system and international value chain (see Annex A in OECD/Eurostat 2005). Such constraints have important implications for science, technology and innovation (STI) policy. For instance, latest available data from firms in African countries show that the innovation barrier most frequently experienced is lack of funds and high costs associated with innovation (AU-NEPAD 2010, 2014). Clearly, this calls for urgent action not only to improve access to credit but also to remove the deficits that push up the costs of innovation. In the rest of this section, we elaborate on some of the specific factors that inhibit innovation on the African continent. Our discussion relates to the economic infrastructure, local institutions, domestic capabilities and the policy context.

3.1. Limited economic infrastructure

The importance of economic infrastructure to innovation and development is well known (Foster and Briceño-Garmendia 2010; Ridley, Yee-Cheong, and Juma 2006; Salami, Kamara, and Brixiova 2010; Yepes, Pierce, and Foster 2009). However, at the global level, there is a significant gap in the amount of infrastructure needed to support economic activities and more so to deliver on the sustainable development goals (McKinsey 2016). The infrastructure gap in Africa is rather appalling. The gap in Africa is estimated to be $31 billion dollars per year, with power generation presenting the most significant challenge although some areas, particularly ICT, have seen a major expansion recently, arguably due to a growing injection of private capital in the ICT sector (Foster and Briceño-Garmendia 2010).

Unsurprisingly, infrastructure network in Africa has increasingly lagged behind what can be found in other developing regions with a huge inequality in terms of rural–urban coverage (Poole and Buckley 2006; Yepes, Pierce, and Foster 2009; You 2008). In fact, Africa's infrastructure deficit is higher than those of other developing countries with similar levels of per capita income, contradicting the notion that the limited

Table 3. Infrastructure endowment of low-income countries in sub-Saharan Africa and other developing regions.

Measure	Measurement unit	SSA low-income countries	Other low-income countries
Density of paved-road network	kilometres per 100 square kilometres	31	134
Density of total road network	kilometres per 100 square kilometres	137	211
Density of fixed-line	Subscribers per 1000 people	10	78
Density of mobile telephone	Subscriber per 1000 people	55	76
Internet density	Subscribers per 100 people	2	3
Electricity generation capacity	Megawatts per 1 million people	37	326
Electricity coverage	% of households with access	16	41
Improved water	% of households with access population	60	72
Improved sanitation	% of households with access	34	51

Source: Yepes, Pierce, and Foster (2009) and Foster and Briceño-Garmendia (2010).

infrastructure in Africa is a reflection of relatively low-income levels (Yepes, Pierce, and Foster 2009). Table 3, for example, compares the low-income countries in sub-Saharan Africa to those of other developing regions, showing that on all the measures of infrastructure presented, the low-income countries in sub-Saharan Africa have lower stock than their counterparts in other developing regions. Current projections on future infrastructure development, however, show that investment in Africa's infrastructure will remain comparatively low even in relation to other developing or emerging economies (McKinsey 2016).

The constraints that limited infrastructure pose are obvious. In general, inadequate infrastructure and poor management of the little available, in most cases by state-owned monopolies, create the need for local firms to generate their own supply. In fact, infrastructure services in Africa are about 100% more expensive compared to other regions which is a reflection of not only diseconomies of scale in production but also high profit margin due to lack of competition (Foster and Briceño-Garmendia 2010). The cost burden forces firms to divert resources that would otherwise be applied for expansion and innovation, thereby increasing the costs of growth and innovation. For instance, inadequate infrastructure has been a major constraint to productivity growth in small-holder farming in East Africa, a sector which accounts for over 75% of employment in this sub region (Salami, Kamara, and Brixiova 2010). Investing more in Africa's infrastructure is critical to overcoming these challenges and to spurring innovation. China's race to become a top innovation performer globally, following after the United States and Japan (Kim 2014), appears as a good lesson for Africa. While there are many determinants of innovation in China (Girma, Gong, and Görg 2008), it seems difficult to delink China's experience from her massive investment in infrastructure over the past two decades. Between 1992 and 2013, China's spending on infrastructure stood at an annual average of 8.6% of GDP, which was 3.6 percentage points higher than North America and Western Europe combined and 5.5 percentage points higher than Africa (McKinsey 2016). Increasing investment in infrastructure while addressing the rural–urban disparity in infrastructure coverage will be an important enabler of innovation (Africa Union 2015; UNECA 2014) and for promoting inclusivity in the innovation process and outcomes (Goyal 2016).

3.2. Weak systems/institutional factors

Strong innovation systems, be it at the national or sectorial level, are crucial for innovation performance. The functioning of an innovation system depends on its components – the organizations/actors and institutions – and relations among the components, which perform various innovation system activities (Edquist 2001; Edquist and Johnson 2005; Freeman 1987; Lundvall 1992). Being an essential component of the innovation system, institution's role and impact are almost definitive (Edquist 2001); they are the rules of the game, determining how the game is played, who plays the game and even whether the game is played (Mudombi and Muchie 2014). The constellation of the characteristics of institutions also matter for innovation as it defines the economic properties of the knowledge produced (Foray 2005). Weak institutions with fragmented constellations of actors tend to constrain interactive learning, hindering innovation (Egbetokun, Siyanbola, and Adeniyi 2007; Iizuka, Mawoko, and Gault 2015; Muok and Kingiri 2015; Oyelaran-

Oyeyinka, Laditan, and Esubiyi 1996) and affecting the potential of external regulation and control (government policy) of negative innovation externalities (Voeten and Naudé 2014). Furthermore, there is ample evidence that shortage of credit is a serious constraint to firm growth (Akoten, Sawada, and Otsuka 2006; Beck and Demirguç-Kunt 2006; Fisman 2001; Le 2012; Nguyen and Luu 2013; Rand et al. 2009).

The consequences of weak systems of innovation are enormous. Mudombi and Muchie (2014) have argued that the institutional set up at the national (and international) levels has been less favourable for any meaningful innovation in Africa. Oyelaran-Oyeyinka, Laditan, and Esubiyi (1996) found that innovation in Nigeria's manufacturing sector has largely been ad hoc and incremental partly due to weak linkages between the firms and public R&D organizations in Nigeria. Through a case study of cassava and maize-processing industries in Nigeria and Kenya, Ndichu et al. (2015) found that innovation and firm learning with respect to energy efficiency in agro-industrial sectors in sub-Saharan Africa (SSA) tend to emanate from informal mechanisms while universities and public research institutes have remained as less important sources of knowledge. Similarly, Osoro et al. (2016, this issue) found that knowledge sources that are external to the firm, particularly R&D, have limited impact on firm-level innovation in Tanzania. Institutional rigidities in Africa countries have also affected the uptake of more appropriate technological innovations (capital goods) from China in favour of those from advanced countries which are largely unsuitable for Africa's factor endowment (Agyei-Holmes 2016, this issue; Atta-Ankomah 2014).

Of related concern are issues of institutional quality including rule of law, control of corruption and voice and accountability. A large literature has addressed the impact of such institutional quality factors on growth and development (e.g. Acemoglu, Johnson, and Robinson 2005; Glaeser et al. 2004; La Porta et al. 1999). Reviewing several iterations of the World Bank's *Doing Business* Report, Davis and Kruse (2007, 1102) pointed out the initial conclusion of regulation in developing countries being more cumbersome, even sometimes completely outdated, in all aspects of business activity. Besides, compared to developed countries, the business registration process is usually long, expensive and often corrupted (World Bank and International Finance Corporation 2006). Many firms therefore prefer to remain in the informal sector, partly to avoid the burden of the formalization process and partly to also avoid the responsibilities such as taxation and regulation that come with being in the formal sector. In addition, many studies have revealed the negative effects of corruption in the form of informal payments on firm growth (Fisman and Svensson 2007; Rand and Tarp 2012; Ufere et al. 2012). In combination, informality and corruption exert a negative influence on firm growth (Rand and Tarp 2012).

3.3. Limited capabilities

Despite the fact that Africa accounts for 12% of the world population, less than 1% of the world's research output comes from Africa (Mwiti 2015). This somehow points to the extent to which global innovative capabilities are skewed, not only to the disadvantage of Africa but also to that of the entire global south. This pattern has historical roots. Developing countries' share in global R&D was as low as 2% in the late 1960s, sparking a UN-led campaign to deepen R&D activities in the developing countries and culminating in the birth of a radical document called the Sussex Manifesto in the early 1970s (Bell 2009; Kaplinsky 2011) that challenged the global division of labour in innovation. Developing countries' share in global R&D has increased since this period, attaining 21% at the beginning of the twenty-first century, although China and South East Asia account for a large part of the increase (Ely and Bell 2009). Correspondingly, East Asian countries such Korea, China, Thailand and Singapore advanced significantly in the twentieth century while Africa has largely missed out (Lee, Juma, and Mathews 2014).

Since the 1970s, our understanding of how innovative capabilities are developed has deepened and transcended an often one-dimensional focus on formal R&D. There has been a recognition that capability development is largely embedded in interactions and feedbacks between R&D, design and production and marketing processes, representing a departure from the linear models of innovation (Bell 2009; Lundvall and Johnson 1994; Von Hippel 2005). This improvement in our understanding has unveiled additional dimensions of the challenges constraining innovation in low-income settings such as Africa. We now know that capabilities built up through interactive learning processes internal to the firm and through interactions between firms and their clients are as crucial as those derived from access to external R&D organizations. (Caloghirou, Kastelli, and Tsakanikas 2004; Cohen and Levinthal 1990; Jensen et al. 2007; Yam et al. 2011). Both internal and external sources of innovation capabilities are conditioned by factors such as institutions (the rules and norms), the state of economic infrastructure, the level and nature of education and the dynamics/relations within systems of innovation (Assink 2006; Mudombi and Muchie 2014; Spielman et al. 2008). As noted earlier, there are significant gaps in all of these elements in the context of Africa countries, even when compared to other developing regions.

3.4. Policy constraints and weak government support

African countries' policy landscape and the support it renders to innovation capability building raise a lot of concern. Iizuka, Mawoko, and Gault (2015) point out several challenges including weak governance systems for policy-making, implementation, monitoring and experimentation; lack of coherence in policy across national, regional and continental levels; and limited continuity, accountability and transparency of policy. Focusing on agribusiness innovation systems in Tanzania, Mpagalile, Ishengoma, and Gillah (2008) showed that there are major laxities in policy implementation, including limited communication of policy to firms within the agribusiness value chains, while some policies regarding trade, energy, land and labour appears counterintuitive in relation to innovation. There are also issues around policy lock-in during implementation. The innovation systems approach has been officially adopted by many developing countries, including those in Africa with science and technology (S&T) policy having evolved to cover innovation (I) policy and focusing more on capability building; however, the practice still tends to follow a conventional innovation paradigm, and fails to address systemic problems and failures (Intarakumnerd and Chaminade 2007). Iizuka, Mawoko, and Gault (2015) provide an assessment of the extent to which STI policy objectives and priorities of Southern and Eastern African countries have been achieved. Their analysis summarized in Table 4 shows that 'S&T' are more advanced in the countries studied compared to 'I' as the

Table 4. ST&I policies of the 11 African countries.

Country	Development vision	S&T policy	ST&I policy	STI policy objectives & priorities					
				Research capacity	Human resources	Network of researchers	ICT	Institutional capacity	Linkages with private sector
Botswana	Vision 2016 (drafted in 1997)	Science and Technology Policy (1998)	National Policy on Research, Science, Technology and Innovation (2011)						
Burundi	Vision 2025 (adopted in 2010)		National Policy on Scientific Research and Technological innovation (2011)						
Ethiopia	Vision 2025 (announced in 2011)	National Science and Technology Policy (1993)	National Science, Technology and Innovation Policy (2012)						
Kenya	Vision 2030 (launched in 2008)	The Science and Technology Act Cap 250 (1977)	Science, Technology and Innovation Act (2013), Draft National Science, Technology and Innovation Policy (2012)						
Malawi	Vision 2020 (launched in 1998)	Science and Technology Act (2003), National Science and Technology Policy (1991 and revised in 2002)	–						
Mauritius	Vision 2020 (launched in 2008)		Draft National Policy and Strategy on Science, Technology and Innovation (2014-2025	Not collecting baseline data on ST&I Indicators					
Namibia	Vision 2030 (adopted in 2004)	Science and Technology Policy (1999)	National Programme for Research, Science, and Technology and Innovation, Draft Innovation Framework (2011)						
Rwanda	Vision 2020 (revised targets in 2012)		National Science, Technology and Innovation Policy (2006), revised in 2014 (not yet approved by Cabinet)						
Tanzania	Vision 2025 (in place since 2000)	National Science and Technology Policy Framework (1985), National Science and Technology Policy revised (1996)	National Science, Technology and Innovation Policy (2013)						
Uganda	Vison 2040 (launched 2013)		National Science Technology and Innovation Policy (2009)						
Zimbabwe	Vision 2020 (adopted late 1980s)	Science and Technology Policy (2002)	Science, Technology and Innovation Policy (2012)						

Colour convention – Achievement of priorities in National STI Policy

0%	25%	50%	75%	100%	not applicable

Source: Iizuka, Mawoko, and Gault (2015).

Note: The degree of progress in the chart only refers to the specific country's plan; hence, these evaluations cannot and should not be used comparatively across countries.

objectives of strengthening linkages with the private sector and building network of researchers are far behind the others.

4. Outline of the special issue

The broad objectives of this special issue are to shed light through sound empirical evidence on different factors outlined above that facilitate or constrain innovation in Africa, and to identify policy options for overcoming the constraints. The first article by Olawale Adejuwon focuses on a structural element in the African innovation ecosystem, that is, brokers. The illustrative sector chosen is small-scale agriculture, a sector that employs the most labour and contributes the most to real GDP in most African countries. The paper argues that the limited development and diffusion of appropriate innovations in the context of small-scale agricultural production in sub-Saharan Africa can be attributed to the lack of cohesiveness among actors within agricultural innovation systems. Actors can, however, be linked through brokerage. The paper identifies brokerage content that is relevant to the African context and recommends brokers who are embedded in the innovation system by their core functions.

The need to make systemic changes to overcome even broader system-wide challenges is the subject of the paper by Andrew Agyei-Holmes. It builds upon the discussion of Adejuwon in the context of the agriculture sector. The specific problem discussed is how agricultural technologies, particularly from China, are imported and diffused within the Tanzanian agriculture sector. The technology transfer process faces challenges related to institutional and systemic weaknesses. Based on firm-, farm- and government-level data on importation, distribution, usage and maintenance of tractors in Tanzania, the paper offers a deeper understanding of the challenges and proposes some pragmatic solutions.

As already discussed above, the innovation process is difficult in many African countries partly due to weak domestic capabilities. African firms often have low levels of absorptive capacity and hence, have difficulties assimilating knowledge developed elsewhere. This paper makes an assessment of the level of absorptive capacity among Nigerian manufacturing and service firms, and links this to product innovation. The paper by Ukpabio et al. assesses the influence of absorptive capacity on firms' product innovation, using innovation survey data on Nigerian manufacturing and services firms. A key result of the paper is that the factors associated with the build-up of absorptive capacity in the two sectors differ; hence, there is no one-cap-fits-all solution to the accumulation of capabilities across sectors in Africa. This result underscores the need for sector-specific policies that will enhance firms' competences and capabilities and drive national competitiveness.

Although patents are widely regarded as an inadequate indicator of innovation particularly in Africa, they nevertheless remain a useful measure. This is so for three reasons, at least. First, patents embody a considerable amount of new knowledge. Second, because they are tangible, patents are some of the most tractable quantities in the innovation process. Third, as a consequence of foregoing reasons, patents offer a nice way to track knowledge flows. These attributes are exploited in the paper by Francesco Lamperti et al. Using patent data and a non-parametric approach, the paper examines persistence of innovation and knowledge flows at the firm level in Africa. This sort of analysis is crucial in order to discriminate between different possible drivers of innovative processes and for guiding public policies aimed at promoting innovation. The paper finds some degree of persistence and a positive impact of knowledge flows from OECD countries.

Beyond knowledge embodied in patents, firms acquire knowledge for innovation from various sources including acquisition of external R&D or new machinery and equipment. This has become a contemporary issue in the economics and management of innovation. The next paper in this issue by Otieno Osoro and colleagues sheds light on the relationship of different external knowledge sources with product and process among a sample of Tanzanian firms, that is, the effect of knowledge sources on firm-level innovation. The analysis reveals, among other things, that product innovation is more constrained by a lack of external knowledge than process innovation. They also show that the joint effect of internal and external knowledge on innovation exceeds the separate effects of internal and external knowledge. This suggest that firms benefit more in terms of innovation by complementing internal knowledge with externally generated knowledge.

The paper by Abdi Yuya and Keun Lee, the last in this special issue, takes the analyses of the preceding paper further by focusing on the knowledge acquired through imported technologies and by participating in international markets. The paper examines how imported technologies and exporting enhance firm-level productivity in the Ethiopian manufacturing sector. The results indicate that exporting, greater use of imported inputs and new capital goods significantly improve productivity and catch-up among firms. The positive productivity effects of imported inputs and new capital goods are higher for exporters than non-exporters. In sum, the findings of this paper suggest that improving access to imported inputs, encouraging investment in new capital goods and strengthening export orientation among manufacturing firms can help accelerate technology transfer and build local innovation capabilities.

5. Issues for further research

The papers in this special issue point to the need for further research in a number of key areas, to deepen our understanding of constraints to innovation in the African context. First, there is a clear need for rigorous analyses on the impact of infrastructure on innovativeness and performance: such analyses are still rare. Datta (2012), Rud (2012) and Ghani, Goswami, and Kerr (2015) lay a formidable groundwork based on Indian data in this regard. Shiferaw et al. (2015) is one of the rare studies in the African context. Another pressing need is for more research on the role of networks and collective action. In this regard, new tools (e.g. dynamic social network analysis as applied in Giuliani 2010) and new data sources (e.g. innovation surveys as championed in Africa by the New Partnership for African Development (NEPAD)) should enable rigorous analyses of networks and interactive learning in Africa. The earlier works of Giuliani and Bell (2005); Oyelaran-Oyeyinka (2005) and Egbetokun (2015) are instructive in this aspect. Poor financing and corruption as barriers to innovation are also under-researched in the African context. It is well known that funding constraints and exposure to corruption inhibit innovation firm performance but the evidence from Africa is very thin. Richer analyses like those by Akoten, Sawada, and Otsuka (2006), Rand and Tarp (2012) and Lorenz (2014) are highly desirable.

In all of the above, the need for effective data collection cannot be overemphasized. The recent efforts under the NEPAD African Science, Technology and Innovation Indicators Initiative (ASTII) are notable, but unless the data are collected longitudinally, sample attrition is discouraged or at least attenuated and the resulting microdata are accessible,[3] progress will be very limited.

Notes

1. These papers were selected after a thorough double-blind review process. Two independent reviewers assessed each paper and several of the papers had to undergo multiple review rounds. We are immensely grateful to all the scholars who gave their time and expertise to the review process.
2. This also partly explains why marketing and organisational changes are at the heart of the innovation process on the continent.
3. The OECD Eurostat Innovation statistics and indicators (http://www.oecd.org/innovation/inno/inno-stats.htm) is an established example to follow. In Africa, a donor-funded project (http://pedl.cepr.org/content/creating-micro-level-dataset-innovation-nigeria) has taken the first steps in this direction by making the data from the existing two waves of innovation surveys in Nigeria openly accessible (https://goo.gl/gYdpLx).

Disclosure statement

No potential conflict of interest was reported by the authors.

ORCiD

Abiodun Egbetokun ⓘ http://orcid.org/0000-0002-2069-7648

References

Acemoglu, D., S. Johnson, and J. A. Robinson. 2005. "Institutions as a Fundamental Cause of Long-Run Growth." *Handbook of Economic Growth* 1: 385–472.

Adebowale, B. A., B. Diyamett, R. Lema, and O. Oyelaran-Oyeyinka. 2014. " Introduction. Special Issue: Innovation and Economic Development in Africa." *African Journal of Science, Technology, Innovation and Development* 6 (5): v–xi.

Africa Union. 2015. "Science, Technology and Innovation Strategy for Africa 2024." Accessed June 18, 2016. http://www.hsrc.ac.za/uploads/pageContent/5481/Science,20Technology20and 20Innovation20Strategy20for20Africa20-20Document.pdf.

Agyei-Holmes, A. 2016. "Technology Transfer and Agricultural Mechanization in Tanzania: Institutional Adjustments to Accommodate Emerging Economy Innovations." *Innovation and Development* 6 (2): 195–211.

Akoten, J. E., Y. Sawada, and K. Otsuka. 2006. "The Determinants of Credit Access and Its Impacts on Micro and Small Enterprises: The Case of Garment Producers in Kenya." *Economic Development and Cultural Change* 54 (4): 927–944.

Assink, M. 2006. "Inhibitors of Disruptive Innovation Capability: A Conceptual Model." *European Journal of Innovation Management* 9 (2): 215–233.

Atta-Ankomah, R. 2014. "Chinese Presence in Developing Countries' Technology Basket: The Case of Furniture Manufacturing in Kenya." PhD thesis, Open University, UK.

AU-NEPAD. 2010. *African Innovation Outlook 2010*. Pretoria: African Union-New Partnership for African Development.

AU-NEPAD. 2014. *African Innovation Outlook II*. Pretoria: African Union-New Partnership for African Development.

Beck, T., and A. Demirguç-Kunt. 2006. "Small and Medium-Size Enterprises: Access to Finance as a Growth Constraint." *Journal of Banking and Finance* 30 (11): 2931–2943.

Bell, M. 2009. *Innovation Capabilities and Directions of Development*. UK: STEPS Centre, Sussex University.

Bhattacharya, M., and H. Bloch. 2004. "Determinants of Innovation." *Small Business Economics* 22 (2): 155–162.

Caloghirou, Y., I. Kastelli, and A. Tsakanikas. 2004. "Internal Capabilities and External Knowledge Sources: Complements or Substitutes for Innovative Performance?" *Technovation* 24 (1): 29–39.

Cohen, W. 2010. "Fifty Years of Empirical Studies of Innovative Activity and Performance." In *Handbook of the Economics of Innovation*, edited by H. B. Hall and N. Rosenberg, 129–213. Amsterdam: North-Holland/Elsevier.

Cohen, W. M., and D. A. Levinthal. 1990. "Absorptive Capacity: A New Perspective on Learning and Innovation." *Administrative Science Quarterly* 35 (1): 128–152.

Datta, S. 2012. "The Impact of Improved Highways on Indian Firms." *Journal of Development Economics* 99 (1): 46–57.

Davis, K. E., and M. B. Kruse. 2007. "Taking the Measure of Law: The Case of the Doing Business Project." *Law and Social Inquiry* 32 (4): 1095–1119.

De Jong, J. P. J., and P. A. M. Vermeulen 2007. "Determinants of Product Innovation." *International Small Business Journal* 24 (6): 587–609.

Edquist, C. 2001. "The Systems of Innovation Approach and Innovation Policy: An Account of the State of the Art." DRUID Conference, Aalborg. 12–15.

Edquist, C., and B. Johnson. 2005. "Institutions and Organizations in Systems of Innovation." In *Systems of Innovation: Technologies, Institutions and Organisations*, edited by C. Edquist, 41–63. London: Routledge.

Egbetokun, A. A. 2015. "Interactive Learning and Firm-Level Capabilities in Latecomer Settings: The Nigerian Manufacturing Industry." *Technological Forecasting and Social Change* 99: 231–241.

Egbetokun, A. A., W. Siyanbola, and A. Adeniyi. 2007. "Indigenous Innovation Capability in Sub-Saharan Africa: A Review of the Nigerian Situation." Proceedings of the Fifth International Symposium on Management of Technology, pp. 1018–1022.

Ely, A., and M. Bell. 2009. *The Original 'Sussex Manifesto': Its Past and Future Relevance*. UK: STEPS Centre, Sussex University.

Ernst, D. 2007. "Beyond the 'Global Factory' Model: Innovative Capabilities for Upgrading China's IT Industry." *International Journal of Technology and Globalisation* 3 (4): 437–459.

Eurostat. 2008. *Science, Technology and Innovation in Europe*. 2008 ed. Luxembourg: Eurostat Statistical Books, Office for Official Publications of the European Communities.

Fisman, R. 2001. "Trade Credit and Productive Efficiency in Developing Countries." *World Development* 29 (2): 311–321.

Fisman, R., and J. Svensson. 2007. "Are Corruption and Taxation Really Harmful to Growth? Firm-Level Evidence." *Journal of Development Economics* 83: 63–75.

Foray, D. 2005. "Institutions and Organizations in Systems of Innovation." In *Systems of Innovation: Technologies, Institutions and Organisations*, edited by C. Edquist, 64–85. London: Routledge.

Foster, V., and C. Briceño-Garmendia. 2010. *Africa's Infrastructure: A Time for Transformation*. Washington, DC: World Bank.

Freeman, C. 1987. *Technology Policy and Economic Performance*. London: Pinter.

Ghani, E., A. G. Goswami, and W. R. Kerr. 2015. "Highway to Success: The Impact of the Golden Quadrilateral Project for the Location and Performance of Indian Manufacturing." *The Economic Journal* 126 (591): 317–357

Girma, S., Y. Gong, and H. Görg. 2008. "Foreign Direct Investment, Access to Finance, and Innovation Activity in Chinese Enterprises." *The World Bank Economic Review* 22 (2): 367–382.

Giuliani, E. 2010. *Network Dynamics in Regional Clusters: The Perspective of an Emerging Economy*. Papers in Evolutionary Economic Geography (PEEG), 1014.

Giuliani, E., and M. Bell. 2005. "The Micro-determinants of Meso-level Learning and Innovation: Evidence from a Chilean Wine Cluster." *Research Policy* 34 (1): 47–68.

Glaeser, E. L., R. La Porta, F. Lopez-de-Silanes, and A Shleifer. 2004. "Do Institutions Cause Growth?" *Journal of Economic Growth*, 9 (3): 271–303.

Goyal, A. 2016. "Conditions for Inclusive Innovation with Application to Telecom and Mobile Banking." *Innovation and Development*. doi:10.1080/2157930X.2016.1187845.

Hadjimanolis, A. 2000. "An Investigation of Innovation Antecedents in Small Firms in the Context of a Small Developing Country." *RandD Management* 30 (3): 235–245.

Iizuka, M., P. Mawoko, and F. Gault. 2015. *Innovation for Development in Southern and Eastern Africa: Challenges for Promoting STandI Policy*. UNU-MERIT Policy Brief (I, 2015).

Intarakumnerd, P., and C. Chaminade. 2007. "Strategy Versus Practice in Innovation Systems Policy: The Case of Thailand." *Asian Journal of Technology Innovation* 15 (2): 197–213.

Jensen, M. B., B. Johnson, E. Lorenz, and B. Å. Lundvall. 2007. "Forms of Knowledge and Modes of Innovation." *Research Policy* 36 (5): 680–693.

Kaplinsky, R. 2011. "Schumacher Meets Schumpeter: Appropriate Technology Below the Radar." *Research Policy* 40 (2): 193–203.

Kim, Y. 2014. "China-Africa Technology Transfer: A Matter of Technology Readiness." CCS Commentary. Accessed June 18, 2016. http://www.ccs.org.za/wp-content/uploads/2014/02/CCS_Commentary_China_Africa_Tech_2014_YK1.pdf.

La Porta, R., F. Lopez-de-Silanes, A. Shleifer, and R Vishny. 1999. "The Quality of Government." *Journal of Law, Economics, and Organization* 15 (1): 222–279.

Le, P. N. M. 2012. "What Determines the Access to Credit by SMEs? A Case Study in Vietnam." *Journal of Management Research* 4 (4): 90–115.

Lee, K., C. Juma, and J. Mathews. 2014. *Innovation Capabilities for Sustainable Development in Africa*. WIDER Working Paper 2014/062. Helsinki, Finland: UN-WIDER.

Lorenz, E. 2014. "Do Credit-Constrained Firms in Africa Innovate Less? A Study Based on Nine African Nations." GREDEG Working Paper Series (GREDEG WP No. 2014-29). http://www.gredeg.cnrs.fr/working-papers.html.

Lundvall, B. A. 1992. *National Innovation System: Towards a Theory of Innovation and Interactive Learning*. London: Pinter.

Lundvall, B. Ä., and B. Johnson. 1994. "The Learning Economy." *Journal of Industry Studies* 1 (2): 23–42.

McKinsey. 2016. "Bridging Global Infrastructure Gaps." McKinsey and Company. Accessed June 18, 2016. http://www.mckinsey.com/industries/infrastructure/our-insights/bridging-global-infrastructure-gaps.

Mpagalile, J., R. Ishengoma, and P. Gillah. 2008. *Agribusiness Innovation in Six African Countries: The Tanzanian Experience.* Agribusiness and Innovation Systems in Africa.

Mudombi, S., and M. Muchie. 2014. "An Institutional Perspective to Challenges Undermining Innovation Activities in Africa." *Innovation and Development* 4 (2): 313–326.

Muok, B. O., and A. Kingiri. 2015. "The Role of Civil Society Organizations in Low-Carbon Innovation in Kenya." *Innovation and Development* 5 (2): 207–223.

Mwiti, L. 2015. "Science, Technology and Innovation in Africa – Not Always Rosy, But It Is about to Be." *Mail and Guardian Africa.* Accessed June 16, 2016. http://mgafrica.com/article/2015-03-18-science-technology-and-innovation-in-africanot-always-rosy-but-it-is-about-to-be.

Mytelka, L. 2000. "Local Systems of Innovation in a Globalized World Economy." *Industry and Innovation* 7 (1): 33–54.

Ndichu, J., J. Blohmke, R. Kemp, J. Adeoti, and A. E. Obayelu. 2015. "The Adoption of Energy Efficiency Measures by Firms in Africa: Case Studies of Cassava Processing in Nigeria and Maize Milling in Kenya." *Innovation and Development* 5 (2): 189–206.

Nguyen, N., and N. Luu. 2013. "Determinants of Financing Pattern and Access to Formal-Informal Credit: The Case of Small and Medium Sized Enterprises in Vietnam." *Journal of Management Research* 5 (2): 240–259.

OECD/Eurostat. 2005. *Guidelines for Collecting and Interpreting Innovation Data: Oslo Manual.* Paris: OECD/Eurostat.

Osoro, O., P. Vermeulen, J. Knoben, and G. Kahyarara. 2016. "Effect of Knowledge Sources on Firm-Level Innovation in Tanzania." *Innovation and Development* 6 (2): 259–280.

Oyelaran-Oyeyinka, B. 2005. "Inter-firm Collaboration and Competitive Pressures: SME Footwear Clusters in Nigeria." *International Journal of Technology and Globalisation* 1 (3/4): 343–360.

Oyelaran-Oyeyinka, B., G. O. A. Laditan, and A. O. Esubiyi. 1996. "Industrial Innovation in Sub-Saharan Africa: The Manufacturing Sector in Nigeria." *Research Policy* 25 (7): 1081–1096.

Poole, N. D., and P. C. Buckley. 2006. *Innovation Challenges, Constraints and Opportunities for the Rural Poor.* Background Paper for the International Fund for Agricultural Development (IFAD), Rome. January. Wye, Kent, UK. Imperial College London.

Rand, J., and F. Tarp. 2012. "Firm Level Corruption in Vietnam." *Economic Development and Cultural Change* 60 (3): 571–595.

Rand, J., F. Tarp, T. T. Coung, and N. T. Tam. 2009. *SME Access to Credit.* MPRA Paper No. 29467. http://mpra.ub.uni-muenchen.de/29467/.

Ridley, T., L. Yee-Cheong, and C. Juma. 2006. "Infrastructure, Innovation and Development." *International Journal of Technology and Globalisation* 2 (3–4): 268–278.

Rud, J. P. 2012. "Electricity Provision and Industrial Development: Evidence from India." *Journal of Development Economics* 97 (2): 352–367.

Salami, A., A. B. Kamara, and Z. Brixiova. 2010. *Smallholder Agriculture in East Africa: Trends, Constraints and Opportunities.* Tunis: African Development Bank.

Shiferaw, A., M. Söderbom, E. Siba, and G. Alemu. 2015. "Road Infrastructure and Enterprise Dynamics in Ethiopia." *The Journal of Development Studies* 51 (11): 1541–1558.

Spielman, D. J., J. Ekboir, K. Davis, and C. M. Ochieng. 2008. "An Innovation Systems Perspective on Strengthening Agricultural Education and Training in Sub-Saharan Africa." *Agricultural Systems* 98 (1): 1–9.

Ufere, N., S. Perelli, R. Boland, and B. Carlsson. 2012. "Merchants of Corruption: How Entrepreneurs Manufacture and Supply Bribes." *World Development* 40 (12): 2440–2453.

UNECA. 2014. *Youth and Innovation in Africa: Harnessing the Possibilities of Africa's Youth for the Transformation of the Continent.* United Nations Economic Commission for Africa. Accessed June 18, 2016. http://www.uneca.org/publications/youth-and-innovation-africa-harnessing-possibilities-africa%E2%80%99s-youth-transformation.

UNU-INTECH. 2004. *Designing a Policy-Relevant Innovation Survey for NEPAD.* Mimeo. Maastricht, The Netherlands: United Nations University Institute for New Technologies.

Voeten, J. J., and W. A. Naudé. 2014. "Regulating the Negative Externalities of Enterprise Cluster Innovations: Lessons from Vietnam." *Innovation and Development* 4 (2): 203–219.

Von Hippel, E. 2005. "Democratizing Innovation: The Evolving Phenomenon of User Innovation." *Journal für Betriebswirtschaft* 55 (1): 63–78.

World Bank and International Finance Corporation. 2006. *Doing Business 2007: How to Reform.* Washington, DC: World Bank.

Yam, R. C., W. Lo, E. P. Tang, and A. K. Lau. 2011. "Analysis of Sources of Innovation, Technological Innovation Capabilities, and Performance: An Empirical Study of Hong Kong Manufacturing Industries." *Research Policy* 40 (3): 391–402.

Yepes, T., J. Pierce, and V. Foster. 2009. *Making Sense of Sub-Saharan Africa's Infrastructure Endowment: A Benchmarking Approach.* Working Paper 1. Washington, DC: Africa Infrastructure Country Diagnostic, World Bank.

You, L. Z. 2008. *Irrigation Investment Needs in Sub-Saharan Africa.* Washington, DC: World Bank.

Bridging gaps in innovation systems for small-scale agricultural activities in sub-Saharan Africa: brokers wanted!

Olawale Oladipo Adejuwon

ABSTRACT

The limited development and diffusion of appropriate innovations in the context of small-scale agricultural production in sub-Saharan Africa can be attributed to the lack of cohesiveness among actors within agricultural innovation systems. Linkages can however be facilitated among actors by brokerage. Although the practice of brokerage is still at an infant stage, available literature recommends with reservations brokers whose core function is brokerage for the sector. In order to identify actors policy-makers can nominate as brokers to fast-track brokerage activities in the sector, this conceptual study; (a) delineates actors in the innovation system into three groups – smallholders, innovating units and funding/policy support institutions; (b) theorizes that effective brokers – are constructively socially evaluated and high in self-monitoring, have high absorptive capacities, possess global connections and excel in their core functions and (c) applies these characteristics on the delineated groups. The study outlines brokerage content to be information, knowledge and funding and recommends brokers who are embedded in the innovation system by their core functions for the sector.

1. Introduction

The failure of agricultural innovation systems to modernize agricultural production and enhance the productivity of small-scale agricultural practitioners in sub-Saharan Africa (SSA) has been a source of concern for policy-makers and development practitioners. In spite of the large investment in agro-based research over the years, production methods among practitioners have remained rudimentary resulting in poverty and threats to food security. Agricultural research in Africa has been characterized as being out-of-touch with rural realities, not focused on small-scale production and not demand-driven and gender sensitive (Sumberg 2005; FAO 2012). This has led some to label innovations for small-scale agricultural activities as being inappropriate and to be the leading cause of lack of diffusion of these innovations among practitioners. Without the diffusion of innovations among practitioners, learning and competence building in the area of agricultural production will not occur.

The failure of extension services to encourage the adoption of innovations in small-scale agricultural activities has been well documented. The conception of the extension

15

institutions that play intermediary roles between research institutes and practitioners in SSA is based on the linear view of innovation where investment in scientific research routinely results in the development and diffusion of innovations. In this view, the extension service provider plays a boundary spanning role between a specialized research institution and practitioners by creating awareness of innovations from the institute. The linear view of innovation has not been linked to economic development. This may be because it neglects important demand-side dynamics necessary for the development and diffusion of innovations (Lundvall 2007). Contemporary views however see innovation as an interactive process among various actors (Lundvall and Borrás 1997). Innovation not only comes from multiple sources, it is also an outcome of interactive learning within and among institutions and different modes of learning (Jensen et al. 2007; Lundvall 2007). The shift away from the linear model to an interactive one has necessitated a review of the role of intermediaries in innovation activities in small-scale agricultural production in SSA. This interactive view, the National Innovation System framework has gained wide spread interest as a tool for the construction and promotion of innovation systems in the developing world. Freeman (1987) defined innovation systems as a network of institutions in the public and private sectors whose activities and interactions initiate, import, modify and diffuse new technologies. The author stresses the importance of interactions within and between organizations as being the foundation for innovation success. It is expected that applying this principle will bring about the development and diffusion of appropriate innovations in small-scale agricultural activities in SSA.

1.1. Peculiarities of innovation systems for small-scale agricultural activities in SSA

The type of interactions required and the institutions needed to drive successful innovation systems in the sector may however be considered unique. Practitioners are among the World's least educated and poorest. This implies that support may be needed in adopting innovations. In addition, this demographic may also hamper scientific modes of innovation by practitioners themselves. Disincentives for private firms to conduct research into ways of solving problems in the sector may exist especially for disembodied innovations (e.g. crop rotation) and those that may be easily reproduced (e.g. improved cultivars). This may make it necessary to develop and fund public research and other support institutions for the sector. Furthermore, innovations for low income earners require detailed consideration for user needs and socio-economic characteristics. Such information may be difficult to acquire due to the informal nature of small-scale sub-Saharan agriculture. Added to this is the lack of political will and executive, moral and financial capacity of the governments of most sub-Saharan countries which has necessitated the intervention of global institutions in addressing problems related to food security on the continent (Adejuwon 2016). A typical agricultural innovation system for small-scale agricultural activities may therefore consist of three major type of actors; the practitioners, individuals and institutions responsible for developing innovations and support organizations that provide funding and policy instruments to support research and adoption of innovations.

However, there are a range of factors that may cause the failure of the actors to interact with each other. This may be due to the some salient characteristics of innovation systems for small-scale agricultural activities. As mentioned earlier, practitioners are mostly uneducated and operate in informal sectors. Learning processes are usually grounded in experience and passed on from forebears or through apprenticeship. Preferred information channels may also be informal and rudimentary. These qualities are in contrast with formal knowledge institutions. Therefore, interactions may only take place between actors with matching technical skills, education and competence (Lundvall 1985). Another source of asymmetries in interactions may occur due to differences in the philosophy guiding the actions of actors in the system. For example the primary purpose of industrial R&D is to grow the firm through the accumulation of knowledge resources such as patents and trademarks while academic research output can be considered as a public good. The formal/informal sector dichotomy prevalent in most sectoral agricultural innovation systems in Africa may also be a source of isolation as these sectors have been described as dual economies (Spring 2009). Isolation may therefore be caused by differences in socio-cultural frames where actors who share similar frames may interact with each other and do not with those they are dissimilar with. Nevertheless, for innovation systems for small-scale agricultural systems to thrive, there must be interactions among actors.

Drawing from social network theory, people have the strongest ties with people they share the same attributes with (Granovetter 1973). If these ties are platforms for interaction, then actors with strong ties would interact with each other and may not with those with whom they have weak ties. This isolation may be likened to the lack of connectedness or structural holes as referred to by Burt (1992). However, information, knowledge and funding necessary for the production and diffusion of appropriate technologies for the sector may be dispersed among actors who have strong as well as weak ties with each other in the innovation system. Therefore, in innovation systems for small-scale agricultural activities in SSA, key actors that have the capability to foster ties among weakly tied actors may be necessary for the effective generation and diffusion of innovations. In social network analysis literature, such actors are usually referred to as brokers. This is not to say that such structural holes do not exist in non-small-scale agricultural innovation systems, they may however be more prominent, resilient and recurring due to the aforementioned peculiar characteristics of the sector. For example, in innovation systems for consumer goods there may be financial rewards for firms who may be willing to take risks by taking up brokerage roles to seek and combine such dispersed information, knowledge and resources in such ways that have not been combined before to create innovations. On the other hand, rent-seeking firms may not be so willing to take such risks due to the aforementioned peculiarities. It is also unlikely that the agricultural extension services based on the linear model can bridge these structural holes in real-world dynamic agricultural innovation systems. Therefore it may be necessary to reconceptualise extension services to a systemic context of innovation in small-scale agricultural activities in SSA.

1.2. Brokers in the context of small-scale agricultural activities in SSA

Brokers have been described as actors who transfer knowledge between organizations that are not directly linked in a network (Nooteboom 2001). They may also be described as intermediary actors who facilitate interactions between actors lacking access to or trust in one another (Marsden 1982; Gould and Fernandez 1989) or diffusers of information between otherwise disconnected groups (Weiss and Jacobson 1955). A broker can also be described as a key actor with ties with a wide range of actors in a system or one who may serve as a bridge between actors who may otherwise not interact with one another (Gould and Fernandez 1989).

Literature is replete with the role, identity and impact of brokers in innovation systems for industrial and public service sectors (e.g. Hargadon 1998; Kauffeld-Monz and Fritsch 2008; Burt and Merluzzi 2013). However, there have been few studies on brokers in innovation systems for small-scale agricultural activities in SSA. In addition the actual practice of brokerage in the sector is still at an infant stage (FAO 2013). Documented experiences are also limited (World Bank 2012). That notwithstanding, there have been suggestions of how brokers may contribute to connecting actors and how they may emerge in the agricultural sector in Africa. Swaans et al. (2014) noted that brokers may connect actors by facilitating innovation platforms. Klerkx, Hall, and Leeuwis (2009) examined brokers in Dutch agriculture and detailed how they emerged in the sector, their main functions, demerits and contributions. The authors identified seven types of brokers in the Dutch agricultural network. These may be narrowed down to two based on how specialized their brokerage functions are. The first are brokers whose core function is brokerage and the second are those who are members of a network of actors and also provide brokerage functions. Klerkx, Hall, and Leeuwis (2009) also identified the various vulnerabilities of brokers in the Dutch sector as; neutrality tensions when brokers are viewed as being partial towards their financiers or group they belong to; functional ambiguity which may arise from the overlapping of traditional functions and brokerage roles and; funding problems which arise from willingness to pay brokers, difficulty in assessing the impact of brokers and public funding impatience.

Following these findings, Klerkx, Hall, and Leeuwis (2009) recommended that brokers that are organizationally detached from existing organizations may be required in agricultural sectors in Africa. They also proposed that like in the Dutch experience, brokers for the sector be allowed to emerge in a self-organised manner. The authors in addition proposed brokers who are not involved in knowledge generation but simply act as a binding force in the innovation system. Though the authors reported that the brokers found in Africa and other developing countries where those who took up brokerage roles in addition to their core functions, they noted that these type of brokers may have restricted manoeuvring space to carry out and maintain brokerage roles. They argued that innovation brokers whose core function is brokerage may be an option to avoid the vulnerabilities mentioned above and have more space to perform their functions. Various institutions have adopted the aforementioned approach in examining and proposing brokerage in agricultural innovations systems in Africa (e.g. World Bank 2012; FAO 2013; FAO 2014). However, Klerkx, Hall, and Leeuwis (2009) noted that the above recommendation also brings with it its own peculiarities of the aforementioned enumerated tensions. In addition, the authors did not differentiate between large and small-scale agricultural activities in developing countries where socio-economic indices and level of production may require marked differences in policy approaches. Klerkx, Alvarez, and Campusano (2014) also note that the modus operandi of brokers may vary from country to country and sector to sector. This raises several questions relating to the issue of brokering and how it can be used to solve the problem of the production and diffusion of appropriate technologies for the sector.

Who then should be brokers in agricultural innovation systems for small-scale agricultural activities? In addition, is there a means whereby brokerage activities in small-scale agricultural innovation systems in SSA can be stimulated to catch-up with those in formal industrial sectors in the North rather than wait for it to evolve? Should brokers also really not be involved in knowledge generation as suggested by Klerkx and colleagues? The purpose of this study is to provide answers to these questions by proposing characteristics of actors whom policy-makers can nominate as prospective brokers for agricultural innovation systems in SSA. For example, it has become common practice to use educated smallholder farmers to diffuse information obtained from phone applications to other smallholders who do not have the ability to use such applications. In addition, the Nigerian government sought out the International Institute for Tropical Agriculture (IITA) to assist in implementing the Presidential initiative on cassava (Nweke 2005). IITA's intermediary role in the development and diffusion of high-yield pest-resistant cassava varieties and processing technologies has been recognized as the major reason behind the success of the initiative in Nigeria (Adejuwon 2016). Though this study is limited by a lack of a field assessment, it is expected that its results may provide profiles of actors that can be promoted in brokerage roles in the sector.

For the purpose of this study, actors in the sector will be grouped along functional lines, that is, the practitioners, innovating units and policy/funding support institutions. This will highlight the presence of structural holes or a lack of network cohesion and the need to make the network more cohesive through the action of a broker. The study takes the approach of a broker (positional actor) who is a member of a group/sub-group in a structured system of other groups/sub-groups. Also, the study assumes that those who have structural network advantage or opportunities to broker will act on it (Burt 2007). The issues of trust and/or tensions of neutrality and ambiguity can be resolved through a broker with the right social attributes (Burt 1980).

In addition to innovation systems literature, this paper draws on social network literature and other strands on social attributes and management to argue that an actor is more likely to occupy a brokerage position and be successful if accorded with high status and other social attributes like reputation and legitimacy by network members, is globally connected, excels in core functions, has a high absorptive capacity (this emphasizes that brokers must be involved in knowledge generation) and is a high self-monitor. It is argued here that actors who are endowed with these attributes are more likely to have access to structural holes and be accepted as brokers. In the following section, the study will theorize from innovation systems literature why the brokerage of information, knowledge and funding are important in the sector. Subsequently, a construction of the likely characteristics of brokers will be presented. This is followed by a review of the three groups enumerated above and a discussion on how these characteristics may apply to the emergence of brokers from the groups. The study will close with the summary, conclusion and recommendations for future research.

2. Proposed brokerage content

For innovations systems for small-scale agricultural activities to thrive, there must be interactions among support institutions, innovating units and the small-scale practitioners. Employing innovation systems literature, Adejuwon, Taiwo, and Ilori (2014) in a study of small-scale oil palm fruit processors in south western Nigeria argued that three levels of interactions may be required to take place among and within these groups of actors for the development and diffusion of appropriate innovations. These are interactions; (a) between innovating units and smallholders; (b) among and between innovating units dependent on science and technology and those that utilize experience or doing, utilizing and interacting (DUI) mode of learning and innovation and; (c) within and among all the groups of actors. Interactions between the innovating units and smallholders will ensure that needs of the latter are taken into consideration in the innovation process. These interactions may come in the order of use of innovation by the smallholders, feedback to the innovating unit(s) responsible for the innovation on its use and collaboration between the two groups (Lundvall 1985). This set of interactions facilitates knowledge flows that may ensure that innovations developed are appropriate and that competence (as a result of mutual learning by interacting in the two groups) grows and productivity of the smallholder increases. It also emphasizes the importance of funding adoption of innovations as this learning process cannot be achieved without the practitioners adopting innovations. The second set of interactions ensures that innovations embody science- and experienced-based knowledge. Innovation may be based on codified scientific and/or experienced-based knowledge. Jensen et al. (2007) reported that firms that adopted both forms of innovation were more successful than those that adopted just one form. This is even more important in rural based small-scale agriculture where certain customs, practices and skill sets that have been acquired over the years can contribute to innovation development and aid user friendliness and diffusion. The third set of interactions is systemic and ensures interactions within and among all the groups of actors in the system. It is necessary to make a distinction between knowledge and information at this point. While knowledge is the transfer and sharing of know-how through intensive, sustained and focused interactions (as typically in the first and second types of interactions above), information can be referred to as facts that may be transmitted through simple communication (Ahuja 2000). Systemic interactions will ensure that information flows among all groups. Lack of awareness of innovations is a reported cause of the dearth of adoption of innovations in SSA. This lack of awareness may also cause unnecessary duplication of research. Ahuja (2000) also emphasizes that information channels between research groups facilitates obtaining information on technical breakthroughs, fresh insights to problems and failed approaches. Information on how to access funds from various support institutions may also be lacking among these groups. Systemic interactions will also ensure that knowledge flows among institutions through platforms such as, postgraduate programmes, conferences, workshops, training programmes, research alliances and so on. Therefore, robust interactions among and within the three tiers may ensure the success of innovation activities.

3. Proposed characteristics of brokers for the sector

3.1. Constructively socially evaluated

Though Burt and Merluzzi (2013) emphasizes the role of status in locating actors in brokerage positions, Deephouse and Suchman (2008) noted that status, reputation and legitimacy share many antecedents, consequences, measures and processes. It is therefore important to examine the other measures as these concepts are intertwined and are a determinant of status.

3.1.1. Status

Washington and Zajac (2005) defined status as a socially constructed, inter-subjectively agreed-upon and accepted ordering or ranking of social actors based on the esteem or deference that each actor can claim by virtue of the actor's membership in a group with distinctive practices, values, traits, capacities or inherent worth. Deephouse and Suchman (2008) noted that status is categorical and specifically reflects position, segregation and rivalry in a group. They add that status generates cliques, esteem and privileges, is honorific, emphasizes cultural capital and deference in a profession. Washington and Zajac (2005) argue that individuals and organizations seek to enhance their social status by associating with actors of high status. The status of an actor may be measured by the number of people (who are themselves widely cited) that have cited the actor as a preferred contact relative to the people that could have cited the person – the expert to whom experts turn (Podolny 1993). Burt and Merluzzi (2013) noted that high status improves the likelihood that an actor will be a successful broker. They went further to state that high status indicates higher chances of engaging in brokerage activities and also dispel audience tensions about the broker's proposed roles. Burt (2005) argues that higher job ranks are associated with less routine work and more political, strategic and bureaucratic authority. He further argues that people in higher ranks are more likely to have access to structural holes, wield greater bureaucratic authority and are more likely to be successful at brokering connections across those holes. Burt (2005) further reported that people in senior ranks are more likely to be accepted as brokers. Burt and Merluzzi (2013) made a comparison between job rank and status in informal settings and argued that just as structural holes are embedded in formal organizations, they can also be found in informal settings. The authors also argued that just as brokerage across structural holes is easily facilitated in higher job ranks it can also be expedited by actors of high social standing in informal settings. High status therefore presupposes access to structural holes in an innovation system.

3.1.2. Legitimacy

Meyer and Scott (1983) describe organizational legitimacy as the degree of cultural support for an organization and argued that it implies the absence of questions about an organization's goals, means, resources and control systems. However, when questions arise, the legitimacy of the organization may be called to question. Some authors have used these questions to develop constructs of legitimacy. These questions may arise due to failure in meeting performance and mission targets (Meyer and Rowan 1977) and lack of conformity with social norms and formal laws (Weber 1978). From the perspective of gaining legitimacy, organizations may become socially responsible, that is, fulfilling some generic obligations to society such as donating to charities (Wood 1991). Suchman (1995) was however one of the first to offer one of the most widely employed definitions of legitimacy in literature. He defined legitimacy as a generalized perception or assumption that the actions of an entity are desirable, proper, or appropriate within some socially constructed system of norms, values, beliefs and definitions. He went further to propose three major dimensions of legitimacy namely; pragmatic, moral and cognitive legitimacy. Other constructs comprise professional legitimacy which refers to professional endorsement of an entity (Suchman 1995) and socio-political legitimacy (Rao 1994) which signifies endorsement by legal authorities, governmental bodies and other powerful organizations. We can surmise from the above that an actor is conferred with legitimacy if it is efficient in its core functions and its activities to achieve this is done in a socially responsible way and in conformity with laws, social norms, culture and practices. Deephouse and Suchman (2008) distinguish legitimacy from all other social evaluations by arguing that it is a taken-for-granted right to act and command within a particular sphere of activity. This taken-for-grantedness may encourage other organizations to associate with the focal actor so as to be seen as a legitimate entity. Deephouse and Suchman (2008) referred to this as legitimacy-enhancing inter-organizational relationships. Because of this, the focal actor may have relationships or ties with more actors than any other in the innovation system. The consequence of these endorsements and resulting inter-organizational ties is that the focal actor is put it in a brokerage position.

3.1.3. Reputation

Fombrun (1996) defines reputation as the net perceptions of a company's ability to meet the expectations of all its stakeholders. Deephouse and Suchman (2008) define it as a generalized expectation about a firm's future behaviour or performance based on collective perceptions of past behaviour or performance. Rather than categorization (status) and conformity (legitimacy), Deephouse and Suchman (2008) noted that reputation is measured on a continuum of best to worst along the dimension being quantified. Furthermore, the authors argue that reputation is rivalrous (increases at the expense of rival's) and differentiating.

Deephouse and Suchman (2008) implied that entry into the categorical distinctions in status hierarchies is a function of reputation and legitimacy. While status is a measure of deference of prominence in a social structure, it is also an indication of audience reactions or evaluations such as legitimacy and reputation. Therefore, high status actors are reputable – trustworthy in relation to past behaviour; and legitimate – pursue goals with conformity to laws and social norms and custom.

> Characteristic 1: Brokers must be constructively socially evaluated in terms of legitimacy, reputation and status.

3.2. High absorptive capacity

Cohen and Levinthal (1990) define absorptive capacity as the ability to recognize the value of new information, assimilate it, and apply it to commercial ends. The authors noted that it is a function of prior related knowledge generated through learning processes such as R&D, production of goods and services and technical training. Through the accumulated knowledge, the firm is able to recognize and assimilate new knowledge in order to be able to use it. The authors further argue that although a firm's absorptive capability is dependent on the absorptive capabilities of individuals in the firm it is however is not the sum total of individual absorptive capabilities. In order for the knowledge of these individuals to contribute to the absorptive capability of the firm it has to be exploited. This can only be made possible through communication flows between individuals and/or units in the firms. Cohen and Levinthal (1990) suggest the use of actors to facilitate flows between individuals and units and between the firm and the environment. The authors referred to these actors as *gatekeepers*. Among the various groups of actors in an innovation system, varied levels of absorptive capability may exist and in different spheres of knowledge. The more varied the knowledge among the groups, the more the capabilities for appropriate innovation. However, the more varied the knowledge, the more defined the boundaries between the groups. This makes knowledge exchange more difficult. In order to be able to translate the information for use between these groups of actors and between the firm and outside the innovation system, an actor with the capacity to assimilate these various forms of knowledge and translate it among the various groups is necessary. This implies that an actor who has high absorptive capacity is required. This high absorptive capacity which requires competence of the technologies appropriate to the innovation system must be accompanied by knowledge of the needs and problems of the sector. This requires some level of embeddedness of the broker in the sector especially as far as tacit knowledge is concerned. Nooteboom (2001) argues that tacit knowledge reduces absorptive capacity for the recipient of knowledge transfer. He notes that one's own tacit knowledge is taken-for-granted as self-evident and is difficult to replace by new knowledge on the basis of rational argument. Nooteboom (2001) argued that in this situation, the transfer of knowledge may only be facilitated by a trusted insider.

Characteristic 2: Brokers must possess high absorptive capacity.

3.3. High self-monitor

By being able to generate affective states and behaviours appropriate to specific situations, high self-monitors are able to relate to different kinds of people in different cliques (Snyder 1974). Oh and Kilduff (2008) noted that in contrast to low self-monitors, the prototypical high self-monitor is willing and able to change self-presentations to appeal to different social circles. This indicates that high self-monitors are likely to be in central positions in social networks because the acquaintances developed are less likely to be related to each other. Low self-monitors on the other hand are more likely to relate to people similar to themselves, thereby limiting their acquaintances to only those people. As the concept of homophily suggests, because similar people are likely to be acquainted, low self-monitors are not likely to be in brokerage positions. Mehra, Kilduff, and Brass (2001) reported high self-monitoring to be related to high performance among supervisors in selected high technology firms. On a firm level analysis, this finding can be related to the literature on the heterogeneity of Top Management Teams (TMTs). Hambrick and Mason (1984) argue that organizations are a reflection of their TMTs. A heterogeneous TMT will endow on a firm a breadth of perspective which is important for effective decision making. For example Hambrick, Seung Cho, and Chen (1996) reported that heterogeneity of TMT in terms of education, industry experience and function had a positive impact on the propensity and magnitude of competitive actions. In the same vein, this paper argues that TMT heterogeneity will have a significant impact on self-monitoring and opportunities for brokerage; that is, heterogeneity in TMT will bring breadth in the variety of actors the TMT is able to relate with.

Characteristic 3a: Brokers who are individuals must be high self-monitors.
Characteristic 3b: On an organizational level, the TMT of organizations to serve as brokers must be heterogeneous in terms of education, background, function and experience.

3.4. Globally connected

The proximity of firms in regional systems of innovation facilitates knowledge generation, transfer and exploitation. However, a lack of connectedness with actors outside the region may lead to recycling the same information and knowledge leading to technically inferior innovations (Kauffeld-Monz and Fritsch 2008) in relation to globally available technical opportunities. Therefore an actor with access to global knowledge may be may be in a position to diffuse globally sourced novel information and knowledge to actors in the regional innovation system. The authors however stipulate conditions for effective brokerage in such a situation. They contend that the broker, apart from been globally connected, must be connected with actors in the region, must hold high absorptive capacities in the relevant knowledge and must be able and willing to transfer such knowledge to the region.

Characteristic 4: Brokers must be globally connected.

3.5. Excels in core functions

Excellence in core functions or performance is essentially a fundamental antecedent or consequence of the aforementioned characteristics.

Characteristic 5: Brokers must excel in their core functions.

4. Characteristics of actors in innovation systems for small-scale agricultural activities in SSA

4.1. Smallholder practitioners

Dixon et al. (2004) described smallholders as those who often cultivate less than 1 ha of land where population densities are high, 10 ha or more in semi-arid areas, or manage up to 10 heads of livestock. Most smallholders usually have other sources of income apart from agricultural activities. Smallholders may also be categorized along the agricultural value chain, for example, processing capacity. An apt description may also be based on production methods which has an impact on volume of output. They may thus be described as those who make use of manual or semi-mechanised methods of production or use varied amounts of hired hands and family members in their operations depending on the level of production. The consumption patterns of the output of smallholders can also be used to categorize smallholders as they may consume a considerable amount of their output. Many studies have also categorized them by socio-demographic indices as being from the lowest income and educational levels and predominantly women.

4.2. Innovating units

Sumberg (2005) identifies three major actors in agricultural research in Africa; the National Agricultural Research Systems (NARS) maintained by African nation states with a national research focus; International Agricultural Research Centres (IARCs) with emphasis on trans-national, sub-regional or continental agricultural research mandates and lastly the Advanced Research Institutes (ARIs) which are located outside the region but engage in research activities relevant to African agriculture. Most of the research institutions in the NARS were inherited from former colonial powers and have since struggled to replace colonial manpower that manned the research institutions and fund research activities (Beintema and Stads 2004). An example of NARS in Nigeria is the National Institute for Oil Palm Research (NIFOR) which has the specific mandate to conduct research into the genetic improvement, production and processing of the oil palm fruit and other palms of economic importance (ARCN 2015). Like all research institutes in Nigeria, its activities are limited by inadequate funding. Between 1992 and 2003, an average of 12.08% of budgeted estimates was approved while 3.54% were actually released by the Nigerian government (PIND 2011). While funding from respective governments for the NARS research institutions has remained low across board (with a probable exception of South Africa) available literature reports that donor funding has been a major source of financial support for SSA research institutions in general (Beintema and Stads 2004). Most IARCs research institutions have however been funded by Consultative Group for International Agricultural Research (CGIAR). An example of this category is the IITA funded by CGIAR which has recorded laudable successes in the development and adoption of high-yielding drought and blight resistant cassava varieties in countries such as Nigeria, Ghana and Benin (Nweke 2005). Sumberg (2005) notes that the ARIS research institutions which are based in Europe and the USA (some are funded by the World Bank, e.g. CGIAR) provide training for agricultural researchers. In other instances they act as contract researchers and collaborators and run field-based programmes. As a whole, research in SSA is mostly done by public research institutions but that is not to say that private organizations, including individuals and especially NGOs are not involved in the research process either in the area of funding or core research. There are also actors that innovate using the experienced DUI mode of learning and innovation. This includes artisans who are involved in producing machines or tools used for production and/or post-harvest activities. These artisans usually learn by apprenticeship and are hardly involved in science-based enquiries.

4.3. Funding and policy support institutions

Zimmerman et al. (2009) noted that good agricultural strategies, programmes and policies are considered essential to launch small-scale agricultural activities in SSA and attract donor interest. Agricultural policy is the exclusive preserve of the governments in the SSA region. Due to the failure of liberalization policies in the 1980s and 1990s, the States still play a considerable role in the enhancement of small-scale agriculture in SSA. However, several factors may affect the impact of government policies in the region. Most importantly, the region possesses one of the weakest institutions for the proper development of small-scale agriculture. For example, Magnusson et al. (2012)

noted that the provision of a functioning healthcare and education systems and rural infrastructure are basic prerequisites for small-scale agricultural development. However, the region continues to lag behind in socio-economic indices. Coupled with this is the influence global agricultural policies may have on the local policy implementation. In addition, a considerable amount of funding and research expertise for small-scale agricultural development comes from outside the region. Therefore, the development of small-scale agriculture may depend on institutions from outside the region.

5. Discussion

The study proceeds to discuss the above characteristics with respect to the groups of actors delineated for the purpose of this study.

5.1. Small-scale practitioners

It may be expected that brokers from this group will be in the higher echelons of education and production volume. Literature on adoption relates higher educational levels with the early adoption of agro-based technologies. This is expected to bring about two major consequences; high production volume (due to technology adoption) and a better than average knowledge of production processes of both labour-intensive and contemporary modes of production. While the former may bring about positive evaluations of reputation for performance by group members, the latter enhances absorptive capacity by the opportunity to compare both methods of production. A combination of technology adoption and corresponding increases in productivity may bring about a reputation for being a good manager of resources, high financial performance and vision. Absorptive capacity which may be enhanced by higher levels of education and varied production processes may be useful in disseminating knowledge on the adoption of technologies. Success at encouraging colleagues to embrace novelty may earn this category of actors a label of advocate especially if these innovations work as stipulated for adoptees. Brokers from this group are expected to be granted legitimacy by conforming to local and customary laws and being a member of an in-group which may be family, clan, village or organization associated to the group/sub-group they represent in the network (Hofstede 1984; Adejuwon 2013). In Africa, status and legitimacy may also be related to age (as many customs and traditions dictate that elders are always deferred to) and/or higher educational qualifications as discussed above. It is also to be expected that success in core activities will have released the broker from the physical aspects of agricultural activities and has left that function to hired hands and/or other family members. This may allow the broker more freedom to engage in brokerage activities. These characteristics plus the advantage of being in a central position opens up opportunities for brokerage. Work processes and routines in the sector are hardly codified and therefore remain tacit. Nooteboom (2001) argues that tacit knowledge is the greatest obstacle to the adoption of innovations. He noted that tacit knowledge is self-evident and therefore not subject to critical reflection and debate. Nooteboom (2001) recommends that to overcome this impediment, insiders or colleagues who are sufficiently different to yield new perceptions and similar enough to make sense to the target audience may be used to change views.[1] Brokers of this group may thus serve as vessels of information on available innovations, their appropriateness in the sector and how they are used. They are also likely to be in a position to inform other small-holders on available funding opportunities since they are expected to be linked to modern information channels. Given that they are more likely to be more educated, they may be able to express feedback to actors in the innovating unit group in a more useful technical language. And because of their standing in the group, they may act as facilitators between funding institutions and the smallholders. Finally, brokers in this group are likely to be opinion leaders whose views may be sought after by policy-makers.

5.2. Innovating units

A major requirement of the innovating units is to attain the goals for which they were set up. This legitimizes the organization. To achieve this, it is necessary to have the required material and human resources necessary for the successful development and diffusion of agricultural innovations. The consequences of this are far reaching in terms of attaining brokerage positions in the innovation system. Having the required resources guarantees transformation into an expert of sorts in chosen fields. This may also attract the best man-power which may ensure a long-run of successes at innovation. Successful innovations signify knowledge of user needs and adequate feedback. In addition, the necessary enhancements of absorptive capacity; R&D and/or technical know-how are ensured. The straggling situation of agro-technological progress in SSA also requires a unit with global connections to transfer modern and different strands of technology to the region. Therefore, a unit with links to global sources of knowledge and high absorptive capacity may be required. This may be facilitated by having one of the best pools of researchers and/or technicians in the field which a unit's reputation is able to attract. It is also important that the actor is not linked to controversial solutions which may tarnish the image of the innovating unit and cause it to lose legitimacy. For example, Mon-santo, a publicly traded American multi-national agrochemical and agricultural biotech-nology corporation has been linked to suicides by farmers in India and law suits in Canada, the USA and Brazil (Common Dreams, 27 March 2013). Both legitimacy and reputation for being good at core functions may enable the organization attain a status which may draw other innovating units to want to affiliate with it. A varied pool of members of TMT may also ensure the versatility required of high self-monitor-firm in dealing with varied groups of researchers, technicians, funding institutions and research areas. All these attributes may attract alliances to the unit because of accumulated exper-tise, thereby stimulating the unit to take up a leading and more bureaucratic role in learn-ing and innovation activities. Being at the centre of innovation activities may afford an innovating unit brokerage opportunities. For example, due to being connected to more research institutes than its peers, an institute may be privileged to more information about on-going research activities in the group. This may present the actor with the oppor-tunity to prevent duplication of research and facilitate collaborations between actors. The ability to solicit and acquire funds also signifies embeddedness with the funding group which may enable the actor facilitate interactions between peers and the funding group and disseminate information on available funding opportunities. For these aforemen-tioned reasons, the actor may be a facilitator of interactions among its peers, smallholders and the funding group and a source of best (research/funding) practices among network members.

5.3. Funding and policy support group

A major requirement of to-be brokers from this group is the ability to raise funds. As can be drawn from the above analysis, this ability can infuse in the actor the capability to influence policy in agriculture as funding conditions may be tied to preferred policy directions especially in SSA. The basic measure of performance in this group may then be achieving success in enhancing the productivity and socio-economic indices of practitioners through innovative funding procedures and successfully influencing national and regional policy documents on agriculture. The former may be measured in terms of returns to contributions or the amount of additional income made by the smallholder relative to the amount of contributions received. Performance in this regard may encourage donors to contribute to actors in this group as positive returns to contributions are assured. This may result in a large pool of funds for the focal actor of this group. It is also important that the actor is not linked to controversy as donors may delegitimize the actor by publicly disassociating from it. This will starve the actor of funds and thereby influence. Furthermore, since most funding may come from outside the region, an actor with links with foreign donor institutions may be required. In this group only one actor may stand out in this regard; The World Bank. In terms of status, the World Bank may be what Deephouse and Suchman (2008) referred to as a one real-world instantiation; that *is an organization that is virtually a population unto itself and incommensurable with other organizations in its domain*. The institution has not only been instrumental in raising funds for economic development in developing countries, it has also been involved in various programmes for improving sustainability of small-scale agricultural activities in SSA through institutions such as CGIAR, International Food Policy Research Institute (IFPRI) and FAO. It may be assumed that the World Bank may be a broker of brokers. However other actors may act as brokers in the regional system of innovation for small-scale agricultural activities. Furthermore, while the World Bank may retain its legitimacy when it departs from legitimate actions, other actors may not be so immune.

Figure 1 shows a summary of characteristics of brokers that may be used as a checklist for appointing brokers and the possibilities of interactions in the sector.

6. Summary and conclusion

The crux of this study was to proffer characteristics of likely brokers for innovation systems for small-scale agricultural activities in SSA. The objective of policy instruments projected from this study will be to fast-track the emergence of brokers in the sector. The characteristics enumerated above are by no means exhaustive but they may serve as a platform for selecting brokers in policy documents. For example, there are other types of social evaluation such as integrity, credibility and accountability.

The main essence of the innovation systems framework is that cohesiveness of networks brings about successful innovations. Diffusion of innovations denotes success of innovation activities. This enhances competence of actors in the innovation system as feedback from users to producers enriches interactive learning opportunities (Lundvall 1985). Rent-seeking brokers whose core function is brokerage may seek to maintain system fragmentation so as to remain relevant in the scheme of things. Non-profit organizations whose core function is brokerage may also be inadequate as they may lack the

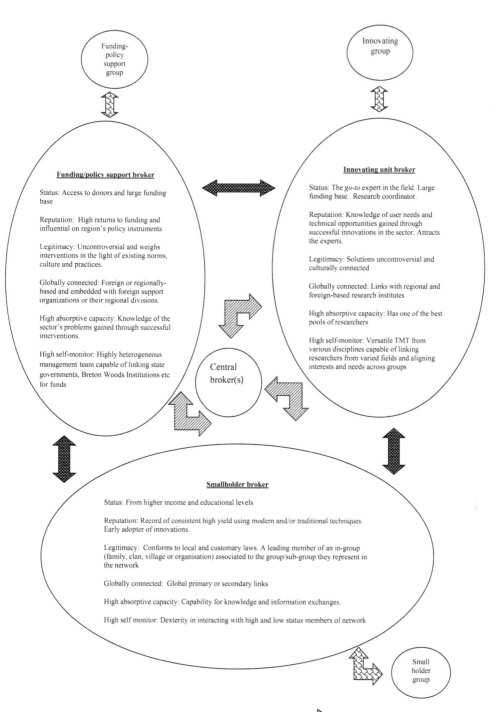

Figure 1. Summary of characteristics of brokers. Key: ⬡⬡⬡⬡⬡⬡⬡➤ Brokerage activities within the broker's own group. ◼◼◼◼◼◼◼➤ Brokerage between groups. ▨▨▨▨▨▨➤ Brokerage activities among all the groups in the sector.

characteristics above. This will limit their access to structural holes, brokerage opportunities and thus success at brokerage activities. Embedded brokers may be necessary for this type of innovation system where resources to pay brokers are scarce. It is also important that brokers be part of the knowledge creation process. Not only does this instil the necessary social evaluations in the broker, it may also alleviate tensions which may arise from trust issues in sharing knowledge. The number of brokers for the sector will however be dependent on the structure of the network on a national and regional basis, the area of focus and objectives.

7. Directions for future research

Future research may operationalize these proposals by identifying the central actors in agricultural innovation systems. Measures of these characteristics will be positively related to number of structural holes the actor may have access to. Structural holes or opportunities to broker are usually measured by the number of actors in the network that are indirectly linked by the broker (e.g. Oh and Kilduff 2008). Status of an actor may be assessed by the number of people that have cited the actor as a preferred contact relative to the number of people that could have cited the person (Podolny 1993), rank or position in an organization and socio-cultural standing in society, for example, age, educational qualifications and alumni. For institutions, specialized rankings such as QS World ranking for universities, European research rankings for research institutions and the Devex list for donor institutions may be used. Legitimacy may be measured by the Janis–Fadner coefficient (Janis and Fadner 1965) of media endorsement which measures the relative proportions of endorsing and challenging comments in a relevant periodical for an organization (e.g. Adejuwon 2013). This can also be measured by number of regulatory enforcement actions (Deephouse 1996). Reputation may be measured by quality of research output, financial performance, extent of diffusion of innovations, vision, leadership and workplace and social responsibility. Absorptive capacity can be measured by R&D intensity and expenditure, responsiveness to learning, human capital, skill level, patents, publications, knowledge of production processes, ability to commercialize new knowledge, experience and level of output (Duchek 2013). Self-monitoring for individuals is measured by the 25-item scale developed by Snyder (1974). Diversity in TMT can be measured by education, industry experience and function (Hambrick, Seung Cho, and Chen 1996). Global connections may be measured by the number of links the actor has outside the national innovation system. Performance in core functions can be measured in terms of sales, production output or productivity on the part of the practitioners. Performance of innovating units may be measured by the diffusion of innovations developed (this implies success of innovation efforts, evidence of interaction with end-users and an understanding of user needs), number of patents and publications. In the case of support institutions, amount of funds raised and returns on funding may be used as benchmarks. The above indicators are by no means exhaustive and are merely suggestions of how the concepts may be measured. In addition, measurement of the concepts may depend on the context of the research to be carried out.

This study is not only limited by a field study but also the involvement of actors along the value chain of small-scale agricultural activities. Signals and feedback on product quality from consumers may determine innovation trajectories. For example large-scale processors of agricultural products may be interested in improving the quality of output of the practitioners and therefore act as brokers between the farmers and knowledge infrastructure and funding facilitators. Future studies may relate the characteristics developed in this study with this class of actors.

Note

1. This program was labelled 'Knowledge bearers in small and medium sized businesses' (KIM) in the Netherlands. It involved training individuals in novel processes and inserting them in SMEs to change perceptions towards innovations (Nooteboom 2001).

Acknowledgment

The author wishes to thank the two anonymous reviewers for their helpful and insightful comments on previous drafts.

Disclosure statement

No potential conflict of interest was reported by the author.

References

Adejuwon, O. O. 2013. "Sources of Organizational Legitimacy in the Nigerian Telecommunications Industry." *African Journal of Business and Economic Research* 8 (2&3): 49–81.

Adejuwon, O. O. 2016. "Building Innovation Systems for Small-Scale Agricultural Activities in sub-Saharan Africa: Key Success Factors." In *Handbook of Research on Driving Competitive Advantage through Sustainable, Lean, and Disruptive Innovation*, edited by X. Wu, A. Koronios, Y. Shou, and L. Al-Hakim, 276–304. Hershey, PA: IGI.

Adejuwon, O. O., K. A. Taiwo, and M. O. Ilori. 2014. "Promoting Technology Adoption in Small Scale Oil Palm Fruit Processing Sector in Southwestern Nigeria: An Innovation Systems Approach." *African Journal of Science, Technology, Innovation and Development* 6 (2): 75–92.

Ahuja, G. 2000. "Collaboration Networks, Structural Holes and Innovation: A Longitudinal Study." *Administrative Science Quarterly* 45 (3): 425–455.

ARCN. 2015. *NIFOR Mandate*. Agricultural Research Council of Nigeria. Accessed January 14, 2015. http://www.arcnigeria.org.

Beintema, N. M., and Gert-Jan Stads. 2004. "Investing in Sub-Saharan African Agricultural Research: Recent Trends." Paper presented at conference on Assuring Food and Nutrition Security in Africa by 2020: Prioritizing Actions, Strengthening Actors and Facilitating Partnerships, The International Food Policy Research Institute, Washington DC, USA, April 1-3.

Burt, R. S. 1980. "Models of Network Structure." *Annual Review of Sociology* 6: 79–141.

Burt, R. S. 1992. *Structural Holes*. Cambridge, MA: Harvard University Press.

Burt, R. S. 2005. *Brokerage and Closure*. Oxford: Oxford University Press.

Burt, R. S. 2007. "Second-hand Brokerage: Evidence on the Importance of Local Structure for Managers, Bankers and Analysts." *Academy of Management Journal* 30 (1): 110–148.

Burt, R. S., and J. Merluzzi. 2013. "Embedded Brokerage: Hubs Versus Locals." In *Research in the Sociology of Organizations*, edited S. P. Borgatti, D. J. Brass, D. S. Halgin, G. Labianca, and A. Mehra. Cambridge, MA: Emerald Group.

Cohen, W., and D. Levinthal. 1990. "Absorptive Capacity: A New Perspective on Learning and Innovation." *Administrative Science Quarterly* 35 (1): 128–152. Special Issue: Technology, Organizations, and Innovation.

Common Dreams. 2013. "Monsanto and the Seeds of Suicide." Accessed July 6, 2015. www. commondreams.org.

Deephouse, D. L. 1996. "Does Isomorphism Legitimate?" *Academy of Management Journal* 39 (4): 1024–1039.

Deephouse, D., and M. Suchman. 2008. "Legitimacy in Organizational Institutionalism." In *The Sage Handbook of Organizational Institutionalism*, edited by C. Greenwood, R. Oliver, K. Suddaby, and K. Sahlin-Anderson, 49–77. Thousand Oaks, CA: Sage.

Dixon, J., K. Taniguchi, H. Wattenbach, and A. Tanyeri-Arbur. 2004. "Smallholders, Globalization and Policy Analysis." Agricultural Management, Marketing and Finance Service (AGSF) Occasional Paper 5, Food and Agriculture Organization of the United Nations, Rome.

Duchek, S. 2013. "Capturing Absorptive Capacity: A Critical Review and Future Prospects." *SBR* 65: 312–327.

FAO (Food and Agriculture Organisation). 2012. *The State of Food and Agriculture, 2010 - 2011. Women in Agriculture: Closing the Gender Gap for Development.* Rome: FAO, United Nations.

FAO (Food and Agriculture Organisation). 2013. *Facing the Challenges of Climate Change and Food Security: The Role of Research, Extension and Communication for Development. Occasional Papers on Innovation in Family Farming.* Rome: FAO, United Nations.

FAO (Food and Agriculture Organisation). 2014. *The State of Food and Agriculture: Innovation in Family Farming.* Rome: FAO, United Nations.

Fombrun, C. J. 1996. *Reputation: Realizing Value from the Corporate Image.* Cambridge, MA: Harvard Business School Press.

Freeman, C. 1987. *Technology Policy and Economic Performance: Lessons from Japan.* London: Pinter.

Gould, R. V., and R. M. Fernandez. 1989. "Structures of Mediation: A Formal Approach to Brokerage in Transaction Networks." *Sociological Methodology* 19: 89–126.

Granovetter, M. S. 1973. "The Strength of Weak Ties." *American Journal of Sociology* 78 (6): 1360–1380.

Hambrick, D. C., and P. A. Mason. 1984. "Upper Echelon: The Organization as a Reflection of its Top Managers." *Academy of Management Review* 9: 193–206.

Hambrick, D., T. Seung Cho, and Ming-Jer Chen. 1996. "The Influence of Top Management Team Heterogeneity on Firm's Competitive Moves." *Administrative Science Quarterly* 41 (4): 659–684.

Hargadon, A. B. 1998. "Firms as Knowledge Brokers: Lessons in Pursuing Continuous Innovation." *California Management Review* 40 (3): 209–227.

Hofstede, G. 1984. "The Cultural Relativity of the Quality of Life Concept." *The Academy of Management Review* 7 (1): 81–94.

Janis, I. L., and R. Fadner. 1965. "The Coefficient of Imbalance." In *Language of Politics*, edited by H. D Lasswell, N. Leites, I. L. Janis, R. Fadner, A. Kaplan, J. M. Goldsen, A. Grey, et al., 153–169. Cambridge, MA: MIT Press.

Jensen, M. B., B. Johnson, E. Lorenz, and B.-Å. Lundvall. 2007. "Forms of Knowledge and Modes of Innovation." *Research Policy* 36 (5): 680–693.

Kauffeld-Monz, M., and M. Fritsch. 2008. "Who are the Brokers in Regional Innovation Systems of Innovation? A Multi-Actor Network Analysis." Jena Economic Research Papers, No 089.

Klerkx, L., R. Alvarez, and R. Campusano. 2014. "The Emergence and Functioning of Innovation Intermediaries in Maturing Innovation Systems: The Case of Chile." *Innovation and Development* 5 (1): 73–91.

Klerkx, L., A. Hall, and C. Leeuwis. 2009. "Strengthening Agricultural Innovation Capacity: Are Innovation Brokers the Answer?" United Nations University Working Paper Series No 2009 – 019.

Lundvall, B.-Å. 1985. "Product Innovation and User-Producer Interaction." Industrial Development Research Series No. 31. Aalborg: Aalborg University Press.

Lundvall, B.-Å. 2007. "Innovation System Research: Where it Came from and where it Might Go." GLOBELICS Working Paper Series no. 2007-01, Global Network for Economics of Learning, Innovation, and Competence Building Systems.

Lundvall B.-Å., and S. Borrás. 1997. "The Globalizing Learning Economy: Implications for Innovation Policy." Report Based on Contributions from Seven Projects under the Program for Research and Technological Development (TSER) Programme DG XII, Commission of the European Union.

Magnusson, U., A. Djurfeldt, T. Håkansson, M. Hårsmar, J. MacDermott, G. Nyberg, M. Stenstrom, K. Vrede, E. Wredle, and J. Bengtsson. 2012. "Critical Research Issues for Future Sub-Saharan African Agriculture." Published by SLU, Framtidenslantbruk/Future Agriculture.

Marsden, P. V. 1982. "Brokerage Behavior in Restricted Exchange Networks." In *Social Structure and Network Analysis*, edited by P. V. Marsden and Nan Lin, 201–218. Beverly Hills, CA: Sage.

Mehra, A., M. Kilduff, and D. Brass. 2001. "The Social Networks of High and Low-Self Monitors: Implications for Workplace Performance." *Administrative Science Quarterly* 46 (1): 121–146.

Meyer, J. W., and B. Rowan. 1977. "Institutionalized Organizations: Formal Structure as Myth and Ceremony." *The American Journal of Sociology* 83 (2): 340–363.

Meyer, J. W., and W. R. Scott. 1983. "Centralization and the Legitimacy Problems of Local Government." In *Organizational Environments: Ritual and Rationality*, edited by J. W. Meyer and W. R. Scott, 199–215. Beverly Hills, CA: Sage.

Nooteboom, B. 2001. *"Problems and Solutions in the Transfer of Knowledge to Small Firms."* Paper presented at the conference of co-operation networks and institutions on regional innovation systems at max Planck Institute, Jena, February 8–10.

Nweke, F. I. 2005. "A Review of Cassava in Africa with Country Case Studies on Nigeria, Ghana, the United Republic of Tanzania, Uganda and Benin." Proceedings of the Validation Forum on the Global Cassava Development Strategy, Vol. 2, 66 pp.

Oh, H., and M. Kilduff. 2008. "The Ripple Effect of Personality on Social Structure: Self-monitoring Origins of Network Brokerage." *Journal of Applied Psychology* 93 (5): 1155–1164.

PIND (Foundation for Partnership Initiatives in the Niger Delta). 2011. "A Report on Palm Oil Value Chain Analysis in the Niger Delta." Abuja: PIND.

Podolny, J. M. 1993. "A Status-based Model of Market Competition." *American Journal of Sociology* 98: 829–872.

Rao, H. 1994. "The Social Construction of Reputation: Certification Contests, Legitimation, and the Survival of Organizations in the American Automobile Industry: 1895–1912." *Strategic Management Journal* 15: 29–44. Special Issue: Competitive Organisational Behaviour.

Snyder, M. 1974. "The Self-monitoring of Expressive Behaviour." *Journal of Personality and Social Psychology* 30: 526–537.

Spring, A. 2009. "African Women in the Entrepreneurial Landscape: Reconsidering the Formal and Informal Sectors." *Journal of African Business* 10: 11–30.

Suchman, M. C. 1995. "Managing Legitimacy: Strategic and Institutional Approaches." *Academy of Management Review* 20: 571–610.

Sumberg, J. 2005. "Systems of Innovation Theory and the Changing Architecture of Agricultural Research in Africa." *Food Policy* 30 (1): 21–41.

Swaans, K., B. Boogaard, R. Bendapudi, H. Taye, S. Hendrickx, and L. Klerkx. 2014. "Operationalizing Inclusive Innovation: Lessons from Innovation Platforms in Livestock Value Chains in India and Mozambique." *Innovation and Development* 4 (2): 239–257.

Washington, M., and E. Zajac. 2005. "Status Evolution and Competition: Theory and Evidence." *The Academy of Management Journal* 48 (2): 282–296.

Weber, M. 1978. *Economy and Society.* Berkeley: University of California Press.

Weiss, R. S., and E. Jacobson. 1955. "A Method for the Analysis of the Structure of Complex Organizations." *American Sociological Review* 20: 661–668.

Wood, D. J. 1991. "Corporate Social Performance Revisited." *Academy of Management Review* 16: 691–718.

World Bank. 2012. *Agricultural Innovation Systems: An Investment Source Handbook.* Washington, DC: World Bank.

Zimmermann, R., M. Brüntrup, S., Kolavalli, and K. Flaherty. 2009. *Agricultural Policies in Sub-Saharan Africa: Understanding CAADP and APRM Policy Processes.* Bonn: German Development Institute.

Technology transfer and agricultural mechanization in Tanzania: institutional adjustments to accommodate emerging economy innovations

Andrew Agyei-Holmes

ABSTRACT

Recent economic growth in Tanzania has been biased towards industry and services, denying farmers potential distributional benefits. Correcting this anomaly requires in part appropriate technologies to raise agricultural productivity. Attempts to either develop local tools or import advanced country technologies had limited benefits. Recent studies suggest that for poor producers in Tanzania, mechanization technologies from emerging economies are more appropriate in relation to their production characteristics. However, being locked-in advanced country technologies means both market and non-market institutions responsible for mechanization technology transfer in Tanzania have evolved to suite machines from the EU, Japan and USA. To accommodate the new market dynamic, where attention is shifting to emerging economies, modifications to the current technology transfer infrastructure are required. Using firm, farm and government level data on importation, distribution, usage and maintenance of tractors in Tanzania, this paper argues that the potential benefits of emerging economy tractors can be greatly enhanced if calculated attempts are made to modify the existing technology transfer and diffusion process.

1. Agricultural technology and poverty in Tanzania

Tanzania recorded an impressive economic growth performance in the noughties, averaging 7% per annum but failed to reduce poverty (NBS 2009). Nearly 40% of the population were considered poor in the same period (NBS 2007). The main explanation offered for this growth-poverty mismatch is that a greater proportion of the progress observed occurred in sectors engaged in by the rich, rather than the poor (Hoogeveen and Ruhinduka 2009; Mkenda, Luvanda, and Ruhinduka 2009). The growth favoured trade and industry; thus although nearly 75% of Tanzania's poor are engaged in agriculture, its growth rate stagnated around 4% (NBS 2007). The consensus is to focus on agriculture as a viable response mechanism to the growth and poverty reduction challenge (Sarris, Savastano, and Christiaensen 2006; Fan, Nestorova, and Olofinbiyi 2010). Admittedly, transforming the agricultural sector into a viable growth pathway requires appropriate mechanization technologies to augment other inputs (Fonteh 2010; Biggs, Justice, and Lewis 2011).

Technological progress and innovation is acknowledged as an important determinant of productivity and growth (Solow 1956). This relationship is well recognized by Tanzanian economic agents and has influenced agricultural policy in diverse ways. For instance, within Tanzania's African Socialism Policy in the 1960s, agricultural mechanization was given prominence. Similarly, the *Kilimo Kwanza* (Agriculture First) Policy in 2009 of agricultural transformation gave significant attention to mechanization. Recognizing the role of technology is necessary, but not sufficient for promoting growth. The selection from a given set of technologies and successfully diffusing them on farms is crucial and places a huge responsibility on the national innovations system.

It is therefore not surprising that successive Tanzanian governments have either facilitated the development of local techniques or the importation of technologies from abroad. First, underpinned by appropriate technology movement principles (Schumacher 1973), projects were undertaken to develop intermediate technologies to fit the Tanzanian context (Carr 1985). Generally supported by acts of charity and without sound understanding of the market these intermediate technologies (mainly small tractors) failed to create the anticipated paradigms (Kaplinsky 1990). Second, collaboration with foreign firms to manufacture farm machinery locally were also unsuccessful (Simalenga 1989). Finally, fuelled by the notion that machines from advanced countries were efficient, the technological gaps created by these failed local efforts were to be filled by importation of farm machinery from advanced countries. With time, it became clear that this conception of efficiency associated with advanced country machines was flawed – they were in fact associated with undesirable social and environmental effects embedded in high cost and labour displacement (ILO 1973; Kaplinsky 1990). Thus after several decades of reliance on advanced country power tillers and tractors, Tanzania succeeded in mechanizing only 13% of all farm lands by 2010 (Lyimo 2011).

Recent developments in the world order of technology generation and usage have opened up new opportunities and widened the choice alternatives for Tanzanians with respect to mechanization technologies. Whilst in the 1970s a mere one-fiftieth of global R&D expenditure were located in developing countries, in the 2000s the figure stood at one-fifth, thanks to China and India (Clark et al. 2009). Several decades of investment in education, training and capital goods sectors in China and India have helped them develop science and technology capabilities for innovation. The characteristics of the emerging economy markets have triggered the development of low cost capital goods (Clark et al. 2009) including tractors and power tillers. Because the nature of these markets are comparable to other developing countries in Sub-Saharan Africa (SSA) like Tanzania, it was anticipated and in fact have been shown that they will produce appropriate technologies that are suitable for production skills, technological capabilities and purchasing power in other low income countries. (Clark et al. 2009). It is therefore not surprising that of all the small tractors used on Tanzanian farms only 5% had Chinese and Indian origin in 2001 but by 2012 the figure had risen to 70% – a clear indication that capital goods from the emerging economies are filling an age old gap (Agyei-Holmes 2014).

Despite these changing paradigms of the source of tractors being imported into Tanzania and current empirical evidence which supports their appropriateness, the technology transfer process has not changed significantly to suite them. Since no two technologies are the same the soft and physical infrastructure developed for the transfer process from the producing country and diffusion within the recipient country might have to necessarily vary to accommodate these differences. Several decades of Tanzania's dependence on advanced country technologies suggests that the framework for technology transfer and diffusion have evolved based on the characteristics of those technologies. As we shall see, emerging economy mechanization technologies differ significantly from the advance country ones – thus relying on the old ways used to import and diffuse advance country machines might not yield the desired results. The actors involved in the technology transfer process in the old order would have developed code of ethics, strategies, set of tacit knowledge and standards over the years to accommodate the characteristics of advanced country mechanization technologies and might be applying same to the new market evolving with emerging economy technologies. In this paper we establish whether these old methods are useful for the new paradigm. If they are not what modifications are needed to enhance an efficient and effective transfer and diffusion of emerging economy tillage techniques? As a precursor to addressing these two research questions, we examine the briefly the distinctiveness of emerging economy tractors and power tillers from the advance country ones.

We situate these discussions within three strands of literature: Technological Choice and Appropriate Technology; Below the Radar Innovations (BRI) and International Technology Transfer (ITT). Current interpretations of the appropriate technology literature suggest that for a technology to be appropriate for the poor, it must combine both Schumacher and Schumpeter tenets (Kaplinsky 2011). This assertion implicitly assumes that once technology is low cost and small scale (Schumacher) in an environment where effective demand exists with numerous entrepreneurs (Schumpeter), then diffusion will occur naturally. The expectation is that since BRI which conforms with the Schumacher and Schumpeter principles are being produced in China and India, other developing countries should naturally benefit. The point of departure of our present paper from the foregoing arguments derives from the importance of absorptive capacity and social capability within any national innovations system in ensuring successful ITT regardless of the nature of technology. We therefore argue that although BRIs could be beneficial to other developing countries, existing technology transfer frameworks present in those developing economies prior to the introduction of the BRIs could inhibit their success.

The rest of the paper is organized into four sections. Section 2 reviews relevant literature. In Section 3 we present a conceptual framework and the data used. In Section 4 an attempt is made to address the two research questions. Section 5 concludes.

2. Technical choice and technology transfer in a changing world order

In any production process including agricultural mechanization, there are infinite possibilities of technically combining labour and capital to produce an output (Farrell 1957; Sen 1968). However, engineering limitations do not allow the attainment of all technically possible combinations of labour and capital (Eckaus 1955). Economically optimal technique choice is therefore constrained by a set of limited engineering production functions (Clark 1985). Depending on the prices of labour and capital in the society under consideration an economically optimal choice of technique can be made with the view of minimizing total cost. Based on market size in which the production process is undertaken, there are also scale considerations to be made (Kaplinsky 1990). Furthermore, the characteristics of consumers affect the quality of products to be produced. Historically, the production technologies were concentrated in advanced countries where capital is relatively abundant. This narrowed the range of economically efficient technologies for labour abundant developing countries (Stewart 1977; Emmanuel 1982).

Stewart (1977) argued that technological development has been such that it creates inappropriate techniques, and leaves underdeveloped and undeveloped the techniques which suites conditions in poor countries. To address the technological needs of relatively poorer households and countries for production and consumption, the appropriate technology movements in the 1970s and 1980s promoted intermediate technologies that were low cost and smaller in scale to meet the infrastructure and skill circumstances of the poor. These movements were generally based on acts of charity. The tenets of the appropriate technology movements led by Schumacher were based on the idea that growth, poverty reduction and distribution in low income countries will be greatly enhanced if producers had access to labour-intensive technologies which were small in scale, and if they produced products which were low cost and accessible to low income consumers (Kaplinsky 2009).

However, the absence of entrepreneurship in low income countries, inadequate skill sets to develop innovation and the lack of effective demand which are the main tenets of capitalism (Schumpeter 1939) made the ideas of the appropriate technology supported by Schumacher very difficult to implement. Producers and consumers in low income countries had unfilled needs, but they lacked what it takes to meet these needs. However, as noted earlier some of these limitations of the appropriate technology movement are being removed, especially in China and India. Entrepreneurship in these two economies have become vibrant, skill sets have improved, incomes and effective demand are also rising as a result of high growth. These changes are enhancing technical change that produces BRI which might go un-noticed. However, because these BRIs combine the tenets of both Schumacher (low cost, intermediate scale) and Schumpeter (capitalism, market driven, effective demand) tenets it provides opportunity for technical change in other developing countries by circumventing the need to use charity as the main engine of technology transfer.

Technology transfer can be described as a broad set of processes covering flows of equipment, know-how and experience between various types of actors (Lema and Lema 2012). Since BRIs are located outside Tanzania their transfer will involve cross border arrangements which constitutes ITT. ITT is a comprehensive term covering mechanisms for shifting information across borders and its effective diffusion into recipient economies. Thus, it refers to numerous complex processes, ranging from innovation and international marketing of technology to its absorption and imitation (Maskus 2004). ITT can be a market-based transaction between unrelated parties or through a non-market mediated approach (Kim 1991). Regardless of the mode of transfer employed the success of the process depends on the absorptive capacity of the recipient country (Mowery and Oxley 1995). The recipient country's ability to recognize new technological opportunities and to capture and integrate new knowledge into the country or firm processes with the aim of increasing competitive advantage is its absorptive capacity (Lane, Salk, and Lyles 2001). For these processes to succeed an effective national innovations system is required. The concept of national innovation systems rests on the premise that efficient linkages among the actors involved in innovation is key to improving technology and innovation performance.

The innovative performance of a country depends to a large extent on how actors within the economy relate to each other as elements of a collective system of knowledge creation and use, as well as the technologies they use (OECD 1997). Which in many ways imply that there should be effective cooperation amongst actors and technologies – and this relationship should not be one-sized fits all. As argued by Abramovitz, the success of the national innovations system to encourage growth depends on the level of social capability. A country's potential for rapid growth is strong when it is technologically backward but socially advanced (Abramovitz 1995). This suggests that the existence of BRI innovations in China and India does not guarantee agricultural development in Tanzania. The Tanzanian society must be adequately prepared to receive the technologies for the anticipated benefits to be achieved – a matter our present study seeks to contribute to. The extent to which agricultural mechanization technology value chains are ready to accommodate new knowledge from emerging economies requires investigation if policy direction is to be influenced positively.

For instance, when Nakandala, Turpin, and Djeflat (2015) investigated technology and management strategies of firms in the rubber products and garments industries in Sri Lanka using the national innovations systems approach, they concluded that firms have heterogeneous capabilities for innovations. And thus for an efficient national innovation system, they proposed a pluralistic policy framework which addresses the needs of each of the participants. Our present study supports this assertion, although in a different light. That is because of the heterogeneity in the characteristics of the technologies which are sourced from advanced countries and emerging economies, we might not be wrong to suggest that policies within the national innovation system to facilitate technology transfer in developing countries should be pluralistic if all sources of technology are to be accommodated.

And in fact rightly so, Walz and Delgado (2012) demonstrate that because there are clear differences between China and India in terms of the importance of electric utilities, they each followed a different form of national innovations system policy to develop their now vibrant wind turbine Industries. Whilst China's achievements were driven by government support, the Indian success story was induced by free markets. They conclude that there is not one successful way of developing the wind turbine industry and that different countries might have to follow different paths. Similarly, we argue that large scale rich farmers in Tanzania sourcing advanced country tractors from the EU, Japan and the USA are in many ways different from small scale capital constrained farmers who source their tractors from India and China. Thus policies to help these two categories of farms to acquire mechanization technologies should be shaped differently within the national innovations system.

It is therefore not surprising that although China was a dominant producer and exporter of considerable solar photovoltaic cells (PV), it was not until 2009 that we saw significant diffusion of the same technology in China (Fischer 2012). Fisher shows that there were barriers related to technology, policy and politics that hindered solar PV use before 2009 and these underlining factors had to be modified to change the status quo. This suggests that a policy environment can prevent an appropriate technology from getting diffused if no effort is made to ensure otherwise.

Additionally, a recent empirical study which examined the diffusion of power tillers demonstrate that the country's innovation system for imported mechanization technologies is deficient and draws attention to some of the social capability and absorptive capacity gaps. They found that at the time of introduction of power tillers, know-how for their use and maintenance existed was limited. Spare parts markets functioned poorly, increasing the travel time required for accessing spare parts several folds. Market failure was also common place and the writers called for policies that will encourage scaling up training for participants in the value chain – a matter which our present study contributes to by expanding the discussions on how the training programmes can be implemented.

3. Conceptual framework and data sources

3.1. Value chains and technology transfer

Farmers in Tanzania can either invest in indigenous technologies (hand hoe or oxen plough) or invest in mechanized technology (power tillers and tractors). Indigenous technologies have proven to be *inefficient*.[1] The output per labour hour, all things being equal improves as one moves from the use of hand hoe, through oxen plough to tractors (and power tillers). If soil structure were conducive, then the 'progressive' farmer might naturally move from the use of hand hoes and oxen ploughs to the use of power tillers and tractors for tillage (Mrema, Baker, and Kaha 2008). Thus the farmer can choose[2] a power tiller or tractor from an advanced country (Matured Market) hereafter, MM or an Emerging Economy hereafter, EE

The choice of an MM or EE have varying implications on employment, output, incomes and capability building of value chain actors[3] (Stewart 1977; Ruttan 2001). That is for any two sources of technologies with varying characteristics, they impact differently on participants in the value chain – thus requiring different strategies at each point in the chain to enhance efficiency and prevent market failure. Figure 1 shows the main types of tillage technologies available to the Tanzanian farmer. Route A on the diagram represents indigenous technologies which are excluded from the present analyses. The paper concentrates on Route B. Under Route B, there is a choice C, to be made between tractors and power tillers with MM or EE origins. There are also actors, D comprising of users (farmers and operators), financial institutions (intermediaries), dealers (importers and distributers) and service providers (spare parts sellers, repairers and local fabricators). Finally, there is government F (in the form of regulation, extension and policy provision), participating to ensure overall efficiency of the system. Each of the actors in the system plays a different role and these roles, depending on the choice made affects the nature of the role to be played and the outcomes so derived, E.

(1) *Dealers (importers and distributors)* import and distribute technologies within the country to sales agents and sometimes directly to farmers. The machines they import are dictated by what manufacturers have on offer, signals from users and their own financial situation. The dealers may borrow from financial institutions to finance the imports or use their own capital.

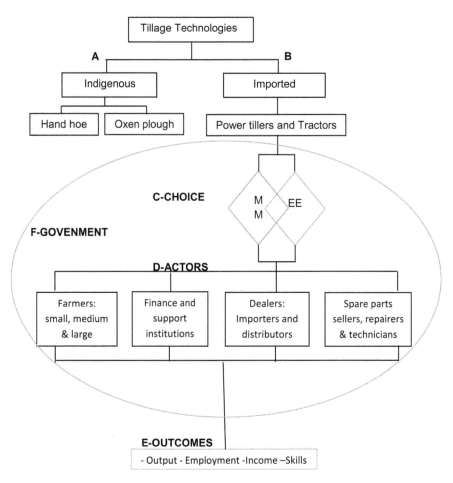

Figure 1. Farm power technology transfer and diffusion in Tanzania.
Source: Agyei-Holmes 2014.

(2) *Farmers* (users) purchase imported machines for tillage. They may borrow from financial institutions. to finance their investments. Large scale farmers sometimes buy their own tractors from abroad, without the help of importers.

(3) Service providers like *repairers* and *spare parts sellers* also work in close collaboration with users and dealers. They provide parts for replacement and also provide regular maintenance and repair when machines break down.

(4) *Banking and finance* institutions provide dealers, users, service providers and government the right financial instruments for purchases and administration of subsidies.

(5) *Government* through its institutions and agents offers a policy framework within which all actors operate. Regulatory, information services provision, taxation, subsidies and standards inspection are the main roles played by the government. Education, training and expertise building through extension activities and traditional school systems are also led by government.

3.2. Data sources and summaries

To address our research questions, we relied on field data collected on value chain actors described in Section 3.1. A mixed method approach was used. First, five field observations were undertaken during the farming season to study the machines whilst in use and examine them for overheating, stress resistance, vibration, noise and fumes released. Second, six focus group discussions and fifteen key informant interviews were carried out with major participants in the value chain. The focus group discussions included people who hire power tillers and tractors, extension and mechanization officers, mechanic apprentices, repairers and women groups. District chief executives, district administrators, extension officers, educational Institution heads, mechanization instructors, spare parts vendors and finance experts across the regions in Tanzania were our main key informants. Third, 225 surveys were conducted with owners of tractors from both MM and EE. For triangulation purposes and to understand the technology transfer process and the supply of spare parts, importers and distributors were interviewed. The main findings from the data sources are compiled for power tillers and tractors from the MM and EE sources (See Table 1).

In general, both tractors and power tillers of MM origin are more durable and more efficient compared with the EE ones. However, whilst MM tractors have averagely higher horsepower, we observe the reverse for power tillers. Similarly, it costs more to buy and operate MM power tillers than the EE ones. On the contrary, although MM tractors are more expensive to procure, the operational costs for EE ones are significantly higher. Additionally, for both tractors and power tillers, it is more difficult to find a repairer for MM machines than EE ones. The travel cost involved in accessing spare parts for power tillers is relatively higher for MM ones. For large tractors, the opposite is true. In terms of employment, power tillers from the EE are more viable than the MM ones and vice versa for tractors. Generally, MM machines are more capital intensive. In terms of profitability, we observe that the MM ones do better when it comes to tractors but fails to do same for power tillers. On the whole MM machines are more environmentally and user friendly than EE ones.

4. Defining and addressing the gaps between the old and new order

As demonstrated in Section 3, there are five major agents along the value chain of mechanization technology transfer in Tanzania. We discuss each of these in turn highlighting some of the challenges posed by the plethora of existing strategies to the effective transfer and diffusion of emerging economy machines. Here we address the two research questions concurrently. That is under each of the five actors we first examine the status quo and lay them side-by-side with the relevant characteristic of the new technology to see if the way in which that particular actor is currently playing its role is useful or otherwise. In instances where they are not, we offer some suggestions for change. Let us begin with dealers.

4.1. Dealers: importers and distributors

There are over 40 companies engaged in the importation and distribution of agricultural machinery in Tanzania.[4] The head offices of these firms are concentrated in Dar es Salaam with a few scattered in regional capitals like Arusha (an important trading and agricultural

Table 1. Differences between MM and EE farm mechanization technologies.

Characteristic differences	Power tillers		Tractors	
	MM	EE	MM	EE
Basic engineering differences				
Horsepower	13.00	15.50	73.00	60.00
Economic life	9.50	3.50	9.00	5.40
Man hours spent per acre (hours)	2.65	3.50	2.00	2.67
Acquisition and operational costs				
Replacement cost (000000TSH[a])	14.50	7.00	62.50	35.00
Cost of repairs per season (000000TSH)	0.50	0.30	5.20	5.80
Cost of spares per season (000000TSH)	0.60	0.35	2.80	5.10
Travel distance for repairs (km)	2.00	0.80	29.60	8.20
Travel distance for purchases (km)	329.00	273.00	252.00	171.00
Warranty (years)	2.00	1.00	3.00	1.00
Contribution to growth				
Acres ploughed per day	3.00	2.40	7.50	6.00
Employment per time (count)	1.00	1.80	2.00	2.00
Total employment in last season (hours)	187.00	200.00	315.00	252.00
Capacity utilization (%)	67.50	40.50	30.00	25.00
Physical ratios and productivity				
Physical ratios (K/L)	0.09	0.04	0.10	0.06
BCR	0.11	0.25	−0.40	−1.13
Pollution and ergonomic indicators[b]				
Vibration	3.06	4.13	2.78	3.02
Noise	2.89	4.27	3.08	3.23
Smoke	2.47	4.00	3.07	3.22
Observations (N)	36	50	36	51

Source: Agyei-Holmes (2014).
Notes: [a]TSH = Tanzanian Shillings; [b]1-lowest; 2-very low; 3-low; 4-neutral; 5-high; 6-very high; 7-highest.

centre); Morogoro (singled out as the grain basket of the country) and; Tanga (home to many cash crop farmers). Generally, older firms focus on MM machines with large scale farmers as their target market whilst the newer firms concentrate EM machines targeting capital constrained farmers.

Data generated from key informant interviews and cross-validation with farmers suggest four important characteristics of the old order of technology transfer with regards to dealership. These include: (a) the nature of machines imported and the extent to which the manufacturers understand the local context; (b) effectiveness of distribution networks and after sales service; (c) supply of spare parts and; (d) one-off importation of a unique brand. We shall discuss these in turn.

First, the question of whether manufacturers of EE tractors understand the characteristics of Tanzanian soils and that a one-sized fit all type of tractor may not be appropriate for all regions is key. Whist soils in the Dodoma region are lighter and easily accommodate tractors from India and China, no matter how low quality the materials used for their fabrication may be, the same cannot be said for soils in the Morogoro Region (Agyei-Holmes 2014). A fact which EE importers must relay back to manufacturers in China and India and if possible bring in their experts to take soil samples for analyses. MM dealers need not worry about this issue because manufacturers from the EU and Japan have subjected their machines for testing and modification to suite almost all soils in SSA. In addition, MM machines as demonstrated in are strong and durable (Table 1) – thus can withstand many soil terrains. So although importers took this feature of tractors for granted in the past, they can no longer do so under the new era of EE machines. As noted by an extension officer:

> ... Chinese machines can't be treated in the old capital goods sense ... they are fragile and care should be taken in terms of where it can be used. I have had a Japanese power tiller for nearly 12 years. Some friends acquired Chinese tillers less than three years ago and they are already damaged under similar soil conditions (Key informant interview with an extension officer in Mbeya 2012)

Second let us consider the distribution networks of the firms responsible for transferring the tractors from source countries into Tanzania. It is a requirement by the Tanzanian regulatory framework for all licensed importers to have a minimum number of distribution agents to facilitate after sales services (Focus group discussion with tractor testing engineers in Arusha, 2012). However, such infrastructure is poorly developed. Dealers argue that it is difficult to comply with this requirement because of the paucity of effective demand. In the words of one dealer:

> ... the highest number of tractors and power tillers I have sold in a year is 60, coming to an average of 2 per region across Tanzania. Imagine I had a sales and service centre in those regions, it would be impossible to finance the housing, labour and taxes associated with it. That is why we ask the owners and users to give us a call when there is a problem; then we can dispatch technicians in a day or two to handle it for them (Key informant interview with a marketing and sales manager of a tractor importing company in Dar es Salaam, 2012).

Although the position of this dealer with MM tractors orientation sounds logical, the actual factor underpinning this posture has to do with the fact that many of their clients are large scale farms which can afford to have their own in-house mechanics, a luxury which small scale farmers cannot afford. The downside to this issue is that newer firms which are importing EE machines seem to be following a similar trend, a situation which must be nipped in the bud if the poor producers who are being targeted for mechanization are to benefit. The second part of the above quotation suggests that upon a phone call a dealer will respond immediately to a farmer. Field evidence suggest otherwise. Sometimes it takes several weeks for the dealer to respond, causing tillage delays. And in fact one of the main foundations for switching from hand hoes to tractors is to make field operations timeous. Thus such delays put the poor farmer's investment in jeopardy. To ensure that the farmer derives maximum benefits from the EE machines, this ought to change. One of the ways through which this problem could be addressed is division of labour by firms spatially. Firms should consider dividing the country into mechanization zones and mandate the strongest firms within particular geographical areas to develop and operate service centres in the corresponding zones. To ensure that their service is universal their mechanics should be given basic training in the repair of other tractor brands that are found in their zone so that if a farmer in their zone has a problem but his or her original supplier is in another zone, they could be given some basic help whilst they wait for permanent support.

Third is the issue of spare parts and how well importers and distributors are supporting the user to get access to them. At the national level every tractor imported for agricultural purposes has both VAT and import duty waived at the time of this research. In addition, for every tractor import a 10% worth of spare parts (in relation to the value of the tractor) can also be brought in without VAT and import duty. Some dealers stop importing more spare parts after this first freight of tax free spare parts even if the farmers who bought the tractors need them. Whilst it is not out of reach for large scale farmers demanding MM machines to place an order on their own for spare parts from the manufacturing company abroad, small and medium scale farmers relying on EE machines have limited capacity to do so. How do we ensure that the poor farmer is not left in a limbo because dealers refused to import spare parts? To start with, we must be made aware that the main reason why government subsidies on spare parts is not perpetual is because of the practice where some businessmen and women undertake to import spare parts specifically for the agricultural sector, enjoy the tax reliefs but yet use those imports for other industries aside from the agricultural sector (Agyei-Holmes 2014).

Consensus gathered from the field engagement with experts suggest that the tax relief could be maintained for continuous importation of spare parts. However, to ensure that there is close monitoring so as to deliver them to farms, the Tanga Port of Tanzania which is relatively less busy compared with the Dar es Salem Port should be used for clearing agricultural machinery and spare parts. In addition, a specific team of the internal revenue service established to follow-up on these spare parts once they enter the country should also be attached to the Tanga Port. This will ensure close monitoring to prevent the spare parts from falling into the hands of the construction industry, for example. There were other key informants who were of the view that, subsidies on tractor spare parts should be completely removed and importers tasked to bring in sufficient stocks as and when farmers need them.

Fourth it is also important to note that there have been instances where dealers who are new entrants in the business come in, import a very unfamiliar brand from the EE and after a year or two disappear from the scene. This leaves farmers who bought such tractors without any support for spares, service or technical advice. For the old order this was not a huge problem since in many instances one could interchange some spare parts across brands and so if one was not available another could be relied upon. To forestall such occurrences specific attempts should be made by the Mechanisation Department of the Ministry of Agriculture and Food Security. Incorporating into the terms of reference when issuing licenses for importers to some regulations concerning steps to be taken before folding-up so that farmers do not suffer unduly will be critical. Once again this has not been a constraint for MM users by their nature, since they have enough capital to scout around the world for such services and spare parts if the dealer fails to provide.

4.2. Service providers: spare parts dealers and repairers

When warranty offered by importers and distributors expires local mechanics and spare parts dealers undertake repairs and maintenance. Many of these repairers are more familiar with MM machines and now beginning to pick up techniques for dealing with EE ones. Because the EE machines breakdown often sometimes their owners misconstrued that the repairers are inefficient. This situation requires regular fora in farming communities to ensure that farmers and repairers have a common understanding of the strengths and weaknesses of the EE machines. Repairer–user conflicts can be reduced if not totally avoided through such a forum. That said the conception that capital goods breakdown less often as the old order of MM had it must be discarded completely or modified so that more mechanics can be trained to address the scale of breakdowns associated with EEs.

Another confusion associated with EE machines but not MM ones is the prevalence of fake spare parts. Until the advent of the EE machines, experts in the field suggest that fake spare parts were not very common. The main challenge is the numerous nature of firms in China and India and the difficulty associated with identifying culprits for appropriate sanctions application. This matter can be curtailed by tighter border controls to ensure that inferior spare parts do not enter Tanzania.

4.3. Intermediaries: finance and support institutions

The sources of capital for purchasing and maintaining farm machinery by the farmer are mainly savings from their farm business and non-farm businesses, loans from family members and sometimes friends. These modes of finance are informal. Some farmers also obtain loans without interest from traders who sell the equipment. Other groups of farmers finance the procurement of their equipment from formal loans obtained from commercial or development banks. These loans may come with intermediaries such as cooperative societies, district assemblies, input support trust funds and special private agricultural support units (See Agyei-Holmes 2014).

The main challenge faced by EE machine buyers is the fact that although their purchasing cost is much lower than MM machines, the qualifying conditions which allows them to obtain credit facilities from financial institutions do not vary to accommodate the price differences. There is a basic requirement by banks for a prospective farmer who wants credit to buy a power tiller to have at least 10 acres of land as a collateral. At the same time the price of an MM power tiller can be as high as three times that of the EE. To ensure fairness and inclusion, this collateral must be proportional to the price of the machine and not a flat rate across board – an adjustment in the value chain required to ease the burden of the poor and smoothen the technology transfer process.

Furthermore, although studies have shown that some EE power tillers are more profitable than MM ones, some financial institutions do not finance their purchases (See Table 1). A similar observation was made in the Mbeya Region where a cooperative society sourcing funds for its members to buy power tillers totally eliminated the possibility for members who wanted EE ones to do so. In an interview with the secretary of the group this is what he had to say:

> … before we agreed to contract loans for our members we tasked a committee to dig into the merits of the two families of machines and they reported to us that the MM ones are better (Key informant interview with a farmer cooperative group secretary in Mbeya, 2012)

These issues need calculated attention to ensure that equal opportunity is given to people who cannot afford the MM machines to source the EE ones if there is room to do so. With the new evidence presented in Table 1, banks and cooperatives should be encouraged to give prospective owners the opportunity to acquire EE machines.

4.4. Users: farmers and machine operators

There are significant differences between the two sets of technologies which require differentiated user approaches to ensure that maximum benefits are derived. First, the notion associated with advanced country tractors and power tillers that capital goods lasts a long period of time should be disregarded. Capital goods are in a sense being converted into variable inputs in the EE sense. That is whilst an average tractor and power tiller from an MM source may be used for 9.5 and 9 years respectively; users of EE machines should condition their minds at the onset that their tractors will last an average of 5 years and their power tillers 3 years. This expectation management does not only put the owner of EE machines at ease but also reinforces the point that within this limited period of time the necessary attention and care should be taken to recoup the investment. MM users might have the luxury of time but EE ones do not.

Second strategies around the purchase of equipment from EE sources must be spot on in terms of timing. With a shorter lifespan, stocks of new EE machines should be taken just before the start of the season. As has been the case for many users there have been instances when the transaction procedures associated with procurement of new machinery has taken so long that they only receive them after the growing season. In such instances capital is locked up for a period of about 10 months. At the same time if the equipment is purchased through a credit facility the financial institution will be demanding monthly instalments. This is particularly a big challenge for EE users who are mostly capital constrained and have a shorter period to pay back loans. When a machine is left idle for a year, the cost implications on one which has a lifespan of 12 years is likely to be less than another which has a lifespan of 3 years.

Third, the robustness of MM machines suggests that even if they are used by inexperienced operators or by operators who are not careful enough, the machine will still be intact. However, because EE machines are fragile, if the operator is careless the farmer might not realize his returns on investment before the machine is scrapped. To ensure this balance, owners of EE machines should insist operators receive the requisite training before handing over the machines to them. Such a training might come at a cost, but cannot be compared with the challenge to be borne if a new tractor or power tiller is destroyed by an incompetent operator.

EE machines are noisy and can damaging the ear. They generate thick smoke and can affect the lungs of users. They also vibrate a lot and can have negative impact on the spine of users especially for power tillers. EE power tillers also overheats easily and creates discomfort for the user. Because of these limitations of EE machines users (operators) must use protective clothing to prevent the likely occupational hazards which are not common place for MM machines.

4.5. Government: policy makers, testing officers and training centres

As a regulator government maintains standards and manage subsidies. Another minor role government institutions play is training and information dissemination. We shall take these in turn and identify the gaps for the new market.

Government testing office for tractors is in Arusha. It has a staff strength of five engineers and other auxiliary staff. All five of these testing officers were trained in Japan at a time when many of the tractors in Tanzania came from MM sources. However, with Chinese and Indian machines becoming popular in Tanzania efforts to understand those markets by training some experts in those countries can be valuable.

Stricter enforcement of standards and information flow between the testing office and potential buyers needs improvement. Current standards testing regimes for imported tractors do not mandate importers to test their machines. Quality problems which face MM machines are minimal compared with EE ones. So although we can afford to overlook this issue for the MM machines, a similar position will not help the EE wave. Changes to this status quo is required to ensure that specifications in machine manuals present the true quality of equipment. Since EE machines fragile, farmers should know the exact quality of what they are buy to prevent surprises during usage. One of the ways to make information about machine quality available to prospective buyers is to give copies of test results on new models of tractors to district mechanization officers for onward distribution to farmers.

Recent proposals to develop a mechanization policy for Tanzania could be a vehicle for addressing regulatory gaps. The policy could be used as a tool for setting quality benchmarks. These bench marks must however be considerate of the fact that demand for higher engineering quality will come with machine price increases. The standards should be moderate, recognizing many users are capital constrained and any benchmark which eliminates EE machines could inhibit access. The development of an accurate benchmarking regime will require strong collaboration amongst officers at the Mechanisation Department, Testing Officers, Project Managers of Financial Institutions, Dealers and Manufacturers (if possible), and Farmer Group Leadership to ensure that the interests of all agents are catered for.

It is also important to flag the point that the two main mechanization training centres visited in Moshi and Morogoro during field work suggest that a greater proportion of the tractors and power tillers being used to train prospective mechanics and operators are advanced country ones. Thus overlooking the fact that the new paradigm is one which should concentrate on emerging economy machines as they are becoming more popular. This matter can be addressed through the administration of the two institutions by electing to procure both MM and EE machines in future when they plan renewing stocks.

5. Conclusion and policy implications

This paper supports the argument that power tillers and tractors from EEs considered to be BRIs have the potential to promote agricultural growth in Tanzania (Clark et al. 2009; Agyei-Holmes 2014). The paper finds that the EEs are in diverse ways different from MM machines and so a modified technology transfer system is required. We thus add to the BRI literature by noting that without the right technology transfer framework and innovation system, their potential benefits could elude Tanzania and in fact other countries in SSA. A positive response to this call will be to pay particular attention to the national innovation systems within which this technology transfer is taking place. Clearly all actors within the chain have absorptive capacity challenges (Lane, Salk, and Lyles 2001) and social capability deficits (Abramovitz 1995) which requires modifications for improvement. The study therefore suggest some considerations for policy.

First, at the importer level dealers must recognize that EE machines are not one-sized fits all and so a lot of consideration should be made to ensure that the right quality of machines is supplied to farmers with the appropriate soil types. The distribution of EE machines should not end at the sales point – distributors must continue to supply spare parts and repair services to users; since unlike MM users, EE users do not have their own resources to cater for these activities. Some of these desirable industry practices must be weaved into the certification process which allows dealers to import tractors so they take them as mandatory. An annual review of dealer performance in relation to the set criteria before renewal of certification to do business could go a long way to help.

Second, with regards to fake spare parts which have become the order of the day since the advent of the EEs, it might serve a good purpose for unannounced visits to warehouses of spare parts importers by appropriate authorities. Stocks which have not been sanctioned by the standards board could be seized to serve as a deterrent to other actors who might be planning to do same – of course these are not novel ideas but if taken seriously we could flush out some of the counterfeit spare parts dealers to save unsuspecting farmers from the ordeal of throwing money down the drain. After all our original objective was to encourage growth and not to take money out of the pocket of farmers. Third, financial institutions must also be encouraged to take the case of small tractors from EEs seriously, since our study shows that they are more profitable than the MM ones. In addition, valuation of requisite collaterals that qualify farmers to borrow for the acquisition of farm machinery requires some parity. The relatively low cost of EE machines must go into the equation. Less should be required of EE buyers since EE tractors are relatively cheaper and consequently reduces the risk of lending all things being equal.

Fourth, at the user level operator training is critical. EE machines are fragile and so at best they should be handled by more experienced operators. If EE machines are to live their full lifespan and provide the anticipated benefits thereof, first time users and inexperienced operators must only be allowed to use them with great caution. Finally, with these new EE technologies coming on board, it is important that the skill sets possessed by government institutions and agents should be tailored to accommodate them. For example, machine testing officers who are locked-in into MM technologies should be given the opportunity to upgrade their knowledge on the EE ones also. Educational institutions should certainly modify their training courses and develop models which deals with the peculiar nature of EE machines. Since many SSA countries have similar socio-economic conditions as Tanzania, they could also draw on some of these suggestions as they attempt to develop their own absorptive capacity and social capability for the transfer and diffusion of EE technologies.

Notes

1. For example, it takes an average man 12 days of 5 hours of intensive work to plough 1 acre with a hand hoe. For the same parcel of land, it takes a pair of oxen with two operators two days of 5 hours' work each. When a power tiller is employed for the same assignment, it takes an average of 3.5 hours with one man. The average tractor ploughs an acre within an hour with one operator (Key informant interview with a mechanisation officer in Tanzania, 2012).
2. Assuming that under our present objective of improving productivity, hand hoe and oxen ploughs are not promising enough.
3. In the same vein the intersection of MM and EE which represents machines which combine characteristics of the two sources will also have varying impacts on output, income, employment and skills.
4. Field interviews with mechanisation experts in Dar es Salaam, 2012

Acknowledgments

I thank the Editors, two anonymous reviewers, Raphael Kaplinsky, Rebecca Hanlin, Joseph Kizulwa, Richmond Atta-Ankomah, David Botchie, George Owusu, Mike Morris, Jacob Salisu, Felix Temu and Jenny Wright. I also acknowledge financial support from The Open University, University of Ghana and Mzumbe University.

Disclosure statement

No potential conflict of interest was reported by the author.

References

Abramovitz, M. 1995. "The Elements of Social Capability." In *Social Capability and Long-Term Economic Growth*, edited by D. Perkins, and B. H. Koo, 19–47. New York: St. Martin's Press.

Agyei-Holmes, A. 2014. "Tilling the Soil in Tanzania: What Do Emerging Economies Have to Offer?" Unpublished PhD thesis, the Open University, Milton Keynes, United Kingdom.

Biggs, S., S. Justice, and D. Lewis. 2011. "Patterns of Rural Mechanisation, Energy and Employment in South Asia: Reopening the Debate." *Economic and Political Weekly* 46 (9). https://www.researchgate.net/publication/50371681_Patterns_of_Rural_Mechanization_Energy_and_Employment_in_South_Asia_Reopening_the_Debate.

Carr, M. 1985. *The AT Reader: Theory and Practice in Appropriate Technology*. Bath: The Pitman Press.

Clark, N. 1985. *The Political Economy of Science and Technology*. Oxford: Basil Blackwell.

Clark, N., J. Chataway, R. Hanlin, D. Kale, R. Kaplinsky, L. Muraguri, and W. Wamae. 2009. "Below the Radar: What Does the Asian Driver Economies: Have to Offer Low Income Economies." Innogen Working Paper No. 69, January.

Eckaus, R. S. 1955. "The Factor Proportions Problem in Underdeveloped Areas." *American Economic Review* 45 (4): 539–565.

Emmanuel, A. 1982. *Appropriate Technology and Underdevelopment*. Chichester: J. Wiley.

Fan, S., B. Nestorova, and T. Olofinbiyi. 2010. "China's Agricultural and Rural Development: Implications for Africa." China-DAC Study Group on Agriculture, Food Security and Rural Development, Bamako, April 27–28.

Farrell, M. J. 1957. "The Measurement of Productive Effiency." *Journal of the Royal Statistical Society* 120 (3): 253–290.

Fischer, D. 2012. "Challenges of low Carbon Technology Diffusion: Insights from Shifts in China's Photovoltaic Industry Development." *Innovation and Development* 2 (1): 131–146.

Fonteh, F. M. 2010. *Agricultural Mechanisation in Mali and Ghana: Strategies, Experiences and Lessons for Sustained Impacts*. Rome: Food and Agricultural Organisation of the United Nations.

Hoogeveen, J., and R. Ruhinduka. 2009. "Lost in Transition? Income and Poverty Reduction in Tanzania Since 2001." Background paper to the Tanzanian Population and Human Development Report 2009, Dar es Salaam.

ILO. 1973. *Mechanization and Employment in Agriculture: Case Studies from Four Continents*. Geneva: International Labour Organisation.

Kaplinsky, R. 1990. *The Economics of Small: Appropriate Technology in a Changing World*. Washington, DC: IT publications.

Kaplinsky, R. 2009. "Schumacher Meets Schumpeter: Appropriate Technology Below The Radar." IKD Working Paper No. 54.

Kaplinsky, R. 2011. "Bottom of The Pyramid Innovation and Pro-Poor Growth." IKD Working Paper No. 62, November.

Kim, L. 1991. "Pros and Cons of International Technology Transfer: A Developing Country's View." In *Technology Transfer in International Business*, edited by T. Agmon, and M. A. von Glinow, 223–239. Oxford: Oxford University Press.

Lane, P., J. E. Salk, and M. Lyles. 2001. "Absorptive Capacity, Learning and Performance in International Joint Ventures." *Strategic Management Journal* 22: 1139–1161.

Lema, R., and A. Lema. 2012. "Technology Transfer? The Rise of China and India in Green Technology Sectors." *Innovation and Development* 2 (1): 23–44.

Lyimo, M. 2011. "Country presentation on Agricultural Mechanisation in Tanzania." Saint Louis: Senegal. Presentation to Workshop on "Boosting agricultural mechanisation in rice-based systems in sub-Saharan Africa".

Maskus, K. E. 2004. "Encouraging International Technology Transfer." UNCTAD-ICTSD Project on IPRs and Sustainable Development, Issue Paper No. 7, UNCTAD-ICTSD.

Mkenda, A., E. Luvanda, and R. Ruhinduka. 2009. *Growth and Distribution in Tanzania: Recent Experience and Lessons.* Dar es Salaam: Interim report to REPOA.

Mowery, D., and J. E. Oxley. 1995. "Inward Technology Transfer and Competitiveness: The Role of National Innovations System." *Cambridge Journal of Economics* 19: 67–93.

Mrema, G. C., D. Baker, and D. Kaha. 2008. *Agricultural Mechanization in Africa: Time for Action.* Vienna, Austria: FAO.

Nakandala, D., T. Turpin, and A. Djeflat. 2015. "Parallel Innovation Policies to Support Firms with Heterogeneous Innovation Capabilities in Developing Economies." *Innovation and Development* 5 (1): 131–145.

NBS. 2007. *LFS 2006, Analytical Report.* Dar es Salaam: National Bureau of Statistics.

NBS. 2009. *Household Budget Survey 2007.* Dar es Salaam: National Bureau of Statistics.

OECD. 1997. *National Innovation Systems.* Paris: Organisation For Economic Co-Operation And Development.

Ruttan, V. W. 2001. *Technology, Growth and Development: An Induced Innovation Perspective.* Oxford: Oxford University Press.

Sarris, A., S. Savastano, and L. Christiaensen. 2006. "The Role of Agriculture in Reducing Poverty in Tanzania: A Household Perspective from Rural Kilimanjaro and Ruvuma." FAO Commodity and Trade Policy Research Working Paper No. 19.

Schumpeter, J. A. 1939. *Business Cycles.* New York: McGraw Hill.

Schumacher, F. 1973. *Small is Beautiful.* London: Blond and Briggs.

Sen, A. K. 1968. *The Choice of Techniques.* 3rd ed. Oxford: Blackwell.

Simalenga, T. E. 1989. "Simulation model to Predict Field Work Days and its Use in Machinery Selection under Tropical Conditions." Unpublished PhD thesis, Copenhagen: Institute of Agricultural Engineering, Royal Veterinary and Agricultural University.

Solow, R. M. 1956. "A Contribution to the Theory of Economic Growth." *The Quarterly Journal of Economics* 70 (1): 65–94.

Stewart, F. 1977. *Technology and Underdevelopment.* Hong Kong: The MacMillan Press.

Walz, R., and J. N. Delgado. 2012. "Different Routes to Technology Acquisition and Innovation System Building?" *China's and India's Wind Turbine Industries, Innovation and Development* 2 (1): 87–109.

Absorptive capacity and product innovation: new evidence from Nigeria

M. G. Ukpabio, A. D. Adeyeye and O. B. Oluwatope

ABSTRACT

This paper assesses the influence of absorptive capacity (AC) on firms' product innovation by relying on pooled cross-sectional data from innovation surveys among Nigerian manufacturing and service firms. The study employs variables such as educational qualification, technology acquisition, intramural R&D and collaboration as proxies for measuring AC. Using the ordinal logit model, our result shows that higher educational qualification is the determinant of product innovation among manufacturing firms while collaboration with knowledge institutions, the determinant among service firms. In addition, the impact of R&D investments on product innovation becomes significant among manufacturing firms when moderated with age. We can thus infer that high-level skilled workers and external collaboration increase the likelihood of introducing new-to-market product innovations among manufacturing and service firms respectively by enhancing the AC of firms. Similarly, R&D investment can only have impact on the ability to introduce new-to-market product innovations as firms mature with age. Since the factors of AC driving the two sectors differ, there is therefore no one-cap-fit-all solution. Hence, there is the need for sector-specific policies that will enhance firms' competences and capabilities and drive national competitiveness. These include state interventions through government policy instruments in areas such as education, training, intellectual property and funding among others. Careful consideration should however be made in introducing these interventions in order to avoid government failure.

1. Introduction

In today's increasing competitive business environment, the need for firms to develop their capability to stay innovative cannot be over emphasized. Innovation is not only important for firms but also has tremendous impact on the overall economy as it enhances national competitiveness and productivity (Muzart 1999; Coad and Rao 2008). While the ability of firms to internalize and utilize external knowledge in its innovation process has been shown to be influenced by its internal capabilities, its application in developing country context has been limited.

The capabilities to create new products or services are likely to result from the acquisition, assimilation and exploitation of new knowledge. These are generally referred to as 'absorptive capacity' (AC) after the work of Cohen and Levinthal (1990). Hence, the degree of novelty – firm, market or world – of firms' innovation is dependent on the level of its AC. In this paper, we measure firms' innovativeness using the product innovation introduced by firms at two levels: firm and market. AC, however, is measured using percentage of staff with a minimum of Bachelor's degree, expenditure on intramural R&D, and technology acquisition, and firms' level of collaboration with external actors (Cohen and Levinthal 1989; Lane, Koka, and Pathak 2006). This study also assessed the influence of AC on the level of innovativeness of firms. The study relies on data from two rounds of innovation surveys covering both manufacturing and service sectors of the Nigerian economy. This presents an opportunity to understand the nature and influence of AC on firms' innovativeness within the Nigerian context, of which exists, to our understanding, little empirical evidence.

In assessing firms' innovativeness, we limit the study to product innovation. We are aware that other types of innovation are also important in firms' overall strategy for growth and competitiveness; however, a firm's competitive advantage depends on its ability to continually develop product solutions that meet the changing needs of the consumer. Also, when firms introduce innovations, the overall objective is meeting their corporate objectives through the introduction of new products or services. Based on the foregoing, we asked questions critical to the understanding of innovation performance in developing countries. These include: Will the degree of novelty of innovation of firms be determined by the level of education of its employees? Does firms' openness to exploitation of external knowledge influence its level of innovativeness? Is there a difference in product innovation in manufacturing and service firms arising from their absorptive capacities?

An important contribution to literature from this study is the analysis of the effect of some moderating variables on firms' AC in developing country context. It has been argued in literature that R&D investment only may not guarantee innovation success unless the roles of certain variables such as age, size, sources of external knowledge and market reach among others are recognized (Hannan 1998; Zahra, Keil, and Maula 2005; Aw, Roberts, and Xu 2009; Criscuolo, Haskel, and Slaughter 2010). For example, previous relationship with market actors such as suppliers, creditors and customers puts older firms in a better position to exploit external knowledge sources for innovation; an advantage that newer firms lack (Hannan 1998; Zahra, Keil, and Maula 2005). Using R&D investment, a widely adopted proxy of AC, we provide empirical evidence of the moderation effect of intervening variables such as age, external collaboration and firms' export capability on the relationship between R&D investments and product innovation.

Our paper proceeds as follows. In Section 2, we review the literature and theoretical frameworks guiding the field of AC and firms' innovation performance. In Section 3, we discuss our methodology and measures and in Section 4, we present and discuss the results. The paper ends with conclusion and some recommendations for policy in Section 5.

1.1. Analytical background: on AC

Knowledge has remained an important resource from which firms' growth can be significantly enhanced through the creative combination of knowledge resources and dynamic managerial capabilities (Spender 1996; Grant 2000; Liao, Fei, and Chen 2007). The resource base view (RBV) emphasizes the importance of organizational knowledge, amongst other characteristics, as the determinant of the variation in the performances of firms (Easterby-Smith, Marjorie, and Tsang 2008). In the RBV, knowledge is seen as the asset stock that underlies firm-level resources, competences and capabilities as well as the basis for competitive advantage in firms (Barney 1991; Leonard-Barton 1992; Hamel and Prahalad 1994; Teece 1998). Knowledge in its key dimensions as postulated by Ambrosini, Bowman, and Collier (2009) includes tacit to explicit knowledge, individual to collective knowledge and architectural to component knowledge. The ability of mangers of firms to understand the key dimensions of knowledge that exist within and outside the firm determines the extent to which firms gain competitive advantage. Drucker in 1965 proposed that knowledge will replace equipment, capital, materials and labour to become the key element in production and two decades after he opined that knowledge resources would be a key determinant of competitive advantage (Drucker 1993). More so, swift changes in business environment has reduced the duration of core competitiveness and as such, firms can only maintain their competitive advantage and innovate by recognizing, acquiring and utilizing knowledge from within and outside the firm (Liao et al. 2010). Thus, the dynamic ability by firms to do this has been subsumed by scholars under the concept of AC (hereafter referred to as AC). The concept of AC has gained significant attention in recent times as knowledge acquisition, assimilation and utilization becomes important for firms growth and survival (Kocoglu, Akgun, and Keskin 2015). AC encompasses combinative capabilities that allow firms to develop new products and processes and achieve sustainable competitive advantage. It involves the ability to assimilate and manage knowledge in order to improve innovation performance and competitive advantage (Moustaghfir 2009) and the lack of this ability can subvert firm's innovation capabilities (Muscio 2007). As noted earlier, Cohen and Levinthal (1989, 1990) pioneered the study on AC, however, other authors such as Zahra and George (2002) reconceptualized the concept as a dynamic capability that influences the nature and sustainability of a firm's competitive advantage. It also introduced the concept of potential and realized AC. While potential AC captures the capabilities that allow firms to recognize and acquire external knowledge, realized AC deals with the exploitation and transformational capabilities.

Over the years, several theoretical and empirical studies have examined the capability that firms possess for AC. These include employees educational qualification (Veugelers 1997; Vinding 2000; Muscio 2007; Ukpabio 2014), R&D Activities (Cohen and Levinthal 1990; Vinding 2000; Daghfous 2004), organizational structure (Kogut and Zander 1992; Lane and Lubatkin 1998; Van Den Bosch, Volberda, and Boer 1999), intra-Organizational Network (Gradwell 2003; Daghfous 2004), prior related knowledge (Kim 1998; Waalkens 2006), machinery/technology acquisition (Vega-Jurado, Gutierrez-Gracia, and de Lucio 2008; Escribano, Fosfuri, and Tribo 2009) and collaboration/linkages (Steensma 1996; Caloghirou, Kastelli, and Tsakanikas 2004; Muscio 2007) among others. Most empirical evidence supports the fact that these dimensions of AC play a significant role in firms' innovativeness and competitive advantage. The most prevalent determinant of AC and innovation in literature is R&D activities (Cohen and Levinthal 1994; Muscio 2007; de Jong and Freel 2012; Fortune and Shelton 2014; Adeyeye et al. 2016). According to this group of scholars, AC is generated by R&D activities. R&D expenditure would likely create competitive advantages as it urges firms to absorb technological knowledge external to the business environment (Veugelers 1997). The act of firms investing in R&D shows that they are keen about assimilating routines and processes and by this they grow knowledge accumulation and enhance their AC (Sanchez-Sellero, Rosell-Martınez, and Garcıa-Vazquez 2013). It is, therefore, believed that R&D expenditure increases the capacity to absorb external knowledge at firm level. R&D activities bring about rapid technological change, increases new knowledge and assimilation of knowledge, which enhances the AC of a firm (Cohen and Levinthal 1990). R&D intensity, overall intangible assets of an employee and industrial gap establishes how well firms absorb external knowledge (Dimelis 2005).

In addition, other studies (Vinding 2000; George et al. 2001; Szogs, Chaminade, and Azatyan 2008; Lee, Liang, and Liu 2010; de Jong and Freel 2012) have considered other internal capabilities such as educational qualification and capabilities developed from external knowledge sources through technology acquisition and external collaboration as important determinants of AC. This is more important for firms in developing countries who suffer from limited R&D capabilities and whose innovation performance is dependent largely on the capabilities and processes within firms. The educational qualification of firms' employees to a large extent plays a crucial role in external knowledge assimilation and utilization for innovation (Oyelaran-Oyeyinka and Adebowale 2012). Studies have revealed that firms whose employees possess higher academic qualification are more likely to assimilate new knowledge and have increased innovative performance (Rothwell and Dodgson 1991; Albaladejo and Romijn 2000) and that the low performance of firms in intramural R&D are perceptible to lack of employees with higher degrees (Ukpabio 2014).

Another determinant of AC is collaboration with external knowledge sources. Formal and informal linkages with actors (universities, research and technology agencies, consultants, suppliers, clients, competitors and government agencies) introduce additional inputs into the learning process which enhances a firm's capacity for knowledge absorption and consequently innovation. It is believed that collaborations are causal factor for innovations as the rate of inventions of firm depends on diversity of the sources of interactions (Romijn and Albaladejo 2002). Firms require knowledge from outside its borders to develop innovations, whether incremental or radical (Freel 2005). Knowledge from external sources can be accessed through external cooperation and technology acquisition. According to Dyer and Singh (1998) in their relational view of AC, they opined that AC of firms is based on social interactions, collaboration and individual relationships. Thus, this viewpoint sees AC as a repetitive process of relational exchange. External collaboration is used by firms to enhance internal capability and shaping competition thereby increasing the firms' competitive advantage. It involves a process wherein firm relating with other firms and actors within their environment (Chipika and Wilson 2006). An important source of knowledge in developing countries is embodied knowledge. Machineries embody new knowledge, blueprints, production and quality control manuals, product and service specifications, and training handouts (Ernst and Kim 2002); hence, the introduction of a new machine in a production process can render entire production processes obsolete. Also, changes to individual pieces of machinery that are embedded into larger configurations of equipment, can have broad repercussions even when the changes may at first glance seem to be isolated. This is because modifications to one machine can affect the operation of other equipment, as well as the duties and skill requirements of staff, and therefore alters the balance of an entire process; hence necessitating the development of new set of skills and capabilities (Robertson, Casali, and Jacobson 2012). In order to build the AC of firms, there is the need to transfuse explicit knowledge into tacit knowledge through training, studying of manuals and blueprints. In most cases, the acquisition of explicit knowledge alone is not sufficient for enterprises to assimilate and use in production, as the translation of explicit knowledge into actual operations requires a significant amount of tacit knowledge. Thus, to augment this, enterprises collaborate with equipment suppliers to develop the capabilities of their engineers and technicians (Ernst and Kim 2002).

1.2. AC and product innovation

Innovation involves new creation of economic significance, which is largely carried out by firms either private or public (Edquist 2008). In developing country context, Mytelka (2000) explained the concept to mean a process by which firms master and implement the design and production of goods and services that are new to them, irrespective of whether they are new to their competitors, their countries or the world. This can take the form of products, processes, marketing strategy or organization structure. Innovation entails the creation or development of new products and processes or services, which is achieved through process of learning, linkage and investment. Therefore, a firm's innovation capacity is linked with learning and technological knowledge, which is translated into a novelty that contributes to creating and enhancing value for the firm (Damanpour 2010). Thus, knowledge transmission, knowledge flows and knowledge spillovers within and across industries and the coordination and integration of knowledge are essential for firms' innovation performance (Malerba 2006). More so, a deeper understanding of the effect of knowledge type on the organization of innovative activities may be achieved in various ways. For instance, a specific dimension of knowledge can be linked with the organization of knowledge production. Example is linking the learning and knowledge environment to the models of innovative activities in a sector. Innovation requires that firms possess requisite knowledge and increasing learning abilities.

In trying to assess the role of AC in innovation, it is important to briefly assess the theoretical underpinning of innovation, learning and competence building in developing country context (Lall 1992; Bell and Pavitt 1993; Katz 1997; Romijn 1999). One of such is the technological capability framework by Sanjaya Lall. The framework highlights the role of technological knowledge and capability in production and innovation function of developing countries (Lall 1992). Due to lack of capability to generate new knowledge through and declining returns on investment in R&D, firms exploit knowledge from open sources such as acquisition of new equipment, machineries and technologies (Chesbrough 2003). The mastery and exploitation of which is a function of the skill, experience and based on a continuous process of learning. The process of innovation in developing countries, therefore, depends on absorbing external knowledge such as technology knowledge, which in turn is a function of a continuous accumulation and exploitation of new knowledge. The extent to which firm-level differences varies in technological effort and mastery, however, varies by industry, firm size and market among others (Lall 1992). Similar to firm-level differences, there exists differences in national technological capabilities.

Countries differ in the way they develop and utilize technologies to drive their productivity and competitiveness. This is influenced by three factors: capabilities, incentive and institutions. Capabilities entail physical investment, human capital and technological effort, while incentives are macroeconomic incentives, incentives from competition and incentives from factor markets. The development of capabilities and the role of incentives express themselves only through specific market and nonmarket institutions. The institutions, especially those external to the firm, are essential to the development of their capabilities. Firms' technological capability when properly developed forms the dynamic capabilities for innovation within the firm. It is the interplay of these that determines how firms learn, master and exploit new technological knowledge at the firm level and how countries strategically deploy their resources over time to achieve industrial growth within a rapidly changing technological environment. In achieving this, Lall identified the role of government. Government has a role in carefully selecting and utilizing state interventions to prevent market failures thereby driving technological growth and development using a combination of different capabilities, institutions and incentives. However, the misuse of such interventions by government may lead to abuses and ultimately lead to government failure (Lall 1992).

The development of new products, however, requires dynamic capabilities or combination of distinctive competencies (Muscio 2007). These dynamic capabilities and competencies are the AC dimensions for developing new products or services (Cohen and Levinthal 1990). These dynamic capabilities, if well developed, increase the level of AC of firm which has a direct impact on firm's product innovation. Product innovation entails diverse organizational strategies as well as unique inputs which results in novel outputs (Martinez-Ros and Labeaga 2009). For instance, Pavitt (1984) posits that the sources of knowledge inputs (intra-firm and inter-firm) for product innovation depend on the internal knowledge (for example, R&D intensity, experience and prior related knowledge) of the firm. A firm through its AC can develop innovative capabilities which will most likely result in innovation performance (Cohen and Levinthal 1990; Fosfuri and Tribo 2008; Ebers and Maurer 2014). Hence, knowledge acquired from external sources, if effectively integrated and exploited through a firm's AC could form the basis for promoting the rate and level of innovation. This in turn could lead to improved performance along with knowledge generation contributing towards firm's future AC. Besides, firm-level characteristics such as firm age, firm size, external cooperation, and engagement in export have a mediating effect on firm's AC and innovation performance (Fortune and Shelton 2014) (see Figure 1). Finally, Becker and Peters (2005) provide evidence that a firm's ability to adapt external knowledge positively influences their innovation output. The relationships between AC and firms' innovativeness have received fairly limited empirical attention, especially in developing country context, thus hindering the testing and practical implications of important theoretical arguments (Fosfuri and Tribo 2008).

1.3. Moderating the R&D-innovation relationship

The literature suggests that firm characteristics such as exporting, age and external cooperation affect the relationship between R&D investments and innovation. Studies have shown that exporting firms engaging in R&D enjoy greater productivity when

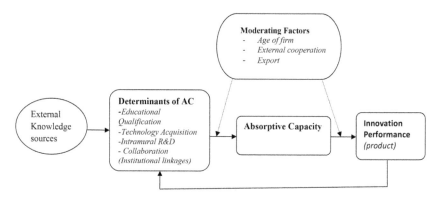

Figure 1. AC and innovation performance: a mediated moderation model. Source: Modified from Fortune and Shelton (2014).

equated with those that do not invest in R&D. For example, Aw, Roberts, and Xu (2009) and Criscuolo, Haskel, and Slaughter (2010) suggest that for exporting firms to be productive, it has to leverage on R&D. There is evidence that older firms experience stronger positive effect of R&D investment on innovative output and performance relative to younger firms. Older firms also demonstrate a stronger indirect effect of R&D investment through innovative output than younger firms (Fortune and Shelton 2014). Consequently, we expect that the relationship between R&D and innovation will depend on firm age. Finally, cooperation moderates the effect of R&D on product innovation as it enables firms to access new knowledge to enhance their intramural R&D. Engagement in external cooperation often offers firms' possibilities to complement the internal R&D resources (Teirlinck and Spithoven 2013).

1.4. Industrial sector in Nigeria

The structure of the Nigerian economy is typical of a developing country. Over half of the GDP is accounted for by the primary sector with agriculture continuing to play an important role. A comparative study of the sectoral contribution to Nigeria's GDP shows that the service sector is becoming the fastest growing sector in Nigeria. Since 2003, the sector has become the fastest growing non-oil sector contributing about 30% of her GDP. This comes amidst declining contribution of the manufacturing sector to GDP and the stagnation of the agricultural sector. The growth in services is due to the liberalization in the telecommunication sub-sector which has attracted significant foreign direct investment and the growth in the wholesale and retail sub-sector (National Bureau of Statistics [NBS] 2011). Despite this, the oil and gas sector, in particular, remains the main source of revenue for the government, accounting for over 95% of export earnings and about 85% of government revenue between 2011 and 2012 (Adeoye 2005).

In Nigeria, the industrial sector is characterized by SMEs which account for about 90% of the firms (Ariyo 2004). They cut across the industrial sector although the majority is agro allied and food processing. They are, however, faced with constraints such as lack of access to fund, technology, basic infrastructure such as electricity, good road, portable water, etc. which limits their capacity to grow and expand rapidly. Consequently, most firms rely on self-supply of electricity by using generators, which escalate their cost of production and erode their competitiveness relative to foreign firms. Today, the Nigerian industrial and manufacturing sector accounts for less than 10% of Nigeria's GDP, with manufacturing capacity utilization accounting for about 67.5% (Egbetokun et al. 2009).

The multinational companies in Nigeria are also important players in the Nigerian industrial sector especially in facilitating access to foreign exchange and foreign technologies. However, as noted by Ozoigbo and Chukuezi (2011), local firms did not benefit from transfer of these technologies due to restrictive intellectual property regimes and license. This is a very sensitive barrier for Nigeria. In Nigeria, as in most African countries, the industrial sector has weak in-house capabilities to undertake R&D. They also have weak linkages with knowledge institutions (Egbetokun et al. 2009; Siyanbola et al. 2012; Adeyeye, Jegede, and Akinwale 2013). These restrain them in their innovation process. To substitute for this, they use different strategies to innovate which include imitation, adaptation and reverse engineering among others. They exploit mainly market and industry sources for information for innovation (Oyelaran-Oyeyinka and Lall 2005; Egbetokun, Adeniyi, and Siyanbola 2012). Their innovations are, therefore, incremental with few firms introducing new-to-market innovations (Bala-Subrahmanya 2006).

2. Methodology

2.1. Data

The data for this study were sourced from a combined pooled cross-sectional sample of Innovation Surveys in Nigeria undertaken in 2008 and 2011 in manufacturing and service sectors. While the 2008 Survey covered the reference period 2005 and 2007, the 2011 covered 2008 and 2010. The surveys were undertaken under the NEPAD ASTII Initiative and were guided by the OECD Oslo Manual. The structure of the questionnaire followed after the community innovation survey questionnaire, adapted to the context of the participating countries. About 1500 firms, each with an employee of a minimum of 10, were sampled in each round. The aggregate response rate was 44% (*see* Table 1 *for sectoral distribution of the sample*). Due to the challenge of getting a comprehensive sampling frame of enterprises in Nigeria, a harmonized frame was developed from the list of enterprises from the NBS, Stock Exchange trading list and business associations list such as the Chambers of Commerce and Industry. In order to ensure a fair geographical and sectoral representation, the firms were stratified and sample selections were made using ISIC Rev. 3.1 in the first round and ISIC Rev. 4 in the second.

The datasets include information on the innovation investments, sources, obstacles and outcomes in the firms as well as detailed firm characteristics including size, human capital, age, qualification, location and export status. The similarity in sampling procedure and information in the two datasets made it possible for merging and analyses. The cross-

Table 1. Sectoral distribution of the sample.

Year	Manufacturing	Services	Total
2008	521	207	728
2011	371	260	631
Total	892	467	1359

sectional data give a better representation of the sectors and enhance broader understanding of key variables influencing innovation in both sectors of the Nigerian economy.

2.2. Measures

2.2.1. Dependent variable

The dependent variable is the product innovation of firms (PRODINNO), measured on an ordered scale ranging from 0 to 2. Product innovation in this context comprises of innovation in goods or services. According to Oslo Manual, it is the introduction of a good or service that is new or significantly improved with respect to its characteristics or intended uses (OECD 2005). The three possible values of the variable depend on the novelty of the product innovation: 0 depicts no innovation; 1, new-to-firm product innovations; and 2, new-to-market innovations. This is similar to the approach used by Vinding (2000); however, the fourth level of novelty, newness to the world was not used in our study because it was not reported by any of the firms sampled. This is not farfetched as studies have revealed that most firms in Nigeria focus more on incremental innovation rather than radical innovation (Egbetokun et al. 2008). In many instances, they lack R&D capabilities, a necessary catalyst for new-to-the world innovation; rather they innovate through modification, imitation and combining existing knowledge in new ways (Arundel, Bordoy, and Kanerva 2008).

2.2.2. Independent variables

The proposed analytical model considers various AC variables as possible determinants of innovation. The first explanatory variable is PERCENTGRAD. It measures the share of employees with a minimum of Bachelor's degree or Higher National Diploma (HND). In Nigeria, government equates the HND to a Bachelor's degree in terms of employment. The level of education of firms' employees significantly influences its knowledge assimilation and R&D capability and ultimately innovative performance (Rothwell and Dodgson 1991; Albaladejo and Romijn 2000; Oyelaran-Oyeyinka and Adebowale 2012). EXTERN is a categorical variable indicating collaborative partner (Vinding 2000). Firms that do not collaborate are assigned the value 0; those with close ties with market actors such as suppliers, clients and competitors take the value 1 while the value 2 is assigned to firms that collaborated with knowledge sources such as consultants, universities or public research institutes. Making use of these partners requires varying level of AC due to their different characteristics and also has different implications on firms' innovative performance. For instance, collaboration with clients can lead to improvement in product innovation (Brockhoff 2003; Chung and Kim 2003). On the other hand, collaboration with research organizations provides firms with knowledge to develop innovations intended to open new markets and segments (Belderbos et al. 2004). Another proxy for AC is the variable MACHEXPEND. This describes the estimated amount expended on the acquisition of machinery, equipment and software to aid innovation activities. Acquisition of new machineries offers enterprises the opportunity to develop new capabilities and skills in their technical staff through training and assimilating knowledge from technical documents and manuals. The objective of this is to develop and transform explicit knowledge into tacit knowledge needed in their operations and production processes (Ernst and Kim 2002). Also, firms' investment in machinery results in improved innovation capabilities which brings about improved competencies of the R&D personnel and enhances the process of production of firms. This leads to our final measure of AC: R&DEXPEND. This is the amount expended on intramural R&D in 2010 by firms which is measured as a proportion of firms' total expenditure. AC is traditionally considered as a positive function of R&D. This is at the core of the work of Cohen and Levinthal because it not only produces new knowledge in the sense of innovations but also contributes to the AC of firms by increasing the skills of the employees who have been involved in the R&D process. This strengthens firms' receptivity to relevant external knowledge (Veugelers 1997). We also introduce three interaction terms reflecting the moderated relationship between R&D investment and firms' product innovation. R&DEXPORT assesses whether investment in R&D increases the ability of firms to absorb external knowledge through trade openness. R&DCOOP is a measure of openness indicating whether the nature of firms' collaborative partners influences the relationship between R&D investment and firms' innovativeness. The last interaction variable, R&DAGE, assesses the effect of age on the relationship between firms' R&D activities and their product innovation.

2.2.3. Control variables

The proposed analytical model considers five control variables. These are SIZE, SECT, AGE, SUBSID and EXPORT. SIZE is constructed as the logarithm of total number of employees. Evidence abounds in literature on the impact of size on firms' performance. While evidence in literature mostly affirms a positive relationship, others such as Kasseeah (2013) posited an inverse relationship. While Segarra-Blasco (2010) attests that size is positively associated with productivity and performance of firms, Falkin (2007) argues that the effects of innovation, as a main determinant for organizational performance differ between large and small-/medium-sized firms. This is because size determines firms' investments in technology acquisition, engagement in R&D, and capability to acquire, assimilate and interpret external knowledge. Accordingly, firm's AC is built cumulatively and is dependent on the AC of its individual employees, therefore, firm size which is represented by the number of employees, exerts an inherent influence on the formation of AC (Cohen and Levinthal 1990). The second control variable SECT takes a binary variable, the value of 1 for service firms and 0 for manufacturing firms. It has been argued that the sector in which firms operate reveals the technological prospect for the industry (Mohnen and Dagenais 2000). The age of firms was also considered as an important control variable, constructed using the year of establishment of the firm (AGE). According to Cohen and Levinthal, AC is built over time and thus it is history dependent. Following this assumption, age becomes a significant variable with moderating impact on firms' AC because younger firms have less experience to learn from when compared with older firms. The study also controls for whether or not the firm is part of a larger group (SUBSID). This is constructed as a binary variable where firms that belong to a group are assigned '1' otherwise, '0'. Firms that belong to a group have access to information and other knowledge resources through their parent companies which gives them advantage in the innovation process (Kang and Park 2012). Consequently, they are able to enhance their AC through the benefits ensuing from this relationship. Finally, we introduce the variable EXPORT, a variable indicating whether firms operate in the international market which is also constructed as a binary variable. Firms' engagement in international market through export activities have been empirically proven to be positively associated with knowledge accumulation and innovation activities (DiPietro and Anoruo 2006; Leon-Ledesma 2005; Salim and Bloch 2009). Also, Salomon and Shaver (2005) opined that firms' innovation capabilities can be enhanced through foreign knowledge gained through their engagement in exporting activities.

3. Results and discussion

For the estimations of our dependent variable, PRODINNO, we used an ordinal logit model due the rank-ordered nature of the variable. In this paper, we achieved two things. First, we investigate how AC influences the PRODINNO, using two rounds of data from Nigeria's innovation survey in both manufacturing and service sectors. Second, using R&D investment as proxy for AC, we investigate how moderating variables such as age, size, collaboration and export capacity of firms influence this relationship.

Comparing the prevalence of product innovation, shows that there is a co-occurrence of good and service innovations in manufacturing and service firms (Table 2)

Descriptive statistics are given in Table 3. Our result shows that about 34% of the firm in our sample belong to service sector. On the average, about 39% of employees in Nigerian enterprises have a minimum of bachelor's degree as academic qualification. Our result also shows that on the average, most of the firms are medium sized and have an average age of 18 years. Similarly, about 21% of the firms are subsidiaries while about 17% of them export their goods. Our result also shows that most of the firms spend more on technology acquisition than undertake R&D. The result as shown in our sample explains the industrial landscape in most developing countries which is characterized by small firms with teething challenges such as high turnover, resource constraints, lack of internal capability to introduce frontier innovations, thereby focusing more on local market rather than competing on the international stage.

Our proxies for AC include external collaboration, R&D investment, investment in machinery and equipment, percentage of staff with academic degree. For Nigerian firms on the average, external collaboration and percentage of staff with bachelor's degree are significant (p-value $<= .05$) while others such as expenditure on machinery and R&D are insignificant (Table 4). The fewer number of firms represented in the regression analysis is attributable to missing observations in the variables of interest (Table 3). This explains similar observations in succeeding tables.

When disaggregated by sector, PERCENTGRAD, a measure of academic qualification is significant at 5% within manufacturing sector, while others, including R&D investment, are insignificant (Table 5). This shows that for one percentage point increase in the share of highly educated staff, the log odds of introducing a new-to-market product innovation

Table 2. Product innovation prevalence among Nigeria enterprises (%).

	2008		2011	
	Manufacturing	Service	Manufacturing	Service
Product innovation				
Enterprise introduced new/significantly improved goods	48.6	38.6	53.8	23.0
Enterprise introduced new/significantly improved services	40.7	62.3	40.5	41.5
Degree of novelty of innovation				
New to market	34.9	29.7	42.5	41.9
Only new to firm	65.1	68.1	90.4	87.2

Table 3. Descriptive results of variables.

Variable	N	Mean	Median	Std. Dev.	Min	Max
PERCENTGRAD	507	39.12	34	26.46	0	99
EXTERN	246	0.29	0	0.65	0	2
MACHEXPEND (million Naira)[a]	332	21.6	0	550.0	0	20,100
R&DEXPEND (million Naira)[a]	120	3.5	0	74.9	0	2700
SUBSID	279	0.21	20	0.40	0	1
SIZE	631	179.64	0	1100.00	8	17,000
SECT	1356	0.34		0.47	0	1
AGE	1023	18.07	0	15.26	1	151
EXPORT	227	0.17		0.37	0	1

Note: [a]1USD = 150 Naira as at the time of the surveys.

is 0.03. This supports previous studies which state that having high-level skilled workers increases the capability of firms to explore external sources of knowledge and assimilate them for production processes (Oyelaran-Oyeyinka and Adebowale 2012). In fact, poor performance in firms' R&D and innovative performance have been attributed to low educational qualification and lack of skilled workers (Albaladejo and Romijn 2000; Ukpabio 2014). Kisaka (2014) argues that education and training improves the entrepreneur's ability to acquire, assimilate and apply already available and new knowledge, which helps SMEs to improve their survival and competitiveness. This is because high level education develops in an employee the mental ability to form independent opinions, establish priorities, understand and discuss the methodology, utilized techniques and their applications. This is an important ingredient in explaining AC which depends on the dynamic characteristics of knowledge and hence leverages on constant and consistent training and education to produce innovative outcomes (van der Heiden et al. 2015). Hence, the higher the level of education, the higher these capabilities needed for innovation. Empirical studies in Nigeria have shown that firms whose employees possess higher academic qualification are more likely to assimilate new knowledge and have increased innovative performance (Oyelaran-Oyeyinka and Adebowale 2012; Ukpabio

Table 4. Ordered logistic regression analysis of product innovation and AC among Nigerian firms.

PRODINNO	Coef.	p-value	[95% Conf. Interval]	
PERCENTGRAD	0.01	.03	0.00	0.02
EXTERN				
None	Benchmark			
Market Sources	1.08	.03	0.11	2.04
Knowledge Institutions	1.26	.03	0.15	2.37
MACHEXPEND (million Naira)	−3.58e−09	.31	−1.05e−08	3.30e−09
R&DEXPEND (million Naira)	−2.83e−08	.39	−9.34e−08	3.69e−08
SUBSID	0.39	.23	−0.26	1.05
SIZE	0.00	.04	0.00	0.00
SECT	−0.02	.00	−0.03	−0.01
AGE	−0.01	.22	−0.04	0.01
EXPORT	−0.85	.21	−2.16	0.47
R&DEXPORT	0.31	.72	−1.36	1.98
R&DAGE	0.33	.01	0.08	0.59
R&DCOOP	−0.52	.36	−1.61	0.58
Numbers of obs	279			
LR χ^2 (12)	58.36			
Prob > χ^2	0.00			
Log likelihood	−235.03			
Pseudo R^2	0.11			

Table 5. Ordered logistic regression analysis of product innovation and AC among Nigerian manufacturing firms.

PRODINNO	Coef.	p-value	[95% Conf. Interval]	
PERCENTGRAD	0.03	.00	0.01	0.05
EXTERN				
None	Benchmark			
Market Sources	0.79	.26	−0.58	2.16
Knowledge Institutions	−0.52	.52	−2.10	−1.06
MACHEXPEND (million Naira)	−6.25e−09	.19	−1.57e−08	3.23e−09
R&DEXPEND (million Naira)	3.39e−08	.46	−5.58e−08	1.24e−07
SUBSID	0.21	.68	−0.80	1.22
SIZE	0.00	.17	−0.00	0.00
SECT	0.04	.26	−0.03	0.09
AGE	−0.01	.60	−0.03	0.02
EXPORT	0.03	.97	−1.66	1.73
R&DEXPORT	−1.68	.13	−3.87	0.51
R&DAGE	0.77	.00	0.36	1.18
R&DCOOP	0.71	.36	−0.82	2.25
Numbers of obs	167			
LR $\chi^2(12)$	67.4			
Prob > χ^2	0.00			
Log likelihood	−111.51			
Pseudo R^2	0.23			

2014). This points to the role of government in using state intervention in education to drive sectoral industrial growth as highlighted by Lall. Incentives to support the rapid production of higher skills through higher education are important to drive technological growth in developing countries. Such incentives include tuition free in science, technology, engineering and mathematics courses from basic to tertiary education, student loans and bursary among others. This will stimulate interest and help to raise the critical mass needed for industrial growth and national competitiveness. Also, incentives should be provided to firms to support training and retraining of their staff in developing skills and competences needed to absorb and assimilate new knowledge in production process. This will assist firms to stay competitive in an environment laden with fast changing and high technology obsolescence.

In assessing the effect of R&D investment, a proxy for AC, on product innovation, we first address how some moderating variables such as age, export and cooperation (R&DAGE, R&DEXPORT and R&DCOOP) affect the relationship. Our result shows that R&DAGE is significant at 5% level despite the fact that R&DEXPEND is not (Table 5). This signifies that the effect of R&D investment on firms' product innovation matures with age, that is, there is a stronger positive effect of R&D investment on product innovation in older firms relative to younger ones. This finding may be explained by the concept of 'liability of newness' (Stinchcombe 1965), which highlights resource constraint, weak ties to external partners, skill, knowledge and technology deficiency as challenges to innovation in newer firms (Teece, Pisano, and Shuen 1997; Zahra, Keil, and Maula 2005). Innovation capabilities take time to develop, and is even more difficult for younger firms as they suffer from lack of trust from external partners whom they could leverage on for knowledge to overcome their internal deficiencies (Lynn, Reddy, and Aram 1996). This result is important for firms in the manufacturing sector in Nigeria, because most of the firms in the sector have few employees with higher academic degrees and as such experience skill gaps.

Our result within the service sector shows that the coefficient of collaboration with external knowledge institutions is significant at 5% (Table 6). Specifically, as firms collaborate with knowledge institutions, such as universities and research institutes, the odds of introducing new-to-market product innovation increases by 82% (i.e $e^{0.6}-1$). This can be explained by the fact that collaboration with knowledge institutions enhances firms' capabilities by opening up new frontiers of knowledge useful in the innovation process. None of the controls or intervening variables moderates the role of R&D on firms' innovation in the service sector.

The role of external collaboration in innovative performance is established in literature. For instance, Badillo and Moreno (2014) argued that firms tend to benefit more from different and increasingly geographically dispersed actors which provide them with new technologies or specialized and novel knowledge that they are unable to find locally. This benefit is, however, dependent on their level of AC. This confirms previous literature that exposure to external partners provides firms with knowledge and information that are useful in the innovation process (Giuliani and Bell 2005; Escribano, Fosfuri, and Tribo 2009). Firms with higher levels of AC can manage external knowledge flows more efficiently, thereby leading to improved innovative performance. They do this by translating external knowledge coming from cooperative agreements into new, specific commercial applications more efficiently than in the absence of this feature (Badillo and Moreno 2014). However, according to Zahra and George (2002), these benefits are not automatic rather they depend on firms' ability to mobilize both the potential and realized AC to acquire and exploit the new knowledge. This is particularly important in developing country context which lacks the capabilities to generate new knowledge through R&D and hence leverage on collaboration for knowledge useful in their innovation process. There is, therefore, the need for state interventions in exploring opportunities provided by loopholes in intellectual properties regimes as a catch-up strategy. The selective and efficient utilization of such interventions may go a long way to assist firms in developing

Table 6. Ordered logistic regression analysis of product innovation and AC among Nigerian service firms.

PRODINNO	Coef.	p-value	[95% Conf. Interval]	
PERCENTGRAD	0.00	.68	−0.01	0.02
EXTERN				
None	Benchmark			
Market sources	0.62	.41	−0.85	2.10
Knowledge Institutions	2.46	.00	0.88	4.04
MACHEXPEND (million Naira)	−1.97e−08	.54	−8.31e−08	4.38e−08
R&DEXPEND (million Naira)	−7.78e−08	.42	−2.70e−07	1.15e−07
SUBSID	0.56	.27	−0.44	1.56
SIZE	0.00	.18	−0.00	0.00
SECT	−0.01	.44	−0.03	0.01
AGE	0.00	.91	−0.05	0.06
Export	−14.98	.99	−2043.30	2013.33
R&DEXPORT	16.29	.99	−2012.03	2044.61
R&DAGE	−0.04	.86	−0.43	0.36
R&DCOOP	−1.11	.21	−2.82	0.61
Numbers of obs	112			
LR χ^2(12)	30.14			
Prob > χ^2	0.00			
Log likelihood	−97.22			
Pseudo R^2	0.13			

countries gain knowledge needed for innovation and thereby enhancing their competitiveness.

The difference in the nature of AC driving product innovation between manufacturing and services may be attributed to the differences in characteristics of services and manufacturing. The service sector is characterized by intangibility, inseparability of production and consumption, interactivity and variability, as well as weak protection of intellectual property (Miles 2005). Drejer (2004) argues that the intangible nature of services means that they are difficult to quantify and taking a technological approach to measure the innovation in services is unlikely to capture the full variety of organizational and relational activities within services that adds to economic progress. Also, Tether (2005) posits that the innovation activities for services tend to put a greater emphasis on soft capabilities, in training and human capital for instance, whereas manufacturing applies a more mechanistic approach, which is more oriented towards the creation of well-defined products and processes. This is confirmed in Nigeria's innovation survey 2011 results that organizational and marketing innovations are more prevalent among service firms in Nigeria than manufacturing with product innovation representing the dominant innovation type among manufacturing firms. Even in implementing product innovation, manufacturing firms introduce more of new or significantly improved products compared to firms in the service sector focusing on new or significantly improved services. Among services, training is the most prevalent innovation activity while acquisition of machinery dominates the manufacturing sector (NACETEM 2011). The inseparability and variability characteristics of services make it important that innovations in the sector is driven by relational factors such as direct interaction between the producer and consumer, hence, at the core of this is the direct exchange of ideas, knowledge, know-how is facilitated, product improvements based on customers' or providers' previous experiences are implemented (Nagy 2013). The nature of services shows that service firms place more emphasis on direct interaction and close collaboration with users to drive innovative performance which is different from technology acquisition prevalent in the manufacturing sector.

4. Conclusion

This study, on the basis of findings discussed above, concludes that AC significantly influences the development of product innovation among Nigerian firms, however, with differences between manufacturing and service firms. For instance, while higher education qualification drives product innovation in manufacturing sector, among service firms, we found association between external collaboration and product innovation. R&D only has influence on innovation among manufacturing firms when interacted with age. Other AC determinants such as intramural R&D and expenditure on machinery had no influence on the survey firms' product innovation as most of the firms do not engage in intramural R&D and their investment in machinery acquisition seems relatively low.

This difference is particularly important for policy as it implies that there is no one-cap-fit-all solution for industrial development in the country. Therefore, there is the need for attention to be paid to sector-specific policies and instruments to drive firms' innovation performance. For example, within the manufacturing sector, attention should be paid to improving the quality of higher education and providing incentives for students to study science-related courses thereby developing a critical mass of potential employees to drive performance of the sector. The recent tuition-free policy of government from primary to university level for students studying any of the science, technology, education and mathematics subjects or courses is a positive move in this direction. In addition, government should introduce fiscal incentives such as tax rebate, soft loans, etc. for manufacturing firms undertaking R&D. This will reduce the burden of funding and short term expectation of return on investment. On the other hand, innovation in the service firms is influenced by firms' collaboration with knowledge institutions. The findings of this study have practical implication for improving performance of firms in Nigeria, especially among SMEs since they constitute majority of the nation's enterprises. Increase in SME's innovation performance may constitute a significant increase in national income. Firms with limited resources like SMEs in Nigeria can invest on their human capital and establish variety of linkages with other organizations as strategy for enhancing innovation performance.

Finally, the need for state interventions through policy instruments of government is particularly an important tool to drive firms' productivity and competitiveness and thereby enhance industrial growth especially in developing country context. These range from policy on education, training, intellectual property and funding among others. It should, however, be stated that there is need for efficient, selective and strategic utilization of these interventions or else, it may have a negative effect which may ultimately lead to government failure.

Acknowledgments

We particularly appreciate the Science, Technology and Innovation (STI) Indicators Project team at NACETEM who produced the data used in this paper. We are also thankful to two anonymous reviewers for their helpful comments.

Disclosure statement

No potential conflict of interest was reported by the authors.

References

Adeoye, F. W. 2005. "Industrial Development in Nigeria in the Context of Globalization." A paper submitted for Presentation at the 45th Annual Conference of the Nigerian Economic Society (NES).

Adeyeye, A. D., O. O. Jegede, and Y. S. Akinwale. 2013. "The Impact of Technology Innovation and R&D on Firms' Performance: An Empirical Analysis of Nigeria's Service Sector." *International Journal of Technological Learning, Innovation and Development* 6 (4): 374–395.

Adeyeye, A. D., O. O. Jegede, A. J. Oluwadare, and F. S. Aremu. 2016. "Micro-Level Determinants of Innovation: Analysis of the Nigerian Manufacturing Sector." *Innovation and Development* 6 (1): 1–14.

Albaladejo, M., and H. Romijn. 2000. "Determinants of Innovative Capability in Small UK Firms." Working Paper, Eindhoven Centre for Innovation Studies.

Ambrosini, V., C. Bowman, and N. Collier. 2009. "Dynamic Capabilities: An Exploration of How Firms Renew Their Resource Base." *British Journal of Management* 20: S9–S24.

Ariyo, D. 2004. "Small Firms are the Backbone of the Nigerian Economy." Accessed January 15, 2011. www.africaeconomicanalysis.org/articles/gen/smalhtml.

Arundel, A., C. Bordoy, and M. Kanerva. 2008. *Neglected Innovators: How Do Innovative Firms that Do Not Perform R&D Innovate? Results of an Analysis of the Innobarometer 2007 Survey, No. 215, INNO-Metrics Thematic Paper.* Brussels: European Commission.

Aw, B. Y., M. J. Roberts, and D. Y. Xu. 2009. *R&D Investment, Exporting, and Productivity Dynamics, NBER Working Paper Series, 14670.* Cambridge, MA: National Bureau of Economic Research.

Badillo, E. R., and R. Moreno. 2014. "Does Absorptive Capacity Determine Collaborative Research Returns to Innovation? A Geographical Dimension." Working Paper 2014/28 1/36, Research Institute of Applied Economics.

Bala-Subrahmanya, M. H. 2006. "Technological Innovations in Indian Small and Medium Enterprises (SMEs) Sector: Does Firm Size Matter?" *International Journal of Innovation and Learning* 3 (5): 499–517.

Barney, J. B. 1991. "Firm Resources and Sustained Competitive Advantage." *Journal of Management* 17: 99–120.

Becker, W., and J. Peters. 2005. "Innovation Effects of Science-Related Technological Opportunities, Theoretical Considerations and Empirical Findings for Firms in the German Manufacturing Industry." *Journal of Economics and Statistics* [Jahrbuecher fuer Nationaloekonomie und Statistik]. Department of Statistics and Economics, Justus-Liebig University Giessen, 225 (2): 130–150.

Belderbos, R., M. Carree, B. Diederen, B. Lokshin, and R. Veugelers. 2004. "Heterogeneity in R&D Co-operation Strategies." *International Journal of Industrial Organization* 22: 1237–1263.

Bell, M., and K. Pavitt. 1993. "Technological Accumulation and Industrial Growth: Contrasts between Developed and Developing Countries." *Industrial and Corporate Change* 2: 157–209.

Brockhoff, K. 2003. "Customers' Perspectives of Involvement in New Product Development." *International Journal of Technology Management* 26 (5/6): 464–481.

Caloghirou, Y., I. Kastelli, and A. Tsakanikas. 2004. "Internal Capabilities and External Knowledge Sources: Complements or Substitutes for Innovative Performance?." *Technovation* 24: 29–39.

Chesbrough, H. 2003. *Open Innovation.* Cambridge, MA: Harvard University Press.

Chipika, S., and G. Wilson. 2006. "Enabling Technological Learning Among Light Engineering SMEs in Zimbabwe Through Networking." *Technovation* 26 (8): 969–979.

Chung, S., and G. M. Kim. 2003. "Performance Effects of Partnership Between Manufacturers and Suppliers for New Product Development: The Supplier's Standpoint." *Research Policy* 32: 587–603.

Criscuolo, C., J. E. Haskel, and M. J. Slaughter. 2010. "Global Engagement and the Innovation Activities of Firms." *International Journal of Industrial Organization* 28: 191–202.

Coad, A., and R. Rao. 2008. "Innovation and Firm Growth in High-Tech Sectors: A Quantile Regression Approach." *Research Policy* 37 (4): 633–648.

Cohen, W. M., and D. A. Levinthal. 1989. "Innovation and Learning: The Two Faces of R&D." *The Economic Journal* 99: 569–596.

Cohen, W. M., and D. A. Levinthal. 1990. "Absorptive Capacity: A New Perspective on Learning and Innovation." *Administrative Science Quarterly* 35: 128–152.

Cohen, W. M., and D. A. Levinthal. 1994. "Fortune Favours the Prepared Firm." *Management Science* 40: 227–251.

Daghfous, A. 2004. "Absorptive Capacity and the Implementation of Knowledge Intensive Best Practices." *S.A.M. Advanced Management Journal* 69 (2): 21–29.

Damanpour, F. 2010. "An Integration of Research Findings of Effects of Firm Size and Market Competition on Product and Process Innovations." *British Journal of Management* 21: 996–1010.

Dimelis, S. P. 2005. "Spillover from FDI and Firm Growth: Technological, Financial and Market Structure Effects." *International Journal of the Economics of Business* 12: 85–104.

DiPietro, W. R., and E. Anoruo. 2006. "Creativity, Innovation, and Export Performance." *Journal of Policy Modeling* 28 (2): 133–139.

Drejer, I. 2004. "Identifying Innovation in Surveys of Services: A Schumpeterian Perspective." *Research Policy* 33 (3): 551–562.

Drucker, P. 1965. *The Future of Industrial Man: A Conservative Approach*. New York: New American Library.

Drucker, P. 1993. *The Post-Capitalist Society*. Oxford: Butterworth-Heinemen.

Dyer, J. H., and H. Singh. 1998. "The Relational View: Cooperative Strategy and Sources of Interorganizational Competitive Advantage." *Academy of Management Review* 23 (4): 660–679.

Easterby-Smith, M., L. Marjorie, and E. Tsang. 2008. "Inter-Organizational Knowledge Transfer: Current Themes and Future Prospects." *Journal of Management Studies* 45: 677–690.

Ebers, M., and I. Maurer. 2014. "Connections Count: How Relational Embeddedness and Relational Empowerment Foster Absorptive Capacity." *Research Policy* 43: 318–332.

Edquist, C. 2008. "Identification of Policy Problems in Systems of Innovation through Diagnostic Analysis." Paper presented in the Prime-Latin America Conference at Mexico City, September 24–26.

Ernst, D., and L. Kim. 2002. "Global Production Networks, Knowledge Diffusion, and Local Capability Formation." *Research Policy* 31: 1417–1429.

Egbetokun, A. A., A. A. Adeniyi, and W. O. Siyanbola. 2012. "On the Capability of SMEs to Innovate: The Cable and Wire Manufacturing Subsector in Nigeria." *International Journal of Learning and Intellectual Capital* 9 (1/2): 64–85.

Egbetokun, A., W. Siyanbola, O. Olamade, A. Adeniyi, and I. Irefin. 2008. "Innovation in Nigerian Small and Medium Enterprises: Types and Impact." MPRA Paper No. 25338. http://mpra.ub.uni-muenchen.de/25338/.

Egbetokun, A. A., W. O. Siyanbola, M. Sanni, O. O. Olamade, A. A. Adeniyi, and I. A. Irefin. 2009. "What Drives Innovation? Inferences from an Industrywide Survey in Nigeria." *International Journal of Technology Management* 45 (1/2): 123–140.

Escribano, A., A. Fosfuri, and J. A. Tribo. 2009. "Managing External Knowledge Flows: The Moderating Role of Absorptive Capacity." *Research Policy* 38 (1): 96–105.

Falkin, M. 2007. "Cross-Country and Cross-Industry Patterns in the Determinants of Innovation Output: Evidence for Countries Based on CIS 3 Micro Data".

Fortune, A., and L. Shelton. 2014. "Age Matters: Disentangling the Effect of R&D Investment in the Global Chemical Products Industry." *Business Management Dynamics* 3 (11): 35–54.

Fosfuri, A., and J. A. Tribo. 2008. "Exploring the Antecedents of Potential Absorptive Capacity and its Impact on Innovation Performance." *Omega* 36: 173–187.

Freel, Mark S. 2005. "Patterns of Innovation and Skills in Small Firms." *Technovation* 25 (2): 123–134.

George, G., S. A Zahra, K. K. Wheatley, and R. Khan. 2001. "The Effects of Alliance Portfolio Characteristics and Absorptive Capacity on Performance: A Study of Biotechnology Firms." *The Journal of High Technology Management Research* 12 (2): 205–226.

Giuliani, E., and M. Bell. 2005. "The Micro-Determinants of Meso-Level Learning and Innovation: Evidence from a Chilean Wine Cluster." *Research Policy* 34 (1): 47–68.

Gradwell, T. 2003. "Outsourcing Knowledge Creation: Don't Give the Game Away." *Specialty Chemicals* 23 (8): 24–25.

Grant, R. M. 2000. "Shifts in the World Economy: The Drivers of Knowledge Management." In *Knowledge Horizons; The Present and the Promise of Knowledge Management*, edited by C. Depress and D. Chauvel, 27–53. Boston: Butterworth-Heinemann.

Hamel, G., and C. K. Prahalad. 1994. *Competing for the Future*. Boston, MA: Harvard Business School Press.

Hannan, M. T. 1998. "Rethinking Age Dependence in Organizational Mortality: Logical Formalizations." *The American Journal of Sociology* 104 (1): 126–164.

van der Heiden, P., C. Pohl, Mansor S. Bin, and J. van Genderen. 2015. "The Role of Education and Training in Absorptive Capacity of international technology transfer in the aerospace sector." *Progress in Aerospace Sciences* 76: 42–54.

de Jong, J. P. J., and M. Freel. 2012. "Remote Collaboration, Absorptive Capacity, and the Innovative Output of High-Tech Small Firms." Paper Submitted to the Druid Society Conference Copenhagen. June 19–21 2012.

Kang, K. N., and H. Park. 2012. "Influence of Government R&D Support and Inter-firm Collaborations on Innovation in Korean Biotechnology SMEs." *Technovation* 32 (1): 68–78.

Kasseeah, H. 2013. "Innovation and Performance in Small- and Medium-Sized Enterprises: Evidence from Mauritius." *Innovation and Development* 3 (2): 259–275.

Katz, J. 1997. *The Dynamics of Technological Learning During the ISI Period and Recent Structural Changes in the Industrial Sector of Argentina, Brazil and Mexico.* Santiago de Chile: CEPAL.

Kim, L. 1998. "Crisis Construction and Organizational Learning: Capability Building in Catching-up at Hyundai Motor." *Organization Science* 9: 506–521.

Kisaka, S. E. 2014. "Impact of Education and Training on Entrepreneurial Behavior in Kenya: An Application of the Resource-Based Theories." *Journal of Education and Practice* 14 (5): 167–173.

Kocoglu, I., A. E. Akgun, and H. Keskin. 2015. "The Differential Relationship Between Absorptive Capacity and Product Innovativeness: A Theoretically Derived Framework." *International Business Research* 8 (7): 108–120.

Kogut, B., and U. Zander. 1992. "Knowledge of the Firm, Combinative Capabilities, and the Replication of Technology." *Organization Science* 3 (3): 383–397.

Lall, S. 1992. "Technological Capabilities and Industrialization." *World Development* 20 (2): 165–186.

Lane, P. J., B. R. Koka, and S. Pathak. 2006. "The Reification of Absorptive Capacity: A Critical Review and Rejuvenation of the Construct." *Academy of Management Review* 31: 833–863.

Lane, P. J., and M. Lubatkin. 1998. "Relative Absorptive Capacity and Inter-Organizational Learning." *Strategic Management Journal* 19: 461–477.

Lee, S. C., H. Liang, and C. Y. Liu. 2010. "The Effects of Absorptive Capacity, Knowledge Sourcing Strategy, and Alliance Forms on firm Performance." *The Service Industries Journal* 30: 2421–2440.

Leonard-Barton, D. 1992. "Core Capabilities and Core Rigidities: A Paradox in Managing New Product Development." *Strategic Management Journal* 13: 111–125.

Leon-Ledesma, M. A. 2005. "Exports, Product Differentiation and Knowledge Spillovers." *Open Economies Review* 16: 363–379.

Liao, S., W. Fei, and C. Chen. 2007. "Knowledge Sharing, Absorptive Capacity and Innovation Capability: An Empirical Study of Taiwan's Knowledge-Intensive Industries." *Journal of Information Science* 33 (3): 340–359.

Liao, S. H., C. C. Wu, D. C. Hu, and K. A. Tsui. 2010. "Relationships Between Knowledge Acquisition, Absorptive Capacity and Innovation Capability: An Empirical Study on Taiwan's Financial and Manufacturing Industries." *Journal of Information Science* 36 (1): 19–35.

Lynn, L. H., N. M. Reddy, and J. D. Aram. 1996. "Linking Technology and Institutions: The Innovation Community Framework." *Research Policy* 25: 91–106.

Malerba, F. 2006. "Innovation and the Evolution of Industries." *Journal of Evolutionary Economics* 16 (1): 3–23.

Martinez-Ros, E., and J. M. Labeaga. 2009. "Product and Process Innovation: Persistence and Complementarities." *European Management Review* 6: 64–75.

Miles, I. 2005. "Innovation in services." In *The Oxford Handbook of Innovation*, edited by J. Fagerberg, R. Mowery, and R. Nelson, 433–458. Oxford: Oxford University Press.

Mohnen, P., and M. Dagenais. 2000. *Towards an Innovation Intensity Index: The Case of CIS 1 in Denmark and Ireland.* Montreal: CIRANO, Scientific Series.

Moustaghfir, K. 2009. "How Knowledge Assets Lead to a Sustainable Competitive Advantage: Are Organizational Capabilities a Missing Link?" *Knowledge Management Research & Practice* 7: 339–355.

Muscio, A. 2007. "The Impact of Absorptive Capacity on SMEs' Collaboration." *Economics of Innovation and New Technology* 16 (8): 653–668.

Muzart, G. 1999. "Description of National Innovation Surveys Carried Out, or Foreseen, in 1997–99 in OECD Non_CIS-2 Participants and NESTI Observer Countries." STI Working Paper Series 1999/1, Paris: OECD.

Mytelka, L. 2000. "Local Systems of Innovation in a Globalized World Economy." *Industry and Innovation* 7 (1): 33–54.

NACETEM 2011. *Nigeria's Innovation Survey 2005–2007.* Ile-Ife: NACETEM.

Nagy, A. 2013. "Approaching Service Innovation Patterns." *European Journal of Interdisciplinary Studies* 5 (1): 39–45.

NBS 2011. "Review of the Nigeria Economy [online]." Accessed May 5, 2013. http://www.nigeriastat. gov.ng

OECD 2005. *Guidelines for Collecting and Interpreting Innovation Data.* 3rd ed. Paris: OECD.

Oyelaran-Oyeyinka, B., and K. Lal. 2005. "Sectoral Pattern of E-business Adoption in Developing Countries." UNU-INTECH Discussion Paper Series 07, United Nations University, INTECH.

Oyelaran-Oyeyinka, B., and B. O. A. Adebowale. 2012. "University – Industry Collaboration as a Determinant of Innovation in Nigeria." *International Journal of Institutions and Economies* 4 (1): 21–46.

Ozoigbo, B. I., and C. O. Chukuezi. 2011. "The Impact of Multinational Corporations on the Nigerian Economy." *European Journal of Social Sciences* 19 (3): 380.

Pavitt, K. 1984. "Sectoral Patterns of Technological Change: Towards a Taxonomy and Theory." *Research Policy* 13: 343–373.

Robertson, P. L., G. L. Casali, and D. Jacobson. 2012. "Managing Open Incremental Process Innovation: Absorptive Capacity and Distributed Learning." *Research Policy* 41: 822–832.

Romijn, H. A. 1999. *Acquisition of Technological Capability in Small Firms in Developing Countries.* London: Macmillan.

Romijn, H., and M. Albaladejo. 2002. "Determinants of Innovation Capability in Small Electronics and Software Firms in Southeast England." *Research Policy* 31 (7): 1053–1067.

Rothwell, R., and M. Dodgson. 1991. "External Linkages and Innovation in Small and Medium-Sized Enterprises." *R&D Management* 21: 125–136.

Salim, R. A., and H. Bloch. 2009. "Business Expenditures on R&D and Trade Performances in Australia: Is There a Link?." *Applied Economics* 41: 351–361.

Salomon, R. M., and J. M. Shaver. 2005. "Learning by Exporting: New Insights from Examining Firm Innovation." *Journal of Economics and Management Strategy* 14: 431–460.

Sanchez-Sellero, P., J. Rosell-Martınez, and J. M. Garcıa-Vazquez. 2013. "Absorptive Capacity from Foreign Direct Investment in Spanish Manufacturing Firms." *International Business Review* 23 (2014): 429–439.

Segarra-Blasco, A. 2010. "Innovation and Productivity in Manufacturing and Service Firms in Catalonia: A Regional Approach." *Economics of Innovation and New Technology* 19 (3): 233–258.

Siyanbola, W.O., A. A. Egbetokun, I. Oluseyi, O. O. Olamade, H. O. Aderemi, and M. Sanni. 2012. "Indigenous Technologies and Innovation in Nigeria: Opportunities for SMEs." *American Journal of Industrial and Business Management* 2: 64–75.

Spender, J. C. 1996. "Making Knowledge the Basis of a Dynamic Theory of the Firm." *Strategic Management Journal* 17: 45–62.

Steensma, H. K. 1996. "Acquiring Technological Competencies Through Inter-Organizational Collaboration: An Organizational Learning Perspective." *Journal of Engineering and Technology Management* 12: 267–286.

Stinchcombe, A. L. 1965. "Social Structure and Organizations." In *Handbook of Organizations*, edited by J. G. March, 142–193. Chicago, IL: Rand McNally.

Szogs, A., C. Chaminade, and R. Azatyan. 2008. "Building Absorptive Capacity in Less Developed Countries. The Case of Tanzania." Circle Electronic Working Papers.

Teece, D. J. 1998. "Capturing Value from Knowledge Assets: The New Economy, Markets for Know-how, and Intangible Assets." *California Management Review* 40: 55–79.

Teece, D. J., G. Pisano, and A. Shuen. 1997. "Dynamic Capabilities and Strategic Management." *Strategic Management Journal* 18: 509–533.

Teirlinck, P., and A. Spithoven. 2013. "Research Collaboration and R&D Outsourcing: Different R&D Personnel Requirements in SMEs." *Technovation* 33 (4): 142–153.

Tether, B. S. 2005. "Do Services Innovate (Differently)? Insights from the European Innobarometer Survey." *Industry and Innovation* 12 (2): 153–184.

Ukpabio, M. G. 2014. "A Study of Technology Acquisition and Absorptive Capacity in Nigerian Commercial Banks." A research Project Submitted to African Institute for Science Policy and

Innovation (AISPI), Obafemi Awolowo University, Ile-Ife, in Partial Fulfilment of the Award of Master of Science in Technology Management.

Van Den Bosch, F. A. J., H. W. Volberda, and M. D. Boer. 1999. "Co-Evolution of Firm Absorptive Capacity and Knowledge Environment: Organizational Forms and Combinative Capabilities." *Organization Science* 10: 551–568.

Vega-Jurado, J., A. Gutierrez-Gracia, and I. F. de Lucio. 2008. "An Analytical Model of Absorptive Capacity." INGENIO (CSIC-UPV) Working Paper Series 2008/2, 1–24.

Veugelers, R. 1997. "Internal R & D Expenditures and External Technology Sourcing." *Research Policy* 26 (3): 303–315.

Vinding, A. L. 2000. *Absorptive Capacity and Innovative Performance: A Human Capital Approach. Department of Business studies — DRUID/IKE Group.* Denmark: Aalborg University.

Waalkens, J. 2006. "Building Capabilities in the Construction Sector: Absorptive Capacity of Architectural and Engineering Medium-Sized Enterprises." PhD Thesis, University of Groningen, Groningen.

Zahra, S., and G. George. 2002. "Absorptive Capacity: A Review, Reconceptualization, and Extension." *Academy of Management Review* 27 (2): 185–203.

Zahra, S. A., T. Keil, and M. Maula. 2005. "New Ventures' Inward Licensing: Examining the Effects of Industry and Strategy Characteristics." *European Management Review* 2: 154–166.

Persistence of innovation and knowledge flows in Africa: an empirical investigation

Francesco Lamperti[ID], Roberto Mavilia[ID] and Marco Giometti

ABSTRACT
This paper investigates the persistence of innovative activities at firm level in Africa. Assessing whether innovation is persistent or not is crucial in order to discriminate between different possible drivers of innovative processes and for guiding public policies aimed at promoting innovation. Using patent data, our aim is to capture some relevant features of innovative activities in the African region. Moreover, we look at the effect of international knowledge flows on the persistence of innovative activities. Employing a non-parametric approach based on transition probability matrices, we find some degree of persistence and a positive impact of knowledge flows from developed countries (OECD).

1. Introduction

In this paper, we study the persistence of innovative activities at the firm level in Africa using patent data. Our aim is to capture and characterize some features of innovative activities in the African continent, and to understand whether knowledge flows from developed countries may have a positive impact on innovative activities.

To the best of our knowledge, there are currently no studies on the persistence of innovative activities at the African level. This is a relevant question, because on the one hand it could have important policy implications, on the other hand it can help shed light on patterns of innovation in developing countries, given that the majority of studies has focused on Western countries. This is one of the few studies that investigate the phenomenon of innovation in Africa employing a cross-country analysis, which allows for a more comprehensive understanding with respect to the majority of other studies that are based on case studies focused on one or few countries.

We aim to address the issue of persistence in the context of the African continent, employing a transition probability matrices (TPM) approach, as in Cefis (2003). Also, we contribute to the literature on international knowledge flows, studying whether such knowledge spillovers from developed countries may have a positive effect on the persistence of innovative outcomes. No study so far has focused on this particular aspect, but it is really important to understand whether international collaborations can help foster the accumulation of technical skills and hence boost the capacity to innovate.

We first assess if there is persistence in innovative activities across the whole sample of firms, and then we study whether the presence of knowledge flows from countries belonging to the Organisation for Economic Cooperation and Development (OECD) has some positive effects on the persistence of innovation among African firms. In particular, we study whether firms whose research teams are formed by inventors coming from developed countries display more persistence in innovative activities with respect to firms whose research teams display only African inventors. We interpret the presence of a foreign inventor as a proxy for knowledge flows among countries, hence we indeed try to assess whether international knowledge flows can have a positive impact on fostering technical abilities relevant for innovation in a developing continent such as Africa. In this context it is relevant to specify that we read cross-regional networking as a phenomenon where knowledge is transferred from one side of the research collaboration to the other and, possibly, vice versa. There is strong evidence in literature that research collaborations across firms and regions are pivotal for acquiring external knowledge (Singh 2005), and promoting the creation of new knowledge (Miguélez and Moreno 2013). Even though the focus is on Europe, Miguélez and Moreno (2013) document the existence of a positive correlation between cross-regional networking and innovation, even though this effect is found to be less relevant than that played by regional labour mobility. In line with the point of view adopted in this paper, Breschi and Lissoni (2009) use patent applications (from certain technological fields biotechnology, organic chemistry, and pharmaceuticals) to show that networking activity across firms (and locations) is in large part responsible for the localization of knowledge flows. With specific reference to the interactions between researchers from developing and advanced countries, Montobbio and Sterzi (2010) suggest that the innovative activity of Latin American countries has largely benefit from R&D that is performed in some OECD country and, in particular, they underline that face-to-face relationships are one of the key drivers of the result. Very recently, Giuliani, Martinelli, and Rabellotti (2016) have found that cross-border inventions between BRICS firms and EU actors are growing, they are more valuable than domestic ones, and constitute an opportunity to accumulate technological capabilities.[1]

We remind that, by focusing on co-invention and patent data, our aim is to capture and characterize some important features of the process of innovation among African firms, and not, for example, to study which are actually the drivers of innovative activities. Our results indicate some degree of persistence, especially when considering a medium- and long-term horizon, and highlight the important role of knowledge flows in fostering innovation: firms whose research team have been formed by one or more inventors coming from OECD countries consistently display higher level of persistence, meaning that their likelihood to keep innovating through time is higher than those.

The rest of the paper is organized as follows: Section 2 presents a review of the literature, Section 3 explains in detail the empirical methodology employed in the paper, Section 4 is dedicated to the analysis of whether there is persistence in innovation among African firms, Section 5 considers the role of knowledge flows and their impact on the persistence of innovative activities, and Section 6 concludes.

2. Motivation and literature review

The notion of persistence corresponds to the firm's ability to innovate in a given period after having innovated in the previous one, and as such can be interpreted in many ways. Malerba, Orsenigo, and Peretto (1997) observe that, if innovation is considered a purely random process, persistence is usually represented by the degree of serial correlation of innovative activities. If instead one thinks of innovation as a concept stemming from interactions between agents, knowledge, and market opportunities, then persistence can be seen as a cumulative process influenced by market forces and by the accumulation of technological competencies. They also note that the ability to innovate once may indeed establish a virtuous circle, either yielding higher profits, which in turn allows higher investments in R&D and hence increases the chance of future innovations, either generating specific knowledge that by accumulating could subsequently lead to other innovations. However, since market feedbacks and cumulativeness are not observable, they suggest that serial correlation at the firm level represents a valid proxy of persistence.

So far, empirical evidence is mixed. Cefis (2003), employing a non-parametric approach based on transitional probability matrices and patent data, on the one hand finds low evidence of persistence at the aggregate level, which also decreases over time. On the other hand, she does find strong evidence of persistence in innovative activities at the firm-level, since great innovators and non-innovators have a high probability of remaining in their state, and persistent innovators generate a disproportionate share of innovative activities. Cefis and Orsenigo (2001) extend the same approach in a cross-country and cross-sector analysis, and obtain results pointing at heterogeneity across industrial sectors and substantially invariant inter-sectoral differences among countries, which in turn suggest that persistence may be a technology-specific phenomenon. Malerba and Orsenigo (1999), using patent data as well, analyse the patterns of innovative exit, entry, and survival. What emerges is that innovative activities are characterized by a high degree of turbulence, a large share of new innovators is given by occasional innovators, and only a few entrants succeed in innovating after their first patent. In case they do, however, their technological performance improves considerably afterwards. This fact, combined with evidence that large innovators tend to remain large for a long time, suggests that innovative activities stem from a relatively stable – and small – core of large and persistent innovators. Peters (2009), who employs a random effects probit model using panel data from German firms, finds a high degree of persistence.

Assessing whether innovation is persistent or not is important for at least two reasons. First, it may help to discriminate between different possible drivers of innovative processes: evidence of persistence would imply that innovation derives from firm-specific technological abilities – which gradually build through time and eventually lead to high barriers to entry – whereas lack of this evidence would suggest that the dynamics of innovation is mainly driven by small uncorrelated shocks – and that new innovators systematically substitute incumbents. Second, it is crucial for determining the efficacy of government policies aimed at promoting innovation: if innovative activities are found to be persistent then policies aimed at stimulating innovation – with the eventual objective of catalysing growth – can be much more efficient and long-lasting, as they would induce a permanent change in favour of innovation.

This last aspect is especially relevant in Africa, where recently there have been many efforts to launch science, technology, and innovation policies with the ultimate objective of boosting economic growth.[2] However, notwithstanding the important role innovation is supposed to play, there are relatively few works that study innovation within the African context. Oye-laran-Oyeyinka, Laditan, and Esubiyi (1996) analyse, through survey interviews, which factors determine the successful or unsuccessful adoption of industrial innovation by firms in Nigeria. They find that the establishment of linkages with other firms – especially foreign companies able to provide the necessary technology – is an important source for inno-vation, whereas the lack of appropriate national infrastructures may be a significant obstacle.

Goedhuys (2007) analyses the learning processes and linkage behaviour of small and large, local and foreign firms active in Tanzania, and how different learning mechanisms affect product innovation. The results indicate that both foreign and local firms are product innovators, although in different ways: local firms exploit the formation of lin-kages with other domestic firms, whereas foreign firms innovate thanks to a higher invest-ment in human capital. Rooks et al. (2005) assess the relative efficiency of South Africa's innovation system, evaluating the responses of more than 600 firms to a questionnaire. Their results point to a substantial similarity in terms of innovative outputs between South Africa and countries belonging to the European Union, with South Africa's invest-ment on innovation generally lower than the European mean. Robson, Haugh, and Obeng (2009), employing a multi-level theoretical framework, study innovation in Ghana, in par-ticular with respect to the characteristics of entrepreneurs, the internal competencies of firms, and firm location. Innovation is found to be positively related to entrepreneur's level of education and to the firm size. Also, innovation is mainly incremental among Gha-naian firms, consisting of introduction of products, services, and processes new to the firm, but not new to the industry as a whole.

More recently, De (2014) evaluates the optimal conditions for innovation within emer-ging economies using a generalized linear framework, focusing in particular on Kenya and Uganda. She finds that in both countries investment on human capital in the form of on-the-job training is a significant predictor of innovation, as well as long-term investments in the firm's internal infrastructure – technology, equipment, and building. Other country-specific variables are found to be important, in particular the competition with the infor-mal sector in Kenya and the access to generators in Uganda. Adeyeye et al. (2016) focus on Nigeria and analyse the influence of firms' innovation activities on the propensity to implement innovations and whether size influences the type of innovation implemented by firms. They show that intramural R&D plays a significant role for innovative processes, whereas the size does not matter. Egbetokun, Mendi, and Mudida (2016) analyse firm-level innovation data from Kenya and Nigeria. In the study, some evidence is found on the existence of complementarities between internal and external technological innovation strategies in the case of Kenya, but not in the case of Nigeria.

Another important question related to innovation is understanding whether international knowledge flows from developed countries have some positive effect on innovative outcomes of firms in developing and less-developed countries, given the implications for economic growth and innovation policies. The importance of knowledge spillovers is well acknowledged in the literature (see, e.g. Griliches 1992). Such spillovers can take place through many chan-nels, either formal methods of communication such as scientific publications or informal person-to-person contacts involving different researchers. To investigate the impact of international knowledge flows and their effects, many studies have focused on international R&D collaborations and cross-border inventions – that is, those involving inventors from foreign countries – and their impact on the quality of innovations.

Two orders of considerations apply. At a theoretical level, there are some authors who argue that such collaborations induce innovations of higher quality through the combination of different skills and knowledge (Levinthal and March 1993; March 1991), whereas others suggest that international collaborations may be not efficient as a consequence of high coordination costs and difficulties in integrating knowledge coming from different research teams (Furman et al. 2005; Grant 1996; Singh 2008). At the empirical level, results are mixed. Branstetter, Li, and Veloso (2014) study Indian and Chinese inventors, finding that cross-border inventions receive more citations – and hence, are more valuable – than patents produced by domestic research teams with no international components. Alnuaimi, Singh, and George (2012) also find that the quality of patents is positively affected by international collaborations. However, their results also underline the research teams' difficulties in the absorption of external knowledge. Hence, it is not clear whether such collaborations may enhance the accumulation of technological competences in developing countries. In addition to that, there is recent evidence showing that the structure of research collaborations in Africa is anything but homogeneous and it is strongly constrained by multifaceted factors such as regional geography, history, culture, and language (Adams et al. 2014). Moreover, Landini, Malerba, and Mavilia (2015) show that also in relatively more advanced regions (Northern Africa) international research collaborations are rapidly changing but, still, they are remarkably weak. In another work focused on the automotive supply industry, Lorentzen and Gastrow (2012) employ case studies from Germany and South Africa and find that the offshoring of knowledge-intensive activities is beginning to appear in an industry that is known more than others for centralizing most such activity close to headquarter locations and always in developed economies.

In such an unclear context, understanding the impact of successful research collaborations between groups of African inventors (working for African firms) and researchers from more-developed countries might be crucial for policy design. For example, in a similar fashion but with different geographical focus, Kim, Lee, and Marschke (2006) construct a dataset containing detailed information about inventors, patents, and firms, and investigate the international transmission of knowledge in the USA. They find that the number of U.S. firms collaborating with researchers with foreign experience has increased, and that those firms have an easier access to non U.S. technological know-how compared to firms that do not collaborate with inventors having foreign research experience. In line with these findings, Alnuaimi, Singh, and George (2012) show that cross-country collaboration improves not just the resulting ideas, but also has a long-term benefit for the involved inventors in terms of continuing to generate higher-impact ideas in the future. Drawing on all these contributions and emphasizing the continuity of the innovation process rather than the quality of its outcome, in the next sections we characterize the persistence of innovation in Africa and the role of cross-border co-invention.

3. Methodology

We investigate the persistence in innovating activities by employing a non-parametric approach based on TPM, as in Cefis (2003). Persistence is defined as the probability of a firm of remaining in its initial state. In particular, we suppose that the distribution of patents across firms at a certain point of time is approximated by a Markov chain. Denoting by F_t the distribution of patents across firms at time t, we assume that its law of motion is time-invariant and described by $F_{t+1} = P \cdot F_t$. There is no particular reason why the law of motion of F_t should be a first-order relation, still it is useful to analyse the dynamic behaviour of F_t. P is a transition probability matrix, whose entries represent the one-step transition probabilities from state i to state j, that is:

$$p_{ij} = P(X_{t+n} = j \mid X_t = i),$$

with $t = 1977, 1978, \ldots, 2014$ and $n = 1, 5, 10$ years. The states are given by number of patents requested by each firm within the considered period. For illustrative purposes, we consider only two states, where state 1 and 2 are given by the firm having zero patents and at least 1 patent, respectively. However, this framework can be easily adapted to any finite number of states; in particular, we will start with the simplest setting with the zero vs. some patent states only and then we will enrich it by considering four categories, namely zero, one, from 2 to 5 patents and more than 5 patents.

Hence, let X_t be a stochastic process approximated by a two-state Markov chain, with transition probabilities:

$$P(X_{t+1} = j \mid X_t = i) = \begin{bmatrix} p & 1-p \\ 1-q & q \end{bmatrix}, \tag{1}$$

where p and q represent the probabilities of remaining in the same state as in the previous period. In case a Markov chain with more than two states would have been considered, one should read the probabilities of remaining in each state on the main diagonal of the matrix in (1). In our illustrative setting, the implied autoregressive process for xt is the following:

$$x_t = (1 - q) + \rho \cdot x_{t-1} + v_t, \tag{2}$$

where $\rho = p + q - 1$. In our framework we say that there is persistence in innovative activities if $\rho > 0$. In particular, if both are equal to 1, there is perfect persistence, whereas if both are less than 0.5 there is the tendency to revert from one state to the other, and hence there is little or none persistence. In the case where $\rho > 0$ but only one of the two elements (p and q) is above 0.5, then we say that there is evidence of persistence but it biased towards one state. An analogous reasoning applies to the case of a Markov chain with more than two states. To provide a reasonably complete characterization of the innovative dynamics and to check the robustness of our results, TPMs are estimated for three different period lengths, that is, 1 year, 5 years, and 10 years. What is particularly relevant in terms of persistence is that it brings the following consequence: when firms have innovated at time t, their probability to keep innovating in the future is higher than what they would have faced in case no innovation at time t.

Given the relative short length of our sample, when we will show the results of our empirical exercise we follow Cefis and Orsenigo (2001) in presenting bootstrapping standard errors for the probability estimates we obtain.[3]

4. Persistence of innovative activities among African firms

4.1. Data

The data we use in this part are drawn from Orbis,[4] and our dataset is a panel of patents requested by 1106 African firms in the period 1977–2014. The total number of patents amounts to 6043. Table 1 shows the composition of our sample of firms in terms of patenting activity.

Note that the number of firms that do not patent has constantly decreased over the years, and that the majority of firms that patent have no more than four patents registered.

Our dataset covers 17 African countries: Botswana, Democratic Republic of Congo, Cote D'Ivoire, Algeria, Egypt, Gabon, Kenya, Liberia, Morocco, Mauritania, Mauritius, Namibia, Nigeria, Seychelles, Senegal, Tunisia, and South Africa. Figures 1 and 2 describe the composition of firms and patents present in our sample in terms of geographical location. Notice that the vast majority of the firms in the sample is located in South Africa, whereas Morocco, Mauritius, and Egypt account for a smaller, but still significant, fraction. This pattern emerges also looking at the composition of the patents, where South Africa clearly outperforms all other countries in terms of patenting activity. This is, clearly, a limitation our data. Notwithstanding it and considered the frequentist statistical basis of the methodology we apply, we think that keeping all the observations (and not focusing on South Africa only) provides more robustness to our results and allows a better examination of aggregate properties of innovation processes in Africa.

From Figure 3 it is possible to see that the patenting activity has persistently increased over the years. Figure 4 shows instead that the composition of patents in our sample is substantially homogeneous in terms of technological sector, with the only two exceptions of textiles and paper, which account for an almost negligible number of patents, and performing operations and transporting, which outperforms the other sectors.

Our dataset has some limitations that are worth to mention now. First of all, we already highlight that even if we are in presence of a panel data of many African countries, data on South Africa are predominant. Still, we are among the first to offer a cross-country analysis of innovation activities in Africa. Secondly, the use of patent data may prevent us from capturing the whole range of innovative outputs that are produced in the continent. The limitations of patent data are well known (Cohen, Nelson, and Walsh 2000; Dernis and Guellec 2002; Frietsch and Schmoch 2006). Patents represent only a portion of innovative activity and none of the latter stage investments entailed in commercializing technology. Patents are of widely varying value to firms. Motivations for patenting vary across industries and technologies; equally important, they change over time and over countries. Firms often choose to keep innovations that are commercially sensitive a secret; the propensity to patent may also vary according to the costs and the competence of patenting; and many patents may never be implemented commercially. Patents may even obstruct innovation on occasion if they slow the diffusion of knowledge or pose prohibitive barriers

Table 1. Number of firms in the sample (by patenting activity).

	Number of patents						
	0	1	2–4	5–9	10–19	20–49	>50
1977–1986	913	82	72	22	11	5	1
1987–1996	838	101	103	31	19	10	4
1997–2006	618	207	199	40	25	16	1
2007–2014	561	296	183	40	16	4	6

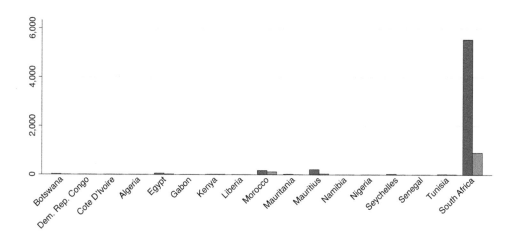

Figure 1. Number of patents and firms per country.

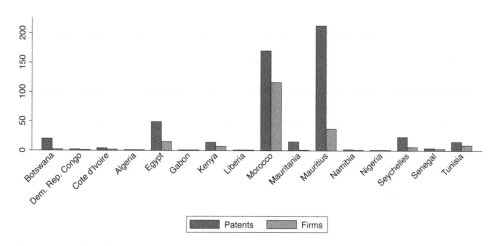

Figure 2. Number of patents and firms per country without South Africa.

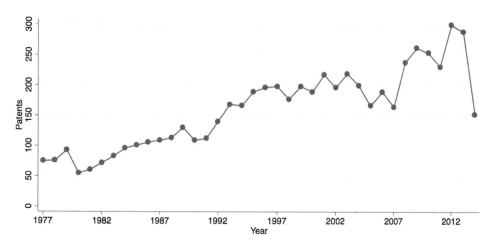

Figure 3. Number of patents per year.

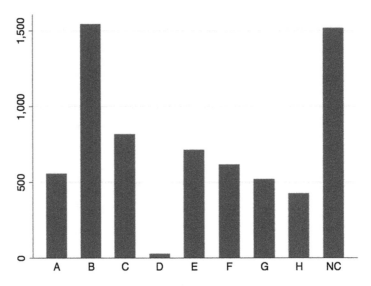

Figure 4. Number of patents, per technological sector (IPC). A: Human Necessities; B: Performing Operations, Transporting; C: Chemistry, Metallurgy; D: Textiles, Paper; E: Fixed Constructions; F: Mechanical Engineering, Lighting, Heating, Weapons; G: Physics; H: Electricity: NC: Not Classified.

to market entry. One important remark is on a limitation of patent statistics in relation to the immature systems of innovation in the international context, as could be Africa.

Patent data, on the other hand, are available for all countries but, as said before, many if not most innovations are never patented, since patents are awarded to inventions, not innovations, and the propensity to patent varies considerably across sectors and levels of economic development. So, as for many other indicators, this gives at best a very partial view of what we wish to measure. However, they constitute the only measure of innovation available for a long time-span as the one we consider in this paper. This is due to a historical lack of reliable data on innovative processes and science and technology indicators, and only recently there have been efforts to produce and obtain them (NEPAD 2014). However, no other data are available on innovative outcomes from 1977 to 2014, and hence the choice of patent data is the only one available to conduct a meaningful analysis on such a long time-span.

4.2. Results

As explained in Section 3, we first rely on the estimation of a two-by-two transition probability matrix to assess whether African firms display persistence in their innovative outcomes, and then we turn to the four-by-four case. Table 2 reports the results of the estimation procedure for the two-by-two case, carried out considering a time-horizon of 1 year, 5 years, and 10 years. The higher coefficients are displayed in the columns 'No Patent', meaning that, irrespectively of being in a state with patents or not, the probability of going to the state 'No Patent' is very high. Note, however, that these coefficients decrease as the considered time-horizon increases, and consequently the probability of going to the state 'Patents' increases.

Table 2. Transition probabilities.

	1 year		5 years		10 years	
	No patent	Patents	No patent	Patents	No patent	Patents
No Patent	0.9253	0.0747	0.7983	0.2017	0.6883	0.3117
	(0.0012)	(0.0012)	(0.0044)	(0.0043)	(0.0088)	(0.0088)
Patents	0.9103	0.0897	0.7563	0.2437	0.6124	0.3876
	(0.0047)	(0.0047)	(0.0106)	(0.0106)	(0.0120)	(0.0120)

Looking at the coefficients $\rho^{(2)}$ with $t = 1, 5, 10$ being the time-horizon under consideration and with the symbol (2) indicating that we are considering the two-state case, we can see that there is some degree of persistence, as all are greater than 0:

$$\rho_1^{(2)} = 0.015$$

$$\rho_5^{(2)} = 0.042$$

$$\rho_{10}^{(2)} = 0.076$$

Considering Table 3 we can observe a similar pattern. If a firm is able to innovate at time t, it has a high probability of not innovating at time $t + 1$, as can be seen looking at the coefficient of the first column, '0 patents'. However, as the time span under consideration increases, we see that these coefficients becomes lower and lower, whereas those in the other columns tend to increase (at least one patent at time $t + 1$). We also observe that a firm that does produce innovation at t has a fair chance to innovate also at $t + 1$, that is,

Table 3. Transition probabilities.

No. of patents	0	1	2–5	>5
1 year				
0	0.9252	0.0479	0.0219	0.0049
	(0.0013)	(0.0010)	(0.0007)	(0.0003)
1	0.9141	0.0622	0.0188	0.0048
	(0.0063)	(0.0050)	(0.0033)	(0.0016)
2–5	0.9105	0.0655	0.0153	0.0087
	(0.0086)	(0.0075)	(0.0050)	(0.0022)
>5	0.9019	0.0607	0.0327	0.0048
	(0.0181)	(0.0151)	(0.0096)	(0.0056)
5 years				
0	0.7989	0.0998	0.0666	0.0347
	(0.0045)	(0.0034)	(0.0032)	(0.0019)
1	0.7693	0.1249	0.0720	0.0339
	(0.0156)	(0.0114)	(0.0088)	(0.0068)
2–5	0.7323	0.1461	0.0887	0.0328
	(0.0178)	(0.0128)	(0.0111)	(0.0080)
>5	0.7717	0.1190	0.0611	0.0482
	(0.0234)	(0.0186)	(0.0142)	(0.0117)
10 years				
0	0.6949	0.1380	0.1044	0.0627
	(0.0088)	(0.0068)	(0.0059)	(0.0049)
1	0.6012	0.1878	0.1368	0.0742
	(0.0188)	(0.0152)	(0.0132)	(0.0095)
2–5	0.5723	0.2070	0.1367	0.0840
	(0.0203)	(0.0181)	(0.0154)	(0.0102)
>5	0.6455	0.1472	0.1371	0.0702
	(0.0289)	(0.0209)	(0.0201)	(0.0149)

8% over 1-year horizon, which however rises to around 25% and 40% over a 5-year and 10-year period, respectively.

Looking at the coefficients $\rho^{(4)}$, where the notation is analogous as previously, we can see that also in this case there is some degree of persistence, as all are greater than 0:

$$\rho_1^{(4)} = 0.008$$

$$\rho_5^{(4)} = 0.061$$

$$\rho_{10}^{(4)} = 0.090$$

These figures indicate that persistence is not high but even not negligible, in line with Cefis and Orsenigo (2001) and Cefis (2003), and it is slightly higher considering a medium and a long time-horizon. This result is mainly driven by the high probability of remaining in a state with no innovative outcomes, which is consistently greater than 0.5. However, in determining the persistence of innovation the relative importance of the transition probabilities changes as the time-horizon changes, with the probabilities of having a positive number of patents being more and more important.

Overall, for longer time spans we observe higher persistence. This result is what we would expect in an environment where firms are characterized by a low patenting activity (see Table 1): even those firms that innovate relatively more are not likely to produce innovative outcomes every year. This is in contrast with the results of Cefis and Orsenigo (2001), who find that persistence is negatively correlated with the length of the time-horizon.

However, this difference is probably due to the fact that they take into consideration advanced countries such as France, Germany, Italy, Japan, the UK, and the USA, whereas we consider developing and less-developed countries. Along these lines, a possible explanation comes from the different patterns of firms' entry, exit, and survival in industrialized and developing countries. Firstly, firm exit is higher in developing countries, thereby leaving increasing persistence once the market selection mechanisms force poor performers out of the market. Secondly, as reported in Bartelsman, Haltiwanger, and Scarpetta (2004), transition economies are characterized by firm entry largely outpacing firm exit, while more balanced patterns are found in other countries. This points to the fact that new firms not only displace obsolete incumbents in the transition phase but also filled in new markets, where faster technological development and lower competition might lead to innovation persistence among first comers. The combination of these two factors might explain why our findings differ from Cefis and Orsenigo (2001).

Finally we also perform the investigation of persistence for the five most densely populated sectors in our sample, and we recall here that we still find evidence of persistence in the majority of them. The interested reader might find the results and more details in the Appendix.

5. The role of knowledge flows

5.1. Data

After having assessed whether there is persistence in innovation among African firms, using a large dataset of firms and patents obtained through Orbis, we now turn to the question of whether knowledge flows from developed countries (OECD members) may have a positive impact on the persistence of innovative activities on African firms.

For this part of the analysis, we rely on a different dataset than the one we use in the previous part. The reason is that in this case we need information on the inventors in the research teams of the firms that applied for a patent. In particular we need the data relative to inventors' country of residence, since in this paper knowledge flows are captured by the presence of at least one foreign inventor – coming from an OECD country – in the research team of a firm. Patent data include stated addresses and country of residence of the researchers. When inventors from different countries collaborate we interpret such collaboration as source of knowledge flows. However, we are not able to distinguish the cases where the inventor is working at an address that is different from what he/she declares as residence. Notwithstanding this limitation, we think that the country of residence reflects at least part of the inventor's background, implying that some knowledge exchange brought by diversity might still take place.

Therefore, our dataset for this part of the analysis is a panel of patents requested by 1048 firms from 1977 to 2012, and it is drawn from the PATSTAT-CRIOS database (Coffano and Tarasconi 2014), a large dataset of patents set up and maintained by The Invernizzi Center for Research on Innovation, Organization, Strategy and Entrepreneurship (I-CRIOS) at Bocconi University. This dataset provides with much more detailed information on patents, which is crucial for this part of the analysis. However, this information is unnecessary for the previous part of the analysis, and therefore we use the dataset obtained from Orbis as it encompasses a substantially higher number of observations, in terms of patents, guaranteeing more reliable estimates. On the other side, we could not use the Orbis dataset in this part, as it does not contain information relative to inventors.

Table 4 shows the composition of our sample in terms of firms, firms' patenting activity, and inventors. The first column displays the number of firms that have at least one patent in the considered period, whereas the others indicate the number of patents in the period, the average number of patents per firm, the total number of inventors, and the average number of inventors per patent. Table 4 also indicates that firms, inventors, and patents increase over time, as well as the average number of patents per firm and

Table 4. Summary statistics.

Period	Firms	Patents	Patents/firm	Inventors	Inventors/patent
1977–1986	186	343	1.84	456	1.33
1987–1996	281	558	1.99	899	1.61
1997–2006	464	1008	2.17	1835	1.82
2007–2012	256	558	2.18	1162	2.08
Total	1050	2467	2.35	4234	1.72

Note: The figures in the last row, 'Total', do not correspond to the sum or the average of the previous rows, except for the column 'Patents', which is actually the sum. This is due to the fact that a firm and an inventor may patent in more than one of the 10-year periods considered here.

Table 5. Firms, patents and inventors (by country of origin).

Country	Patents	Inventors	Firms
Algeria	5	4	5
Botswana	1	3	1
Burkina Faso	2	6	2
Cameroon	1	1	1
Democratic Republic of Congo	1	0	1
Egypt	34	54	25
Ethiopia	2	1	2
Gabon	2	1	1
Ghana	1	1	2
Kenya	8	16	8
Liberia	11	1	7
Madagascar	5	10	3
Mali	5	0	1
Mauritius	83	1	33
Morocco	42	69	35
Namibia	12	6	9
Niger	1	0	1
Nigeria	2	3	2
Senegal	1	0	1
Seychelles	99	8	39
Sierra Leone	10	2	7
South Africa	2087	3051	830
Tanzania	1	1	1
Togo	2	0	1
Tunisia	46	71	26
Zimbabwe	4	4	4
OECD		799	
Total	2468	4167	1048

the size of research teams, showing both a higher propensity to innovate and a rise in the collaborations within research efforts.

Table 5 shows instead the composition of our sample in terms of geographical location. It displays all the African countries present in our sample. The row for 'OECD' indicates the number of inventors that have been in a research team of one of the African firms present in our sample. Also in this case South Africa outperforms the other countries in terms of number of firms, patents, and inventors. With regards to the number of inventors in our sample, it has overall increased over the years, as can be seen from Figure 5, which also shows the evolution of the average number of inventors that have worked for a patent application.

Figure 6 displays, for each year, either the number of firms that in that year have had in their research teams an inventor coming from an OECD country for the first time (bars), either the share of firms that have at least one OECD inventor in the considered year out of the total number of firms in the same year (line). The pattern that we can observe suggests that there have been more and more inventors coming from OECD countries over the years, and that the share of firms has increased as well.

5.2. Results

For this part of the analysis we rely on the methodology already explained, first considering two states of the world – 'No patent' and 'Patent' – and then four states – 0, 1, 2–5, and more than 5 patents. We begin by estimating transition probabilities over the full

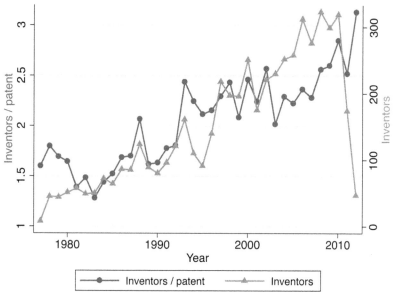

Figure 5. Number of inventors per year.

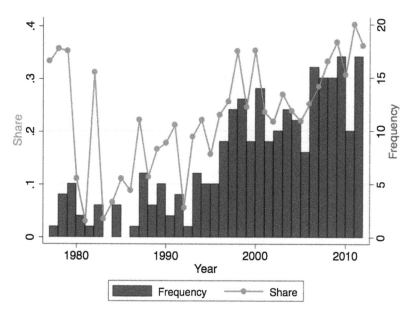

Figure 6. Number of firms with OECD inventors.

sample, then we carry out the estimation procedure considering the firms that in at least one year have had at least one inventor coming from an OECD country, and subsequently considering all the other firms. We eventually compute the ρ coefficients as before, and see whether these coefficients differ across the two different samples.

Table 6 reports the results for the firms that have had at least one inventor from an OECD country ('OECD' column) and for all the other firms ('Africa' column), in case

Table 6. Transition probabilities (two states of the world).

	Full Sample		Africa		OECD	
	No patent	Patents	No patent	Patents	No patent	Patents
1 year						
No Patent	0.9627	0.0373	0.9656	0.0344	0.9533	0.0467
	(0.0005)	(0.0005)	(0.0005)	(0.0005)	(0.0011)	(0.0011)
Patents	0.8082	0.1918	0.8955	0.1045	0.6559	0.3441
	(0.0096)	(0.0096)	(0.0125)	(0.0125)	(0.0171)	(0.0171)
5 years						
No Patent	0.8350	0.1650	0.8433	0.1567	0.8144	0.1856
	(0.0051)	(0.0051)	(0.0055)	(0.0055)	(0.0093)	(0.0093)
Patents	0.7929	0.2071	0.8175	0.1825	0.7027	0.2973
	(0.0113)	(0.0113)	(0.0124)	(0.0124)	(0.0244)	(0.0244)
10 years						
No Patent	0.6765	0.2665	0.7445	0.2555	0.7057	0.2943
	(0.0085)	(0.0085)	(0.0094)	(0.0094)	(0.0162)	(0.0162)
Patents	0.6124	0.3235	0.6912	0.3088	0.6170	0.3830
	(0.0134)	(0.0134)	(0.0159)	(0.0159)	(0.0270)	(0.0270)

two states of the world are considered. The results for the full sample in the two-by-two matrix are comparable to the ones obtained in the previous section with the data drawn from Orbis, despite some slight differences that are due to the lower number of observation. Still, the same pattern emerges: there is some degree of persistence and as the time-horizon under consideration increases, the relative importance of the Patent–Patent coefficient goes up as well. Looking at the results obtained for the 'Africa' sample and the 'OECD' sample, it is possible to observe that the coefficients in the No Patent–No Patent cells are similar, but there is a clear difference for the Patent–Patent cells, indicating that the presence of a foreign inventor in a firm's research team, and hence the presence of some kind of knowledge flows, correlates with a higher probability of remaining in an innovation state.[5]

Table 7 reports the results of the estimation conducted over the two subsamples considering four different states of the world.[6] What emerges is comparable to what already inferred in the two-by-two transition probability matrix, that is, a similarity of the coefficients of the 0–0 cells, and a substantial difference in the transition probabilities of remaining in an innovation state. In particular, we note that the coefficients corresponding to permanence in the highest innovation state (more than 5 patents over the considered time-span), are much higher for the 'OECD' sample irrespectively of considering a time period of 1, 5, or 10 years; in some cases the coefficient for the 'OECD' sample is even almost seven times higher than the one for the 'Africa' sample (for the 1-year period).

Looking at the coefficients for two-by-two case $\rho_t^{i,2}$, with $t = 1, 5, 10$ being the time-horizon and $i \in \{ AF, OECD \}$ indicating the sample, we can see that there is some degree of persistence across both samples:

$$\rho_1^{AF,2} = 0.070 \quad \rho_1^{OECD,2} = 0.297$$

$$\rho_5^{AF,2} = 0.026 \quad \rho_5^{OECD,2} = 0.112$$

$$\rho_{10}^{AF,2} = 0.053 \quad \rho_{10}^{OECD,2} = 0.089$$

Table 7. Transition probabilities (four states of the world).

No. of patents	Africa				OECD			
	0	1	2–5	>5	0	1	2–5	>5
1 year								
0	0.9656	0.0307	0.0034	0.0002	0.9532	0.0010	0.0100	0.0008
	(0.0006)	(0.0005)	(0.0002)	(0.0001)	(0.0010)	(0.0009)	(0.0006)	(0.0002)
1	0.9254	0.0486	0.0237	0.0023	0.7826	0.1114	0.0870	0.0190
	(0.0141)	(0.0141)	(0.0030)	(0.0010)	(0.0205)	(0.0212)	(0.0086)	(0.0033)
2–5	0.7381	0.1349	0.0952	0.0317	0.5210	0.1856	0.2156	0.0778
	(0.0363)	(0.0223)	(0.0348)	(0.0076)	(0.0276)	(0.0207)	(0.0341)	(0.0117)
>5	0.3846	0.3077	0.2308	0.0769	0.1923	0.0385	0.2885	0.4808
	(0.0955)	(0.0932)	(0.0774)	(0.1162)	(0.0356)	(0.0280)	(0.0403)	(0.0465)
5 years								
0	0.8136	0.1574	0.0255	0.0035	0.7987	0.1297	0.0565	0.1511
	(0.0034)	(0.0031)	(0.0013)	(0.0005)	(0.0060)	(0.0049)	(0.0033)	(0.0019)
1	0.9297	0.0392	0.0294	0.0016	0.7297	0.1622	0.0811	0.0270
	(0.0189)	(0.0185)	(0.0037)	(0.0010)	(0.0323)	(0.0334)	(0.0123)	(0.0071)
2–5	0.7168	0.1770	0.0708	0.0354	0.6026	0.1025	0.1795	0.1154
	(0.0386)	(0.0197)	(0.0393)	(0.0089)	(0.0432)	(0.0211)	(0.0459)	(0.0191)
>5	0.4706	0.1176	0.1765	0.2353	0.2683	0.0488	0.1463	0.5366
	(0.0853)	(0.0482)	(0.0504)	(0.0882)	(0.0451)	(0.0205)	(0.0305)	(0.0489)
10 years								
0	0.6210	0.3113	0.0582	0.0100	0.5690	0.2575	0.1269	0.0466
	(0.0076)	(0.0070)	(0.0029)	(0.0012)	(0.0145)	(0.0099)	(0.0087)	(0.0047)
1	0.9511	0.0262	0.0192	0.0035	0.7686	0.1074	0.0826	0.0413
	(0.0164)	(0.0165)	(0.0031)	(0.0012)	(0.0368)	(0.0376)	(0.0143)	(0.0084)
2–5	0.8036	0.1340	0.0357	0.0268	0.7612	0.1045	0.0746	0.0597
	(0.0380)	(0.0183)	(0.0412)	(0.0077)	(0.0492)	(0.0192)	(0.0527)	(0.0161)
>5	0.55	0.2	0.15	0.1	0.2368	0.1579	0.1842	0.4211
	(0.0887)	(0.0534)	(0.0462)	(0.1006)	(0.0418)	(0.0323)	(0.0335)	(0.0575)

Following the same notation, we can now consider the coefficients in the four-by-four case:

$$\rho_1^{AF,4} = 0.186 \quad \rho_1^{OECD,4} = 0.771$$

$$\rho_5^{AF,4} = 0.159 \quad \rho_5^{OECD,4} = 0.677$$

$$\rho_{10}^{AF,4} = -0.2171 \quad \rho_{10}^{OECD,4} = 0.172$$

These results show evidence of persistence in both samples, although it is much higher for the OECD one. Also, we notice that the only case where we observe absence of persistence is obtained using a 10-year windows and only African research groups ('Africa' sample). These findings highlight the positive impact exerted by knowledge flows in fostering the persistence in innovative activities, as the coefficients obtained for the OECD sample are consistently higher than those obtained for the Africa sample either considering two states of the world either considering four. This positive effect we find in this paper suggests that there could be a significant increase in the ability to innovate persistently in case firms employ inventors and researchers coming from developed countries (OECD), possibly due to knowledge transmission made possible by intra-firm and interpersonal relationships, captured in our paper by the presence of at least one OECD inventor in the firm's research team. This result is in line with the very recent work of Giuliani, Martinelli, and Rabellotti (2016), who find that cross-border inventions engaging researchers from the European Union and developing countries allow the latter to accumulate technological capabilities and access frontier knowledge. Moreover, we find evidence coherent with Montobbio and Sterzi (2010), confirming that face-to-face relationships between inventors are important mechanisms of knowledge transmission. Finally, the positive association between international co-invention and innovative performance emerging from our exercise is consistent with Branstetter, Li, and Veloso (2014), which look at international collaborations focusing on the quality of innovation rather than its persistence.

6. Conclusions

Studying the persistence of innovation in a panel of African countries is a complete novelty in the literature. Our firm-level study is a first attempt to capture and analyse the presence of such peculiarity of innovative activities in the African continent. By employing a non-parametric approach based on TPM we are able to assess, on one hand, whether there is persistence or not across a large sample of African firms. To do so, we take into consideration more than 1000 firms and a total number of about 6000 patents. On the other hand, this approach allows us to further investigate the effect of international knowledge flows, measured by the presence of researchers from OECD countries in the inventors' group, on the persistence of innovative activities. Our focus on co-invention allows to differentiate from previous research, which concentrated on more conventional means of technology transfer from advanced to developing countries, such as imports, exports, and FDI (Adegbite and Ayadi 2011; Archibugi and Pietrobelli 2003; Lall and Narula 2004). Results point out, quite clearly, the presence of some degree of persistence, implying that firms that manage to innovate are more likely to repeat in the future than they would not have innovated. Obviously enough, the share of non-patenting firms in two subsequent periods is higher than the corresponding for patenting firms. However, widening the time-horizon under consideration, the relative importance of firms that constantly patent increases, indicating that those starting to innovate keep on doing it, even though such process requires some time (more than one year). In addition, we find a positive association between international knowledge flows and higher persistence. More specifically, firms having groups of inventors that include an OECD researcher exhibit higher persistence of innovative activities than those with only African researchers and, remarkably, their likelihood to keep patenting trough time is substantially higher.

This, clearly, leads to some crucial policy implications. Recently, indeed, there have been many efforts to design and to implement science, technology, and innovation policies in Africa. All those policy measures were launched with the aim of boosting economic growth. Therefore, our findings can help shed lights on the efficacy of such policies. In particular, our results go towards the direction of promoting innovation policies and enhancing research collaborations with OECD inventors.

Being more precise, if developing and African countries in particular, want to build technological capabilities to catch up with the advanced countries, cross-border patenting activity represents an efficient means that could be promoted by tax reductions or other fiscal incentives for companies involved in international co-patenting. With specific reference to firm-level actions policy should be directed to encourage African firms' participation in global R&D networks, by funding and facilitating technical visits abroad, conference attendance, and sponsoring for internships for foreign engineers and researchers in domestic enterprises. A final policy recommendation regards public investment in technical universities and research facilities as well as structures for technological transfer (e.g. Science Parks), which might attract foreign (OECD) researchers to conduct projects therein, and which are proved to be effective policy instruments in inducing and supporting innovation (see, e.g. Lamperti, Mavilia, and Castellini 2015, and references therein). To conclude, we remind that this study does not look at the determinants of persistence; however, such aspects can constitute a line for future research.

Notes

1. In addition, we remind the interested reader that there are several studies pointing to person-to-person interaction and close location as determinant factors in the diffusion of knowledge (Almeida and Kogut 1999; Cohen, Nelson, and Walsh 2002; Von Hippel 1988; Zucker, Darby, and Armstrong 2002), and research teams are characterized by both.
2. In 2005 the African Ministerial Council on Science and Technology adopted 'Africa's Science and Technology Consolidated Plan of Action', which encompasses the African Union's agenda in terms of science, technology, and innovation policies. Within this agenda, the UNESCO launched an 'African Science, Technology and Innovation Policy Initiative', with the aim to develop national science, technology, and innovation policies for all those African countries still without one, in collaboration with national governments. See also the valuable contribution of Mudombi and Muchie (2014).
3. In particular we used 250 re-samples, iteratively set each transition probability as a single statistic, estimate its distribution and computed bootstrapping standard errors accordingly.
4. Bureau van Dijk Electronic Publishing. (2009). Company Report: BASF SE.
5. A strong remark applies here. A detailed statistical investigation of the direction of causality between international (OECD) collaborations and innovation persistence goes beyond the purposes of this study. We limit ourselves to the detection of associations emerging from the joint analysis of the two phenomena and we interpret them according to evidences already documented in the literature.
6. We estimated also the transition probabilities for the full sample, without splitting it into the two subsamples 'Africa' and 'OECD'. Results are available from the authors upon request.

Acknowledgments

The authors wish to express their gratitude to the anonymous reviewers and the special issue editors for their constructive comments and useful suggestions. This work has been partially funded by "Istituto di Ricerca per l'Innovazione e la Tecnologia nel Mediterraneo", Reggio Calabria (Italy). The authors would like to thank Daniela Marra for excellent research assistantship. Any unreferenced errors, ambiguities, misconceptions will clearly be labelled as the fault of the authors by default.

Disclosure statement

No potential conflict of interest was reported by the authors.

ORCiD

Francesco Lamperti ⓘ http://orcid.org/0000-0003-4862-646X
Roberto Mavilia ⓘ http://orcid.org/0000-0002-9030-0079

References

Adams, J., K. Gurney, D. Hook, and L. Leydesdorff. 2014. "International Collaboration Clusters in Africa." *Scientometrics* 98 (1): 547–556.

Adegbite, E. O., and F. S. Ayadi. 2011. "The Role of Foreign Direct Investment in Economic Development: A Study of Nigeria." *World Journal of Entrepreneurship, Management and Sustainable Development* 6 (1/2): 133–147.

Adeyeye, A. D., O. O. Jegede, A. J. Oluwadare, and F. S. Aremu. 2016. "Micro-level Determinants of Innovation: Analysis of the Nigerian Manufacturing Sector." *Innovation and Development* 6 (1): 1–14.

Almeida, P., and B. Kogut. 1999. "Localization of Knowledge and the Mobility of Engineers in Regional Networks." *Management Science* 45 (7): 905–917.

Alnuaimi, T., J. Singh, and G. George. 2012. "Not with My Own: Long-term Effects of Cross-country Collaboration on Subsidiary Innovation in Emerging Economies Versus Advanced Economies." *Journal of Economic Geography* 12 (5): 943–968.

Archibugi, D., and C. Pietrobelli. 2003. "The Globalisation of Technology and its Implications for Developing Countries: Windows of Opportunity or Further Burden?" *Technological Forecasting and Social Change* 70 (9): 861–883.

Bartelsman, E., J. Haltiwanger, and S. Scarpetta. 2004. "Microeconomic Evidence of Creative Destruction in Industrial and Developing Countries." Policy Research Working Paper Series 3464, The World Bank.

Branstetter, L., G. Li, and F. Veloso. 2014. "The Rise of International Co-invention." In *The Changing Frontier: Rethinking Science and Innovation Policy*, edited by Adam Jaffe and Benjamin Jones, 135–168. Chicago, IL: University of Chicago Press.

Breschi, S., and F. Lissoni. 2009. "Mobility of Skilled Workers and Co-invention Networks: An Anatomy of Localized Knowledge Flows." *Journal of Economic Geography* 9 (4): 439–468.

Cefis, E. 2003. "Is There Persistence in Innovative Activities?" *International Journal of Industrial Organization* 21 (4): 489–515.

Cefis, E., and L. Orsenigo. 2001. "The Persistence of Innovative Activities: A Cross-countries and Cross-sectors Comparative Analysis." *Research Policy* 30 (7): 1139–1158.

Coffano, M., and G. Tarasconi. 2014. "CRIOS - Patstat Database: Sources, Contents and Access Rules." CRIOS Working Paper. Center for Research on Innovation, Organization and Strategy, Bocconi University.

Cohen, W. M., R. R. Nelson, and J. P. Walsh. 2000. "Protecting Their Intellectual Assets: Appropriability Conditions and Why U.S. Manufacturing Firms Patent (or Not)." Working Paper 7552, National Bureau of Economic Research.

Cohen, W. M., R. R. Nelson, and J. P. Walsh. 2002. "Links and Impacts: The Influence of Public Research on Industrial R&D." *Management Science* 48 (1): 1–23.

De, R. 2014. "Optimal Conditions for Innovation: Firm-level Evidence from Kenya and Uganda." Presented at the 9th Annual African Economic Conference, Addis Abeba, Ethiopia.

Dernis, H., and D. Guellec. 2002. "Using Patent Counts for Cross-country Comparisons of Technology Output." *STI Review* (27): 129–146.

Egbetokun, A., P. Mendi, and R. Mudida. 2016. "Complementarity in Firm-level Innovation Strategies: A Comparative Study of Kenya and Nigeria." *Innovation and Development* 6 (1): 87–101.

Frietsch, R., and U. Schmoch. 2006. "Technological Structures and Performance as Reflected by Patent Indicators." In *National Systems of Innovation in Comparison*, edited by U. Schmoch, C. Rammer, and H. Legler, 89–105. Netherlands: Springer.

Furman, J., M. K. Kyle, A. Cockburn, and R. M. Henderson. 2005. "Public & Private Spillovers: Location and the Productivity of Pharmaceutical Research." *Annales d'Economie et de Statistique* (79–80): 165–188.

Giuliani, E., A. Martinelli, and R. Rabellotti. 2016. "Is Co-invention Expediting Technological Catch Up? A Study of Collaboration between Emerging Country Firms and EU Inventors." *World Development* 77: 192–205.

Goedhuys, M. 2007. "Learning, Product Innovation, and Firm Heterogeneity in Developing Countries; Evidence from Tanzania." *Industrial and Corporate Change* 16 (2): 269–292.

Grant, R. M. 1996. "Prospering in Dynamically-competitive Environments: Organizational Capability as Knowledge Integration." *Organization Science* 7 (4): 375–387.

Griliches, Z. 1992. "The Search for R&D Spillovers." *Scandinavian Journal of Economics* 94: S29–S47.

Kim, J., S. J. Lee, and G. Marschke. 2006. "International Knowledge Flows: Evidence from an Inventor-firm Matched Data Set." Working Paper 12692, National Bureau of Economic Research.

Lall, S., and R. Narula. 2004. "Foreign Direct Investment and Its Role in Economic Development: Do We Need a New Agenda?" *The European Journal of Development Research* 16 (3): 447–464.

Lamperti, F., R. Mavilia, and S. Castellini. 2015. "The Role of Science Parks: A Puzzle of Growth, Innovation and R&D Investments." *The Journal of Technology Transfer* 1–26. doi:10.1007/s10961-015-9455-2.

Landini, F., F. Malerba, and R. Mavilia. 2015. "The Structure and Dynamics of Networks of Scientific Collaborations in Northern Africa." *Scientometrics* 105 (3): 1787–1807.

Levinthal, D. A., and J. G. March. 1993. "The Myopia of Learning." *Strategic Management Journal* 14 (S2): 95–112.

Lorentzen, J., and M. Gastrow. 2012. "Multinational Strategies, Local Human Capital, and Global Innovation Networks in the Automotive Industry: Case Studies from Germany and South Africa." *Innovation and Development* 2 (2): 265–284.

Malerba, F., and L. Orsenigo. 1999. "Technological Entry, Exit and Survival: An Empirical Analysis of Patent Data." *Research Policy* 28 (6): 643–660.

Malerba, F., L. Orsenigo, and P. Peretto. 1997. "Persistence of Innovative Activities, Sectoral Patterns of Innovation and International Technological Specialization." *International Journal of Industrial Organization* 15 (6): 801–826.

March, J. G. 1991. "Exploration and Exploitation in Organizational Learning." *Organization Science* 2 (1): 71–87.

Miguélez, E., and R. Moreno. 2013. "Research Networks and Inventors' Mobility as Drivers of Innovation: Evidence from Europe." *Regional Studies* 47 (10): 1668–1685.

Montobbio, F., and V. Sterzi. 2010. "Inventing Together: Exploring the Nature of International Knowledge Spillovers in Latin America." *Journal of Evolutionary Economics* 21 (1): 53–89.

Mudombi, S., and M. Muchie. 2014. "An Institutional Perspective to Challenges Undermining Innovation Activities in Africa." *Innovation and Development* 4 (2): 313–326.

NEPAD. 2014. *African Innovation Outlook 2014*. Pretoria: NPCA.

Oyelaran-Oyeyinka, B., G. O. A. Laditan, and A. O. Esubiyi. 1996. "Industrial Innovation in Sub-Saharan Africa: The Manufacturing Sector in Nigeria." *Research Policy* 25 (7): 1081–1096.

Peters, B. 2009. "Persistence of Innovation: Stylised Facts and Panel Data Evidence." *The Journal of Technology Transfer* 34 (2): 226–243.

Robson, P., H. Haugh, and B. Obeng. 2009. "Entrepreneurship and Innovation in Ghana: Enterprising Africa." *Small Business Economics* 32 (3): 331–350.

Rooks, G., L. Oerlemans, A. Buys, and T. Pretorius. 2005. "Industrial Innovation in South Africa: A Comparative Study." *South African Journal of Science* 101 (3–4): 149–150.

Singh, J. 2005. "Collaborative Networks as Determinants of Knowledge Diffusion Patterns." *Management Science* 51 (5): 756–770.

Singh, J. 2008. "Distributed R&D, Cross-regional Knowledge Integration and Quality of Innovative Output." *Research Policy* 37 (1): 77–96.

von Hippel, E. 1988. *The Sources of Innovation*. New York, NY: Oxford University Press.

Zucker, L. G., M. R. Darby, and J. S. Armstrong. 2002. "Commercializing Knowledge: University Science, Knowledge Capture, and Firm Performance in Biotechnology." *Management Science* 48 (1): 138–153.

Appendix

In this appendix we perform the estimation of transition probabilities for five different industries, considering a two-state Markov process. We exploit the same dataset used in Section 4, whose data are taken from Orbis, which has information also on the major industrial sector firms operate in. Figures A1 and A2 report, respectively, the number of firms and the number of patents by the firm's major industrial sector. In our analysis in this appendix we have considered only the five sectors that display the highest number of observations in terms of patents and firms, as the estimation of transition probabilities is meaningful only in presence of a sufficiently large sample. The five sectors for which we performed the estimation are Chemicals, Machinery, Metals, Primary Sector, and Wholesale & Retail Trade, which are the sectors with the highest number of observations (excluding 'Other services', which is a residual concept).

Results are presented in Table A1. What emerges from the table by looking at the coefficients in the main diagonal for each sector and time windows, is a heterogeneous picture. In all sectors but 'Primary Sector' – which does not show evidence of persistence for any time windows – we observe some degree of persistence for some of the time intervals under consideration. For example, the results for the sector 'Metals' point to persistence over 1- and 10-year windows, but no persistence over 5-year horizon; the other sectors, despite different magnitudes, display persistence over all the time-horizons under consideration. This heterogeneity is in line with Cefis and Orsenigo (2001). Finally, we underline that, as a characterizing feature, the estimated probability of keep innovating after an innovation is quite similar across the industries where persistence is found in the aggregate picture and across the various horizons, with the exception of the 10-year one, where 'Metals' exhibit a slightly larger coefficient that the other classes. Even though further and more detailed research would be needed, the heterogeneity in the presence of persistence across industries seems to be accompanied by some uniformity in the estimated of the transition probabilities characterizing the innovation process of sector where persistence is positively found.

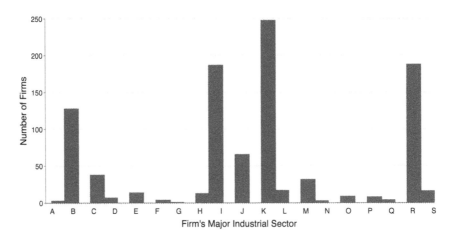

Figure A1. Number of firms, per firm's major industrial sector.

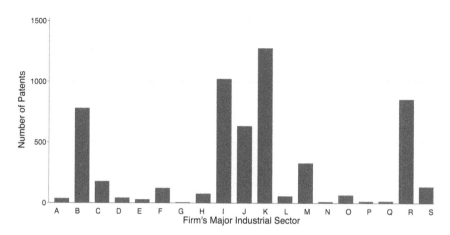

Figure A2. Number of patents, per firm's major industrial sector. A: Banks; B: Chemicals, rubber, plastics, non-metallic; C: Construction; D: Education, Health; E: Food, beverages, tobacco; F: Gas, Water, Electricity; G: Hotels, restaurants; H: Insurance; I: Machinery, equipment, furniture, recycling; J: Metals, metal products; K: Other Services; L: Post, Telecommunications; M: Primary Sector; N: Public Administration, Defence; O: Publishing, Printing; P: Textiles, Wearing apparel, Leather; Q: Transport; R: Wholesale and retail trade; S: Wood, Cork, Paper.

Table A1. Transition probabilities estimated for 5 different industries.

	Chemicals		Machinery		Metals		Primary sector		Trade	
	No patent	Patents	No patent	Patents	No patent	Patents	No patent	Patents	No patent	Patents
1 year										
No Patent	0.9273	0.0727	0.9341	0.0658	0.9121	0.0879	0.9057	0.0943	0.9437	0.0563
	(0.0035)	(0.0035)	(0.0028)	(0.0028)	(0.0049)	(0.0049)	(0.0088)	(0.0088)	(0.0025)	(0.0025)
Patents	0.8971	0.1029	0.8969	0.1031	0.8868	0.1132	0.9675	0.0325	0.9310	0.0690
	(0.0154)	(0.0154)	(0.0125)	(0.0125)	(0.0186)	(0.0186)	(0.0275)	(0.0275)	(0.0132)	(0.0132)
5 years										
No Patent	0.8180	0.1820	0.8257	0.1743	0.7678	0.2322	0.7230	0.2770	0.8566	0.1434
	(0.0124)	(0.0124)	(0.0094)	(0.0094)	(0.0178)	(0.0178)	(0.0275)	(0.0275)	(0.0092)	(0.0092)
Patents	0.7212	0.2788	0.7134	0.2866	0.7652	0.2348	0.8939	0.1061	0.7209	0.2791
	(0.0298)	(0.0298)	(0.0247)	(0.0247)	(0.0404)	(0.0404)	(0.0508)	(0.0508)	(0.0282)	(0.0282)
10 years										
No Patent	0.7156	0.2844	0.7358	0.2642	0.7067	0.2933	0.6602	0.3398	0.7811	0.2190
	(0.0197)	(0.0197)	(0.0163)	(0.0163)	(0.0299)	(0.0299)	(0.0483)	(0.0483)	(0.0148)	(0.0148)
Patents	0.6685	0.3315	0.6241	0.3759	0.5607	0.4393	0.6731	0.3269	0.6178	0.3822
	(0.0359)	(0.0359)	(0.0312)	(0.0312)	(0.0504)	(0.0504)	(0.0679)	(0.0679)	(0.0303)	(0.0303)

Effect of knowledge sources on firm-level innovation in Tanzania

Otieno Osoro, Patrick Vermeulen, Joris Knoben and Godius Kahyarara

ABSTRACT
This paper analyses the impact of different sources of knowledge on product and process innovation in Tanzania using firm-level data. We specifically analyse the separate impacts of internal knowledge, external knowledge and the combined impact of both types of knowledge on firms' product and process innovation decisions. The analysis reveals that the purchase of machinery, equipment or software, year of firm establishment, the sector a firm belongs to, and internal research and development impact on product and process innovation. Product innovation is more constrained by a lack of external knowledge than process innovation. External research and development do not affect product or process innovation and the joint effect of internal and external knowledge on product innovation exceeds the separate effects of internal and external knowledge on innovation. Furthermore, external knowledge acquisition and firm spending on internal research and development affect product and process innovation more effectively for older firms and firms in the services sector. Finally, the interaction of external and internal knowledge raises chances of undertaking product and process innovation with internal and external knowledge having greater impact on innovation when internal and external knowledge complement each other than when utilized separately.

1. Introduction

Innovation is a process of translating ideas or inventions into goods or services with economic value. Knowledge is a prerequisite for innovation as innovation involves the generation, exploitation and manipulation of new forms of knowledge by firms to create new products (Katila and Chen 2008; Schulze and Hoegl 2008). There are two main sources of knowledge for innovation, namely internal and external sources of knowledge (Lundvall 1988; Cohen and Levinthal 1990). The former involves the development and utilization of knowledge within a firm's boundaries while the latter involves the acquisition of new knowledge from external sources.

External knowledge acquisition is useful only if a firm possesses an existing base of knowledge enabling it to utilize such knowledge. A firm's capacity to utilize external knowledge is commonly conceptualized as its absorptive and transformative capacity with the former being the ability to recognize and exploit technological opportunities developed outside the firm (Cohen and Levinthal 1990; Zahra and George 2002) and the latter being the ability to continually redefine a product portfolio based on technological opportunities or skills within a firm (Garud and Nayyar 1994).

The objective of this study is to determine the extent to which different knowledge sources contribute to a firm's innovation performance. Specifically, the study analyses the direction and magnitude of impact of internal and external knowledge sources on firms' innovative performance and the joint impact of factors influencing innovative performance. The study uses cross-sectional data from the Tanzania Enterprise Survey (ES) 2013 and an Innovation Follow-up Survey conducted in 2014. The study finds product innovation to be more constrained by a lack of external knowledge than process innovation. Furthermore, internal and external knowledge have greater impact on innovation when complementing each other than when utilized separately. Finally, external knowledge acquisition and firm spending on internal research and development affect product and process innovation more effectively for older firms and firms in the services sector.

2. Theoretical framework

Schumpeter explained innovation in the context of 'creative destruction' where entrepreneurs had incentives to pursue new innovations to replace old ones in response to declining profit margins resulting from copying innovations (Schumpeter 1912). Various other models have been put forward to explain the relationship between knowledge sources and innovation, such as the linear innovation model of innovation and the interactive model of innovation. The linear model asserts investment in research and development is the main driver of innovation performance with a direct link between research and development expenditures, innovation and productivity gains (Arrow 1962). The interactive model (Nelson and Winter 1982; Baptista and Swann 1998; Cooke and Morgan 1998) on the other hand asserts innovation does not only result from investment in research and development, but also from knowledge acquisition from production activities and through firms' ability to acquire knowledge by developing links with other firms.

Empirical research on innovation has focused on technological learning processes influencing innovation and the conditions for successful innovation. Various studies have examined the role and impact of internal and external sources of knowledge on innovation (Malerba 1992; Lowe and Taylor 1998; Portelli and Narula 2003; Edquist 2004; Szogs 2004; Cassiman and Veugelers 2006; Laursen and Salter 2006; Vega-Jurado, Gutiér-rez-Gracia, and Fernández-de-Lucio 2008). Internal knowledge is key for the enhancement of the ability to use external knowledge and increases a firm's potential to identify opportunities, which in turn has a positive effect on innovation (Zahra and George 2002). Similarly, external sources of knowledge positively affect innovation by enhancing firms access to new opportunities, enabling development of new competences and improving firm-level technical efficiency (Vega-Jurado, Gutiérrez-Gracia, and Fernández-de-Lucio 2008; Keshari 2013). The relation between the ability to acquire new knowledge and innovative performance has been established frequently in the literature (see also Laursen and Salter 2006; Kasseeah 2013).

Malerba (1992) concluded that external and internal knowledge sources were substitutes that firms could adapt as innovation strategies. Other studies emphasized the role of internal competency in utilizing external knowledge, implying complementarity between internal and external knowledge (Lundvall 1988; Cohen and Levinthal 1990). Egbetokun, Mendi, and Mudida (2016) find evidence of complementarities between internal and external technological innovation strategies in Kenya but not in Nigeria. These studies suggest that apart from generating innovation, internal knowledge also improves a firm's capacity to identify and utilize external knowledge for generating innovation. Other studies investigated the relationship between internal and external knowledge more specifically, finding that firms with significant involvement in internal research and development had greater external links and greater capacity to acquire and utilize external knowledge sources (Lowe and Taylor 1998; Edquist 2004).

Various studies have investigated the link between knowledge and innovation in Tanzania. Using a case study of two manufacturing firms in Tanzania, Portelli and Narula (2003) found technological upgrading occurred in Tanzania as a result of foreign investment with its magnitude determined by capabilities within the industrial base in Tanzania. Szogs (2004) and Mahemba and De Bruijn (2003), however, point out that there is only a limited transfer of knowledge between firms in Tanzania. Using firm level data on product innovation and learning in Tanzanian manufacturing and commercial farming, Goedhuys (2007) found that larger and foreign-owned firms invested significantly more in human and physical capital than local small and medium enterprises (SMEs), but these collaborated more intensively with other local firms on product development, marketing and on the input market and upgrade technology.

Although knowledge is an important aspect of innovation, it must be complemented by other factors to successfully achieve innovation. These factors pertain to structural and process characteristics involving firm size, firm age, market structure and factors, and human, organizational and financial resources (Dewar and Dutton 1986; Audretsch and Acs 1987; Moch and Morse 1997; Hurley and Hult 1998; Floyd and Wooldridge 1999; Greene, Brush, and Hart 1999). Other scholars identify information and knowledge management and collaboration with other agents as factors impacting innovation through their effect on structural and process characteristics of firms (Hagedoorn and Narula 1996; Freeman 1998).

As such, the empirical literature reveals the complementary nature between internal and external knowledge in Tanzania via the role of internal competence in utilizing external knowledge, improvement of a firm's capacity to identify and utilize external knowledge for generating innovation, and enhanced external links. Furthermore, larger and foreign-owned firms in Tanzania invested significantly more in human and physical capital than SMEs which however had greater local collaboration on product development, marketing, and on the input market and upgrade technology. However, firm size did not affect any type of innovation in manufacturing firms in Nigeria (Adeyeye et al. 2016).

The study adds value to previous studies by also examining market factors that are not analysed in most studies that examine factors impacting innovation. The market factors are market share enhancement motives for engaging in innovation and cost reducing motives for engaging in innovation. The former increases market share directly, while the latter does this indirectly through the fact that relatively low cost innovations are more competitive and can potentially lead to better performance in the market. Market factors also give an indication of the extent in which firms take into account business aspects when undertaking innovation.

3. Research context and methodology

3.1. Research context

In the national innovation system of Tanzania, the Ministry of Education, Science, Technology, and Vocational Training is responsible for the innovation policy. The ministry spearheads the formulation and implementation of science, technology and innovation policies in the country by formulating and reviewing science, technology, innovation and research policies, guidelines and standards in the country, and monitoring and evaluation of implementation of policies, guidelines and standards. Tanzania furthermore has a Commission for Science and Technology (COSTECH) that coordinates science, technology, and innovation activities in the country and advises the Government on all matters relating to science, technology and innovation.

Given the structure of Tanzania's innovation system, the country's regulatory and institutional structure can be conducive for facilitating innovation upgrading. The innovation system in Tanzania, however, suffers from lack of means and resources for development and promotion of science, technology and innovation, which hinders the further development of innovation activities in the country. There are several reasons for this. First, the government has significantly reduced funding of organizations involved in innovation. This has led these organizations to depend on marketing their services and technologies to survive, which subsequently results in the increased tendency of organizations to introduce unapplied innovations.

Second, the lack of resources for development of innovation in Tanzania has increased the significance of overseas development assistance (ODA) and foreign direct investment (FDI) in development of knowledge and innovation through various bilateral and multilateral programmes. Such programmes can however be insufficient, scattered and poorly coordinated in a manner that fails to adequately support innovative activities in the country. The fact that ODA and FDI come from abroad can lead to supplier-driven support of innovation activities with some programmes being driven by donors' self-interest. Furthermore, ODA and FDI support tends to go more to large enterprises at the expense of smaller enterprises.

As the majority of firms in Tanzania are SMEs, it is imperative for potential SME participants to have access to education to enhance their knowledge and skill acquisition. Most SME participants obtain knowledge from vocational education, which makes vocational education crucial for knowledge creation and innovation in the country. In light of this, the Tanzanian Government established the Vocational Education Authority (VETA) in 1994 to oversee the vocational education training and education system in Tanzania. VETA does this by providing, coordinating, regulating and promoting vocational education and training in the country. The importance of vocational education and training for SMEs, and the economy in general, led the Government to introduce a Skills Development Levy to finance vocational education and training through VETA. The Skills

Development Levy is 6% of the payroll of employers with four or more employees and is an important feature of the innovative performance of SMEs in Tanzania.

3.2. Data

The study employs cross-sectional data from the World Bank, namely the Tanzania Enterprise Survey (ES) 2013 and an Innovation Follow-up Survey conducted in 2014. The former provides a wide range of firm-level variables including information on recruitment, training and R&D practices within the firm. The innovation follow-up survey provides evidence on the nature, role and determinants of innovation in Tanzania. The objective of the World Bank Enterprise Survey and its innovation follow-up was twofold; obtaining feedback from enterprises on the state of the private sector and building a panel to facilitate tracking of changes in the business environment over time. The Innovation Follow-up Survey focused on the main innovation activities undertaken by firms from fiscal year 2010 through 2012 hence only firms established between 2010 and 2012 are included in the study. The follow-up survey involved a subset of Enterprise Survey respondents randomly selected to make up a final sample of 75% of the original Enterprise Survey with the objective of collecting data on innovation and innovation-related activities.

Observations from non-innovating firms are not used in the analysis because the study's dependent variables are firm's attempts to develop innovative products (PROD) and processes (PROC) and not firm development of innovative products and processes because innovation is more of a process rather than an instantaneous event. Observations from non-innovating firms are therefore not utilized in the analysis because such firms have not made any attempt at innovation.

3.3. Variables

3.3.1. Dependent variables

The study focuses on product and process innovation. However, since innovation is a process rather than an instantaneous event, we must not just consider the innovative products or processes themselves, but also the attempt to develop innovative products and processes. In light of this, the dependent variables are measured as a firm's attempts to develop innovative products (PROD) and processes (PROC) that are dummy variables.

3.3.2. Independent variables

There are various knowledge sources embodying different types of knowledge. Knoben and Oerleman (2010) distinguish between firm internal, external business knowledge, external technological knowledge and external codified knowledge, noting that utilization of different types of knowledge result in different outcomes with regards to firm innovativeness. In light of this classification of knowledge, we include the following sources of knowledge: firm internal knowledge (firm funding of internal research and development – IRD); business knowledge (recruitment of staff for innovation purposes – RECRUIT) and staff training (TRAIN), external technological knowledge (firm funding of external research and development (ERD), firm purchase of equipment, machinery or software (PEQP) and purchase of intangible technology (PINT). ERD, PEQP and PINT are external sources of knowledge while IRD, RECRUIT and TRAIN are internal sources of knowledge.

Apart from the variables pertaining to sources of knowledge at the firm level other independent variables for the study pertain to motives for pursuing innovation (cost reducing motives for engaging in innovation – MCOST) and market share enhancement motives for engaging in innovation (MSHARE), the sector of the economy a firm belongs to (SECTOR), that is, a manufacturing dummy, firm innovative experience (EXP) in terms of number of years since introduction of an innovative product/process by a firm, and firm age (AGE) that controls for variation in ability of different firms to innovate. IRD, ERD, PEQP, PINT, RECRUIT, TRAIN, SECTOR, MCOST and MSHARE are all dummy variables while EXP and AGE are continuous variable.

3.4. Empirical specification

We model the impact of the sources of knowledge and their interactions on innovation separately because although external knowledge is important for innovation, its magnitude of importance is determined by a firm's absorptive and transformative capacity (Cohen and Levinthal 1990; Garud and Nayyar 1994; Zahra and George 2002). Absorptive and transformative capacity is acquired mostly through IRD and thus indicates a firm's pre-existing knowledge that can be utilized to identify, assimilate, and exploit external knowledge (Edquist 2004; Vega-Jurado, Gutiérrez-Gracia, and Fernández-de-Lucio 2008).

Various studies have examined the role and impact the different sources of knowledge on innovation (Malerba 1992; Lowe and Taylor 1998; Portelli and Narula 2003; Edquist 2004; Szogs 2004; Cassiman and Veugelers 2006; Laursen and Salter 2006; Vega-Jurado, Gutiérrez-Gracia, and Fernández-de-Lucio 2008). All these studies except one (Vega-Jurado, Gutiérrez-Gracia, and Fernández-de-Lucio 2008) have modelled internal and external together to show the impact of sources of knowledge on innovation. However, since a firm's capacity to absorb external knowledge to undertake innovation and the effectiveness of external knowledge to stimulate innovation depends on a firm's pre-existing knowledge level, the study models internal and external knowledge separately before modelling them together to simulate the impact of pre-existing knowledge levels on innovation before external knowledge acquisition and the impact of external knowledge on innovation assuming a non-existent internal knowledge base.

Modelling internal and external knowledge separately before modelling them together isolates the separate effects of internal and external knowledge on innovation from their combined effects on innovation, which provides a better context to the impact of both sources of knowledge on innovation then when they are modelled together. This can provide a more accurate picture of the relative importance of different knowledge sources on innovation processes.

Six binary logit models are used to achieve the objectives of the study in line with Vega-Jurado, Gutiérrez-Gracia, and Fernández-de-Lucio (2008). Given the objectives of the study, we use the following empirical models.

$$\text{PROD} = \beta_0 + \beta_1 \text{ERD} + \beta_2 \text{PEQP} + \beta_3 \text{PINT} + \beta_4 \text{MCOST} + \beta_5 \text{MSHARE} + \beta_6 \text{EXP} + \beta_7 \text{SECTOR} + \beta_8 \text{AGE}, \tag{1}$$

$$PROD = \beta_0 + \beta_1 IRD + \beta_2 TRAIN + \beta_3 RECRUIT + \beta_4 MCOST + \beta_5 MSHARE$$
$$+ \beta_6 EXP + \beta_7 SECTOR + \beta_8 AGE, \tag{2}$$

$$PROD = \beta_0 + \beta_1 ERD + \beta_2 PEQP + \beta_3 PINT + \beta_4 IRD + \beta_5 TRAIN + \beta_6 RECRUIT$$
$$+ \beta_7 MCOST + \beta_8 MSHARE + \beta_9 EXP + \beta_{10} SECTOR + \beta_{11} AGE, \tag{3}$$

$$PROC = \beta_0 + \beta_1 ERD + \beta_2 PEQP + \beta_3 PINT + \beta_4 MCOST + \beta_5 MSHARE,$$
$$+ \beta_6 EXP + \beta_7 SECTOR + \beta_8 AGE, \tag{4}$$

$$PROC = \beta_0 + \beta_1 IRD + \beta_2 TRAIN + \beta_3 RECRUIT + \beta_4 MCOST + \beta_5 MSHARE$$
$$+ \beta_6 EXP + \beta_7 SECTOR + \beta_8 AGE, \tag{5}$$

$$PROC = \beta_0 + \beta_1 ERD + \beta_2 PEQP + \beta_3 PINT + \beta_4 IRD + \beta_5 TRAIN + \beta_6 RECRUIT$$
$$+ \beta_7 MCOST + \beta_8 MSHARE + \beta_9 EXP + \beta_{10} SECTOR + \beta_{11} AGE. \tag{6}$$

Models (1) and (4) analyse the impact of external knowledge on a firm's product innovation and process innovation activities respectively ignoring internal knowledge capacity. Models (2) and (5) analyse the impact of internal knowledge on a firm's product innovation and process innovation activities ignoring its external knowledge capacity, and Models (3) and (6) analyse the extent to which internal knowledge impacts product innovation and process innovation respectively and its effect on external knowledge in influencing innovation. Apart from identifying impact of knowledge sources on innovation performance, estimation results from Models (1) to (6) also facilitate better identification of the relationship between internal and external sources of knowledge with regards to its impact on innovation.

4. Results

4.1. Descriptive statistics

Discussion of features characterizing the data used for the study is necessary before discussing the empirical results in order to identify patterns in the data. Table 1 summarises statistics of the variables used in the models. The correlation coefficients in Table 1 reveal a far higher correlation between product and process innovation and IRD compared to product and process innovation and ERD with process innovation having a higher correlation with internal R&D and external R&D than product innovation. This may hint at greater impact of internal knowledge than external knowledge on innovation. Both product and process innovation have higher correlations with external technological knowledge than with business knowledge indicating firms may have a preference for buying technology over investing in IRD to produce new technology. There is a significant correlation between internal knowledge (IRD) and external knowledge (ERD and PEQP) as well as a significant correlation between business knowledge (TRAINING) and ERD. This may indicate complementarity between internal knowledge

Table 1. Descriptive statistics and correlation coefficients of variables used in the models.

	Mean	SD	PROD	IRD	TRAIN	RECRUIT	ERD	PEQP	PINT	MCOST	MSHARE	EXP	SECTOR	AGE
PROD	0.21	0.41												
PROC	0.29	0.45	0.46	0.45	0.23	0.10	0.17	0.41	0.08	-0.01	-0.08	-0.27	-0.15	0.04
IRD	0.22	0.41	0.40											
TRAIN	0.25	0.43	0.13	0.35										
RECRUIT	0.23	0.42	0.11	0.27	0.14									
ERD	0.04	0.18	0.15	0.43	0.17	0.21								
PEQP	0.40	0.49	0.32	0.42	0.51	0.08	0.25							
PINT	0.15	0.36	0.14	0.19	0.24	0.20	0.20	0.27						
MCOST	0.27	0.44	0.16	-0.09	0.02	-0.02	-0.14	-0.11	-0.04					
MSHARE	0.55	0.44	0.04	0.18	0.26	-0.10	0.12	0.31	0.23	-0.06				
EXP	1.32	0.58	-0.31	-0.07	-0.07	-0.14	-0.13	-0.08	-0.13	-0.08	-0.02			
SECTOR	0.50	0.50	-0.35	0.01	0.05	-0.12	-0.08	-0.02	-0.04	-0.22	0.20	0.20		
AGE	12.92	9.66	0.08	-0.10	0.20	0.06	0.007	0.04	-0.04	-0.10	-0.14	-0.10	0.20	

and external knowledge in impacting product innovation (Mohnen and Roller 2005; Cassiman and Veugelers 2006).

Most of the firms began pursuing innovation in 2010 or 2011 and have thus had adequate time to at least attempt to undertake product and process innovations. About half of the sampled firms are involved in manufacturing. Table 1 reveals that only about a fifth of the sampled firms undertake or attempt product innovation with 8% more of firms engaging in process innovation. The average age of firms is about 13 years indicating most firms have the potential to undertake innovation by virtue of having a potentially adequate knowledge base. Firms invest about seven times more in internal knowledge and business knowledge than in external knowledge as well as investing more in external technological knowledge via purchase of equipment, machinery or software and tangible technology than in business knowledge through staff recruitment and training. Market factors are important considerations for firms in making innovation decisions. Over half of the firms perceive increased market share as a reason for undertaking product innovation, while decreased costs are the reason for more than a quarter of the firms to undertake innovation.

4.2. Regression analysis

Tables 2 and 3 show the logit model estimation results for Models (1)–(3) and (4)–(6) respectively. Chi-square values for all the models reveal we can reject the null hypothesis that all parameters beside the constant are equal to zero implying the explanatory variables in the models can adequately explain variation in product and process innovation. Furthermore, Pseudo R^2 values for the six models are sufficiently high further indicating changes in product innovation significantly result from changes in the explanatory variables.

4.3. Impact of external knowledge on innovation

Models 1 and 4 show that firm expenditures on ERD and purchasing intangible technology do not influence product or process innovation. Purchase of equipment, machinery or software, however, increases a firm's chances of pursuing both product and process innovation, which increases the chances of pursuing process innovation more than product innovation. External knowledge in Tanzania thus emanates more from buying items than from acquisition of external knowledge to supplement internal knowledge in producing innovative products, as such external knowledge enhances their capacity to absorb new knowledge, which is in line with findings from Cohen and Levinthal (1990).

Purchasing machinery, equipment and software is more common than investing in external knowledge to enhance internal knowledge to undertake innovative processes probably because of low levels of technological capability that constrain firms' capacity to undertake adequate IRD. This finding is consistent with Szogs (2004).

Models 1 and 4 also show the more innovative experience firms have, the higher the chances of undertaking product and process innovation. This indicates firms with less innovative experience mostly engage in innovation by the production of items already existing in the market or by adaptation of existing processes because of the need for time to establish themselves in the market before innovating. Firms must establish

Table 2. Logit estimation results of product innovation.

	Model 1		Model 2		Model 3	
	Coeff	dy/dx	Coeff	dy/dx	Coeff	dy/dx
ERD	0.40	0.1			-1.63	-0.35
PEQP	1.66***	0.39			1.57**	0.37
PINT	-0.30	-0.07			-0.02	-0.005
IRD			3.33***	0.61	3.57***	0.63
TRAIN			-0.36	-0.09	-1.22	-0.29
RECRUIT			-0.63	-0.15	-0.57	-0.14
MCOST	-0.66	-0.16	-0.52	-0.13	-0.58	-0.14
MSHARE	0.02	0.004	-0.03	-0.07	.006	0.02
EXP	-0.73**	-0.18	-0.91**	-0.23	-0.97**	0.24
SECTOR	-1.47**	-0.35	-1.92***	-0.45	-2.08***	-0.48
AGE	0.02	0.005	0.04	0.009	0.05	0.01

Model 1:
Number of obs = 89
LR $\chi^2(8)$ = 29.82
Prob > χ^2 = 0.0002
Log likelihood = −46.776347
Pseudo R^2 = 0.2417
Probability of positive outcome = 0.492

Model 2:
Number of obs = 89
LR χ^2 (8) = 40.38
Prob > χ^2 = 0.0000
Log likelihood = −41.494095
Pseudo R^2 = 0.3273
Probability of positive outcome = 0.509

Model 3:
Number of obs = 89
LR χ^2 (10) = 46.06
Prob > χ^2 = 0.0000
Log likelihood = −38.656666
Pseudo R^2 = 0.3733
Probability of positive outcome = 0.514

Note: * $p < .10$; ** $p < .05$; *** $p < .01$.

Table 3. Logit estimation results of process innovation.

	Model 4		Model 5		Model 6	
	Coeff	dy/dx	Coeff	dy/dx	Coeff	dy/dx
ERD	0.69	0.17			-1.38	-0.29
PEQP	1.99***	0.45			1.61**	0.38
PINT	-0.85	-0.20			-0.93	-0.22
IRD			2.84**	0.58	3.00***	0.60
TRAIN			0.42	0.11	-0.05	-0.01
RECRUIT			-0.62	-0.15	-0.56	-0.13
MCOST	-0.17	-0.04	0.10	0.02	0.06	-0.01
MSHARE	-0.06	0.01	0.02	-0.006	0.06	0.02
EXP	-0.75**	-0.18	-0.84**	-0.21	-0.89**	-0.22
SECTOR	-0.48	-0.13	-0.82	-0.20	-0.87	-0.21
AGE	0.001	0.001	0.018	0.04	0.02	0.004

Model 4: Number of obs = 89, LR $\chi^2(8) = 25.35$, Prob > χ^2 = 0.0014, Log likelihood = -48.557312, Pseudo R^2 = 0.2070, Probability of positive outcome = 0.437

Model 5: Number of obs = 89, LR $\chi^2(8) = 30.29$, Prob > χ^2 = 0.0002, Log likelihood = -46.091116, Pseudo R^2 = 0.2473, Probability of positive outcome = 0.456

Model 6: Number of obs = 89, LR $\chi^2(11) = 38.16$, Prob > χ^2 = 0.0001, Log likelihood = -42.156618, Pseudo R^2 = 0.3116, Probability of positive outcome = 0.455

Note: *$p < .10$; **$p < .05$; ***$p < .01$.

themselves in the market prior to engaging in innovation processes because innovation attempts must be accompanied by adequate internal technological capacity acquired through IRD, training and recruitment (Cassiman and Veugelers 2006). However, firms tend to prioritize business sustainability by focusing on quick win activities over long-term ones, such as investments in internal knowledge. It is only after business stability is attained that firms may desire to venture into innovation. Firm age however does not impact innovation in Tanzania. This finding differs from various findings (Klepper 1996; Kim and Marschke 2005) that younger firms innovate more than older firms. The insignificance of firm age on innovation may imply that factors leading to younger firms being more innovative than older firms such as turnover of innovators from older firms, lower per capita cost of innovation for smaller firms, and higher success of first products relative to products introduced later are less pronounced in Tanzania.

Belonging to the manufacturing sector reduces the chances of a firm undertaking product innovation while it does not influence the chances of a firm undertaking process innovation. The size of the service sector is more than four times that of the manufacturing sector in Tanzania, which implies a higher likelihood of product innovation occurring in the service sector than the manufacturing sector. Furthermore, service firms require less capital than manufacturing firms because production in the service sector tends to be less costly than in the manufacturing sector. Product innovation in the service sector thus tends to be less costly than in the manufacturing sector. This is similar to findings by Baldwin and Gellatly (2004) who found service firms require less financial resources to innovate because they tend to have less financial barriers to innovation than manufacturing firms. Furthermore, belonging to the manufacturing sector does not impact chances of a firm undertaking process innovation, probably because undertaking process innovation is usually cheaper than undertaking product innovation.

Finally, Models 1 and 4 show that market factors do not influence a firm's decision to undertake product or process innovation, which implies that once firms are established, their objective is to gain a foothold in the market through adapting to the situation in the market rather than through introducing innovative products or processes that follows establishment in the market.

4.4. Impact of internal knowledge on innovation

Model 2 shows the impact of internal knowledge of product innovation ignoring external knowledge sources. It shows that internal knowledge accumulated from firm spending on IRD is significant in a firm's decision to undertake product innovation, while business knowledge and codified knowledge does not influence such a decision with it having a slightly higher impact on product innovation than on process innovation. Innovation processes in Tanzania are thus more driven by the internal development of knowledge rather than the internal development of processes and skills.

Firm age does not influence the impact of internal knowledge on innovation indicating younger firms differ slightly with larger firms with respect to attributes that lead to greater impact of internal knowledge on innovation pertaining to innovation costs, better accommodation of innovators, and fresher ideas.

Tanzanian firms preference to generate knowledge through investing in IRD more than through training and staff recruitment is probably because output of IRD tends to be more sustainable than knowledge generated through training and staff recruitment. This is because knowledge obtained from staff training and recruitment may be depleted or totally lost in the face of employee turnover. Such sustainability is essential as it creates knowledge that enhances capacity to utilize external knowledge by increasing a firm's ability to identify and take advantage of technological opportunities emanating from other firms by generating knowledge to do so. This is in line with Zahra and George (2002) who identified knowledge creation as essential for perpetual enhancement of capacity to utilize external knowledge by increasing a firm's ability to identify and take advantage of technological opportunities emanating from other firms.

The insignificance of business knowledge and codified knowledge in influencing product and process innovation in firms in terms of training and recruitment may be a result of the fact that firms in the sample have little innovative experience with the most experienced commencing innovative activities in 2010. Such firms first need to develop an internal knowledge base that can effectively enable them to acquire or develop further knowledge. Development of an internal knowledge base is better under-taken by investing in IRD than on business and codified knowledge, which are more effec-tive only after development of an adequate internal knowledge base hence, the influence of IRD on product innovation when external knowledge is ignored consistent with Goedhuys (2007) and Portelli and Narula (2003).

The chances of a firm undertaking product innovation is higher in Model 2 than Model 1, while the chances of a firm undertaking process innovation is higher in Model 5 than Model 4 implying internal knowledge (ignoring external knowledge) has greater impact on both product and process innovation than external knowledge (ignoring internal knowledge). Since external knowledge is usually more advanced than internal knowledge, greater impact of the latter in innovation is an indication of low absorptive capacity of local firms. This is in line with findings by Semboja and Kweka (2001) and Lane and Lubatkin (1998).

4.5. Joint consideration of external knowledge sources and internal knowledge sources

Estimation results from Models 3 and 6 show the impact of external knowledge on firms' product and process innovation activities given firms' internal knowledge levels. The same variables that are significant in explaining product innovation in Models 1 and 2 are also sig-nificant in Model 3. At the same, the variables that are significant in explaining process inno-vation in Models 4 and 5 are also significant in Model 6, namely purchase of machinery, equipment or software, year of firm establishment, sector firm belongs, and IRD for product innovation and the same variables except sector firm belongs to for process inno-vation. Marginal effects however, reveal much about the joint consideration of external and internal knowledge in influencing product innovation.

First, the impact of firm spending on IRD in Models 3 and 6 exceed that in Models 2 and 5. This indicates that external knowledge complements internal knowledge slightly more for product innovation than it does for process innovation. It furthermore indicates that the more developed a firm's internal knowledge base, the more effective external knowledge sourcing is in facilitating innovation. This finding is consistent with that of Mohnen and Roller (2005) and Cassiman and Veugelers (2006) who found complementarity between internal knowledge and external knowledge in impacting product innovation.

Therefore, despite the less experience of sampled firms in undertaking innovation, they have reasonable absorptive capacity necessary for effective utilization of external knowledge. This finding is consistent with Portelli and Narula (2003) who found magnitude of technological upgrading from external knowledge in Tanzania to be determined by capabilities within the industrial base. The fact that the sampled firms belong to the private sector implies they have a say on the nature of external knowledge acquired based.

Firms having a say on the nature of external knowledge acquired is important as it implies that firms can acquire external knowledge based on internal knowledge capabilities which is necessary for raising technological capabilities through product innovation. This enhances the capacity to adequately utilize external knowledge and thereby takes depth of existing internal knowledge into account, which was identified by Wangwe (1983) and Wangwe et al. (2014) as necessary for raising the level of technological capability in Tanzania.

Second, the impact of purchase of machinery, equipment or software on a firm's decision to undertake product and process innovation in Models 3 and 6 are lower than in Models 1 and 4 indicating lower influence of purchase of machinery, equipment or software in the presence of internal knowledge.

Although the impact of an independent variable shows the magnitude of its impacts on a dependent variable, it is calculated holding values of other independent variables constant. However, various variables may jointly affect the innovation processes implying the effect of a variable may fall short of revealing its actual impact on innovation. We can obtain better insight on the impact of different knowledge sources on innovation by analysing the impact of variation of two independent variables together because such analysis can reveal issues that the analysis of a single variable cannot. We undertake such analysis by analysing the predictive margins of two independent variables on product and process innovation, that is, joint impact of two variables on innovation.

The impact of purchase of machinery, equipment or software on a firm's decision to undertake product and process innovation can be explained in the context of the

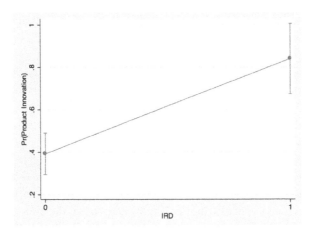

Figure 1. Predictive margins of PEQP and IRD for product innovation.

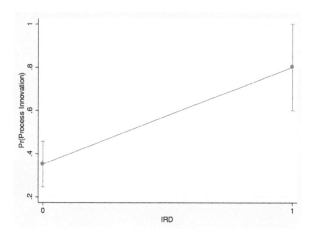

Figure 2. Predictive margins of PEQP and IRD for process innovation.

relationship between purchase of machinery, equipment or software and firm spending on IRD. Figures 1 and 2 show the predictive margins of PEQP and IRD for product innovation and process innovation respectively.

Figures 1 and 2 show the effect of the purchase of machinery, equipment or software on a firm's product and process innovation activities to depend on a firm's internal knowledge base emanating from its IRD activities. The increased impact of IRD can explain the lower effect of purchase of machinery, equipment and software on product and process innovation because firms may undertake such purchases not only to facilitate product or process innovation but also to facilitate development of its internal knowledge base via enhanced IRD outputs.

IRD and purchase of machinery, equipment, and software thus complement each other in product innovation processes. Figures 1 and 2 however, reveal that the impact of purchase of machinery, equipment or software given a firm's level of internal knowledge base

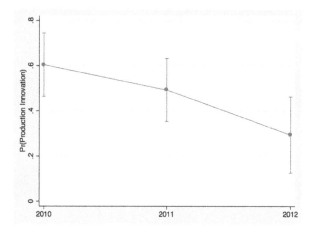

Figure 3. Predictive margins of YEAR and PEQP for product innovation.

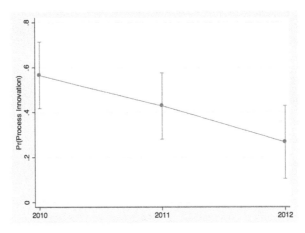

Figure 4. Predictive margins of YEAR and PEQP for process innovation.

is far larger for product innovation than it is for process innovation indicating product innovation is more constrained by a lack of external knowledge than process innovation.

Third, the impact of YEAR and SECTOR on innovation in Model 3 exceeds those in Models 1 and 2 implying the joint consideration of external and internal knowledge enhance the impact of these explanatory variables on a firm's product innovation activities. Figures 3–5 show the predictive margins of YEAR and PEQP for product and process innovation respectively and SECTOR and PEQP for product innovation.

Figures 3–5 show that external knowledge acquisition through purchase of machinery, equipment and software is more effective in facilitating product innovation for older firms and firms in the services sector than for relatively younger firms and firms in the manufacturing sector while external knowledge acquisition through purchase of machinery, equipment and software facilitates is more effective in facilitating process innovation for older firms with the sector a firm belongs to not impacting process innovation. This may be explained by the fact that older firms have begun to undertake measures to develop an internal knowledge base that can effectively enable them to acquire external

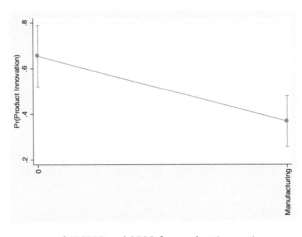

Figure 5. Predictive margins of SECTOR and PEQP for product innovation.

knowledge or invest in IRD that enhances the probability of undertaking product innovation.

Purchase of machinery, equipment and software furthermore enhances services firms likelihood of undertaking product innovation probably because of their lower capital needs relative to manufacturing sector firms, which make them less costly with respect to financial resources to innovate compared to manufacturing firms. Availability of such resources implies service sector firms are more likely to have more developed internal knowledge bases in a shorter period than manufacturing firms that lead to greater impact on product innovation than for manufacturing firms. Figures 6 and 7 show the predictive margins of YEAR and IRD for product and process innovation respectively and SECTOR and IRD for product innovation.

Figures 6–8 reveal that firm spending on IRD has greater impact on a firm's product and process innovation activities the more innovative experience a firm has. Furthermore, being in the service sector enhances the impact of firm spending on IRD on product innovation. This may be because older firms have had more time to develop their internal knowledge base and are thus in a better position to identify and utilize technological opportunities emanating from outside the firms. In terms of the sector in which product innovation occurs, services sector firms have lower capital needs relative to manufacturing sector firms which make them less costly with respect to financial resources to innovate than manufacturing firms resulting in them facing less financial barriers.

The chances of a firm undertaking product innovation in Model 3 exceeds those in Model 1 and Model 2 indicating external knowledge sources complement internal knowledge sources by raising the likelihood of firms to undertake product and process innovation. This is because apart from external knowledge being utilized to undertake innovation, it is also utilized to enhance the internal knowledge base required to effectively identify and utilize external knowledge for innovation. The chances of a firm undertaking process innovation in Model 6 exceeds the chances of undertaking process innovation in Model 4, but is slightly lower than the chances of undertaking process innovation in Model 5 indicating a firm's internal knowledge base plays a greater role than external knowledge in enhancing process innovation. This finding is consistent with Goedhuys (2007) who

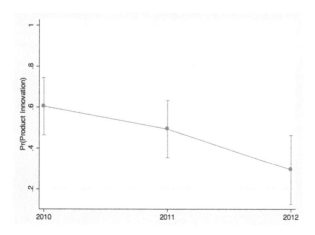

Figure 6. Predictive margins of YEAR and IRD for product innovation.

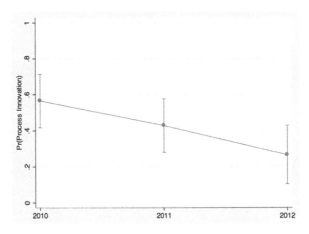

Figure 7. Predictive margins of YEAR and IRD for process innovation.

found local firms in Tanzania focused more in internal knowledge creation to offset weak linkages with foreign firms.

5. Summary and conclusion

The study has several key findings. First, innovation by Tanzanian firms is determined by both internal and external knowledge along with firm characteristics such as the age of a firm and the sector it belongs to with external knowledge complementing internal knowledge slightly more for product innovation than it does for process innovation.

Second, technology purchase is the main external source of knowledge in Tanzania while firm investment in external knowledge does not influence product and process innovation. The main source of internal knowledge in Tanzanian firms, on the other hand, is firm spending on IRD. Furthermore, development of an internal base of knowledge is better undertaken by investing in IRD than on business and codified knowledge, which require a well-developed internal knowledge base.

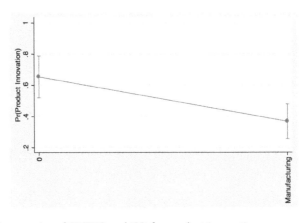

Figure 8. Predictive margins of SECTOR and IRD for product innovation.

Third, the impact of internal knowledge on innovation in isolation is greater than the impact of external knowledge on innovation in isolation indicating poor absorptive capacity of firms that limit their capacity to identify and exploit external technological opportunities. The joint impact of external and internal knowledge raises chances of firms to undertake product and process innovation indicating external knowledge complements internal knowledge in innovation in Tanzanian firms.

Fourth, the impact of technology purchase on a firm's decision to undertake product and process innovation in models where internal and external knowledge are considered to jointly impact innovation is lower than in models where internal and external knowledge are not analysed jointly, indicating lower influence of technology purchase in the presence of internal knowledge.

On the whole, the study found factors affecting innovation to be purchase of machinery, equipment or software, year of firm establishment, sector a firm belongs to, IRD and the sector a firm belongs to. Product innovation is more constrained by lack of external knowledge than process innovation implying product innovation requires a more developed internal knowledge base than process innovation. External knowledge acquisition and firm spending on IRD facilitates product and process innovation more effectively for older firms and firms in the services sector. Finally, internal and external knowledge have greater impact on innovation in Tanzanian firms when they complement each other than when they are utilized separately by firms.

6. Limitations

There are a few limitations that we would like to highlight. First, data for the paper provided information only on innovative activities of firms between 2010 and 2012. This made it impossible to analyse the sustainability of innovativeness of firms and dynamics of knowledge acquisition. Second, the data used did not reveal firms prior innovation history, which would have indicated basis for firm innovation and the importance of prior innovation to current innovation over time. Third, the data prevented analysis of the mechanisms of making knowledge acquisition decisions that could have revealed factors driving such decisions. (A final limitation of using of cross-sectional data is potential endogeneity emanating from unobserved variables that may affect a firm's decision to innovate. The study addresses this limitation by incorporating several control variables in the models to condition out the part of the error that is correlated with the endogenous regressors (firm age and the sector a firm belongs to).

These limitations, however, lead to several issues for future research. One area for future research can focus on analysing knowledge acquisition by firms over a longer period of time to analyse the sustainability of firm innovativeness and knowledge acquisition dynamics. Analysis of prior innovation history and basis of previous innovation is another area for future study that can help identify the basis of knowledge acquisition decisions and their impact on current innovation. Another area for future research is an analysis of the impact of knowledge sources on innovation by sectors, size of firms and the nature of human capital in firms in order to determine the impact of these factors on knowledge acquisition and innovation.

Acknowledgments

We would like to thank the special issue reviewers for their valuable comments and especially guest editor Abiodun Egbetokun for his guidance and support.

Disclosure statement

No potential conflict of interest was reported by the authors.

Funding

This paper was conducted within the framework of Tilburg University's research project 'Enabling Innovation and Productivity Growth in Low Income Countries' (EIP-LIC/PO 5639), funded by the UK's Department for International Development (DFID).

References

Adeyeye, A. D., O. O. Jegede, A. J. Oluwadare, and F. S. Aremu. 2016. "Micro-level Determinants of Innovation: Analysis of the Nigerian Manufacturing Sector." *Innovation and Development* 6 (1): 1–14.

Arrow, K. 1962. "The Economic Implications of Learning by Doing." *The Review of Economic Studies* 29 (3): 155–173.

Audretsch, D., and Z. J. Acs. 1987. "Innovation, Market Structure and Firm Size." *Review of Economics and Statistics* 69 (4): 567–575.

Baldwin, J. R., and G. Gellatly. 2004. *Innovation Strategies and Performance in Small Firms.* Cheltenham: Edward Elgar.

Baptista, R., and P. Swann. 1998. "Do Firms in Clusters Innovate More?" *Research Policy* 27 (5): 525–540.

Cassiman, B., and R. Veugelers. 2006. "In Search of Complementarity in the Innovation Strategy: Internal R&D and External Knowledge Acquisition." *Management Science* 52 (1): 68–82.

Cohen, W. M., and D. A. Levinthal. 1990. "Absorptive Capacity: A New Perspective on Learning and Innovation." *Administrative Science Quarterly* 35 (1): 128–152.

Cooke, P., and K. Morgan. 1998. "The Creative Milieu: A Regional Perspective on Innovation." In *The Handbook of Industrial Innovation*, edited by M. Dodgson and R. Rothwell, 26–31. Cheltenham: Edward Elgar.

Dewar, R. D., and J. E. Dutton. 1986. "The Adoption of Radical and Incremental Innovations: An Empirical Analysis." *Management Science* 32 (11): 1422–1433.

Edquist, C. 2004. "Systems of Innovation: Perspectives and Challenges." In *The Oxford Handbook of Innovation*, edited by J. Fagerberg, D. Mowery, and R. Nelson, 181–208. Oxford: Oxford University Press.

Egbetokun, A., P. Mendi, and R. Mudida. 2016. "Complementarity in Firm-level Innovation Strategies: A Comparative Study of Kenya and Nigeria." *Innovation and Development* 6 (1): 87–101.

Floyd, S. W., and B. Wooldridge. 1999. "Knowledge Creation and Social Networks in Corporate Entrepreneurship: The Renewal of Organizational Capability." *Entrepreneurship, Theory and Practice* 23 (3): 123–143.

Freeman, C. 1998. "The Economics of Technical Change." In *Trade, Growth and Technical Change*, edited by D. Archibugi and J. Michie, 16–54. Cambridge: Cambridge University Press.

Garud, R., and P. R. Nayyar. 1994. "Transforming Capacity: Continual Structuring by Intertemporal Technology Transfer." *Strategic Management Journal* 15 (5): 365–385.

Goedhuys, M. 2007. "Learning, Product Innovation and Firm Heterogeneity in Tanzania." *Industrial and Corporate Change* 16 (2): 269–292.

Greene, P., C. Brush, and M. Hart. 1999. "The Corporate Venture Champion: A Resource-Based Approach to Role and Process." *Entrepreneurship, Theory and Practice* 23 (3): 103–122.

Hagedoorn, J., and R. Narula. 1996. "Choosing Organizational Modes of Strategic Technology Partnering: Interorganizational Modes of Cooperation and Sectorial Differences." *Strategic Management Journal* 14 (5): 371–385.

Hurley, R. F., and G. T. Hult. 1998. "Innovation, Market Orientation and Organization Learning: An Integration and Empirical Examination." *Journal of Marketing* 62 (3): 42–54.

Kasseeah, H. 2013. "Innovation and Performance in Small and Medium-sized Enterprises: Evidence from Mauritius." *Innovation and Development* 3 (2): 259–275.

Katila, R., and E. L. Chen. 2008. "Effects of Search Timing on Innovation: The Value of Not Being in Sync with Rival." *Administrative Science Quarterly* 53 (4): 593–625.

Keshari, P. K. 2013. "Technological Determinants of Firm-level Technical Efficiency in the Indian Machinery Industry." *Innovation and Development* 3 (2): 223–238.

Kim, J., and G. Marschke. 2005. "Labor Mobility of Scientists, Technological Diffusion, and the Firm's Patenting Decision." *RAND Journal of Economics* 36 (2): 298–317.

Klepper, S. 1996. "Entry, Exit, Growth, and Innovation over the Product Life Cycle." *American Economic Review* 86 (3): 562–583.

Knoben, J., and L. Oerleman. 2010. "The Importance of External Knowledge Sources for the Newness of Innovations of South African Firms." *International Journal of Innovation and Regional Development* 2 (3): 165–181.

Lane, P. J., and M. Lubatkin. 1998. "Relative Absorptive Capacity and Interorganizational Learning." *Strategic Management Journal* 19 (5): 461–477.

Laursen, K., and A. Salter. 2006. "Open for Innovation: The Role of Openness in Explaining Innovative Performance Among U.K. Manufacturing Firms." *Strategic Management Journal* 27: 131–150.

Lowe, J., and P. Taylor. 1998. "R&D and Technology Purchase through Licence Agreements: Complementarity Strategies and Complementarity Assets." *R&D Management* 28: 263–278.

Lundvall, B.-Å. 1988. "Innovation as an Interactive Process: From User-producer Interaction to the National System of Innovation." In *Technical Change and Economic Theory*, edited by Dosi et al., 349–369. London, NY: Pinter Publishers.

Mahemba, C. M. M., and E. J. De Bruijn. 2003. "Innovation Activities by Small and Medium Sized Manufacturing Enterprises in Tanzania." *Creativity and Innovation Management* 12 (3): 162–173.

Malerba, F. 1992. "Learning by Firms and Incremental Technical Change." *The Economic Journal* 102 (July): 845–859.

Moch, M., and E. Morse. 1997. "Size, Centralization and Organizational Adoption of Innovations." *American Sociological Review* 42 (5): 716–725.

Mohnen, P., and L.-H. Roller. 2005. "Complementarities in Innovation Policy." *European Economic Review* 49 (6): 1431–1450.

Nelson, R., and S. Winter. 1982. *An Evolutionary Theory of Economic Change*. Cambridge, MA: Harvard University Press.

Portelli, B., and R. Narula. 2003. "Foreign Direct Investment through Acquisitions and Implications for Technological Upgrading: Case Evidence from Tanzania." Paper presented at the University of Oslo, Oslo, Norway, May 2003.

Schulze, A., and M. Hoegl. 2008. "Organizational Knowledge Creation and the Generation of New Product Ideas: A Behavioral Approach." *Research Policy* 37 (10): 1742–1750.

Schumpeter, J. A. 1912. *The Theory of Economic Development, tenth printing, 2004*. New Brunswick, NJ: Transaction Publishers,.

Semboja, H. H., and J. P. Kweka. 2001. "The Form and Role of Industrial Innovativeness in Enhancing Firms' Productivity: The Case of Selected Manufacturing Firms In Tanzania." In *The Industrial Experience of Tanzania*, edited by A. Szirmai and P. Lapperre, 153–170. New York: Palgrave.

Szogs, A. 2004. "The Making of Innovation Systems in Least Developed Countries. Evidence from Tanzania," Paper presented at the DRUID Summer conference on industrial dynamics. innovation and development, Denmark, June 14–16.

Vega-Jurado J., A. Gutiérrez-Gracia, and I. Fernández-de-Lucio (2008). "External Knowledge Sourcing Strategies and In-house R & D Activities: Their Effects on Firms' Innovative Performance". INGENIO Working Paper Series. Working Paper No. 2008/7.

Wangwe, S. M. 1983. "Industrialization and Resource Allocation in a Developing Country: The Case of Recent Experience in Tanzania." *World Development* II (6): 483–492.

Wangwe, S., D. Mmari, J. Aikaeli, N. Rutatina, T. Mboghoina, and A. Kinyondo. 2014. "The Performance of the Manufacturing Sector in Tanzania: Challenges and the Way Forward". UNU-WIDER, WIDER Working Papers, WP/2014/085.

Zahra, S., and G. George. 2002. "Absorptive Capacity: A Review, Reconceptualization, and Extension." *Academy of Management Review* 27 (2): 185–203.

Embodied technology transfer and learning by exporting in the Ethiopian manufacturing sector

Abdi Yuya Ahmad and Keun Lee ⓘ

ABSTRACT

This paper examined the role of imported inputs, new capital goods and exporting on firm performance using micro data collected over 2000–2011 from manufacturing firms with 10 and above permanent employees in Ethiopia. Performance was measured in terms of labour productivity, total factor productivity (TFP) and TFP catch-up. In this paper, we argue that technologies embodied in imported inputs and new capital goods and export orientation are the crucial sources of learning and innovation, which enhance performance of firms in less-developed countries. The hypotheses developed along this argument were econometrically tested by applying a dynamic panel data technique. Results indicate that exporting, greater use of imported inputs and new capital goods significantly improved the productivity and TFP catch-up of firms. The positive productivity effects of imported inputs and new capital goods appeared to be higher for exporters than non-exporters. New capital goods were seen to play a greater role in embodied technology transfer than imported inputs. The findings generally suggest that improving access to imported inputs, encouraging investment in new capital goods and strengthening export orientation among manufacturing firms can help accelerate technology transfer and build local innovation capabilities towards Ethiopia's desired structural transformation.

1. Introduction

International trade plays a crucial role in the process of structural transformation of developing countries (Bernard et al. 2007; Schiff and Wang 2010) through enhancing diffusion of technologies (Aghion and Jaravel 2015) as the main driver of innovation and productivity growth in most countries (Keller 2004). Effective diffusion of technologies in a globalizing world creates convergence (Aghion and Jaravel 2015) through accelerating structural transformation as was witnessed by the success of East Asian economies especially in expanding their production and exports of electronics and telecommunication equipment (Freeman 2011). Increased share of manufactured goods in total export and opening domestic markets for imported goods and foreign investment were among the major success factors for China (World Bank 2012).

Exporting manufactured goods can improve firm performance in many ways, including increased competition, technology or knowledge spillovers following improved information flows, overseas supplier–customer relation, widened market opportunities, scale economies and export-related policy incentives (Wagner 2002; Bernard and Jensen 2004; Van Biesebroeck 2005; Kugler and Verhoogen 2009). However, empirical findings have remained mixed and vary with country contexts and methodologies, making cross-country comparisons and even cross-study comparisons for one country difficult (Wagner 2007). Evidence shows that firms from developing countries generate more benefits from exporting compared to firms from developed countries. In Africa, both multi-country studies (Mengistae and Pattillo 2004; Van Biesebroeck 2005; Bigsten and Söderbom 2010) and country cases such as Bbaale (2011) for Uganda, and Bigsten and Gebreeyesus (2009) for Ethiopia suggest that exporting increases firm productivity. However, there exist asymmetric results even within a country. In the case of Ethiopia, for instance, Siba and Söderbom (2011) failed to confirm evidence of 'Learning by exporting' unlike Bigsten and Gebreeyesus (2009).

Importing also increases firm performance through improving access to better quality capital and intermediate goods produced in advanced countries. These goods are known to be the major source of innovation and productivity in less-developed countries (Paul and Yasar 2009). Particularly, intermediate inputs increase productivity through improving product quality and reducing cost of production (Kasahara and Rodrigue 2008). They also play greater role in international diffusion of technology than exporting (Keller 2004). Increasing dominance of intermediate goods in international trade (Subramanian and Matthijs 2007) suggests its growing importance in facilitating technology transfer. Despite this fact, not enough studies exist on the impacts of imported inputs in developing countries (Wagner 2012; Damijan and Kostevc 2015).

In the sub-Saharan Africa (SSA) context, we know only the work of Bigsten, Gebreeyesus, and Söderbom (2013), which showed that reducing import tariff increased the productivity of input importers. However, this study ignored the potential interactions between exporting and importing in addition to their separate effects on productivity (Kugler and Verhoogen 2008, 2009; Aristei, Castellani, and Franco 2012). Foster-McGregor and Isaksson (2014) provided the first ever evidence on the role of importing, exporting and two-way trade on productivity of firms in 19 SSA countries. However, the estimated effects cannot be free of bias arising from endogeneity due to using cross-sectional data. Moreover, not controlling heterogeneity among countries, mainly, with respect to their levels of development (Wagner 2012), absorptive capacity (Augier, Cadot, and Dovis 2013; Yasar 2013) and market concentration (Jacob and Meister 2005) can lead to biased estimates. Particularly, ignoring the effect of market concentration was seen to inflate firm productivity in Africa (Gelb, Meyer, and Ramachandran 2014). To the best of our knowledge, no studies in SSA have yet considered analysing the productivity effect of new capital goods with importing and exporting. Studies in Ethiopia have largely focused on the impact of exporting but their findings have remained inconclusive.

Against this backdrop and the theoretical underpinnings from international trade literature, this paper examines the role of trade on the performance of manufacturing firms in Ethiopia. It tries to answer three major questions. (1) Does greater use of imported inputs improve firm performance? (2) Is there transfer of technologies embodied in capital goods? (3) Is there evidence of learning from exporting? To answer these, data from the annual census of large and medium manufacturing firms over 2000–2011 are analysed with a combination of dynamic panel data econometrics and matching techniques. Performance is measured with labour productivity, total factor productivity (TFP) and TFP catch-up.

Regression results indicate that imported inputs, new capital goods and exporting have positive significant effects on all measures of performance. Results of the matching technique also confirm all the effects but not that of imported inputs on TFP. The productivity effects of imported inputs and new capital goods appear to be higher among exporters than non-exporters. This study contributes both theoretically and empirically in four ways. First, unlike previous studies, it examines how international trade affects the productivity of Ethiopian firms in relation to diffusion of technologies borrowing the idea that 'Convergence towards the upper end of the productivity spectrum can equally be seen as a process of diffusion … ' (Gelb, Meyer, and Ramachandran 2014). It shows the strong learning potential that underlies importing, exporting and investing in capital goods. Second, the study rigorously proves that new capital goods play greater a role in embodied technology transfer than imported inputs. Third, it provides strong evidence of 'learning by exporting' not only in terms of the direct productivity effect of exporting but also indirectly through enhancing returns out of using more imported inputs and new capital goods. Finally, it is the first study in SSA to have assessed firm-level learning in terms of intra-industry catch-up along with TFP and labour productivity. Using catch-up variable gives a better view of performance from the evolutionary theory perspective.

The rest of the paper is organized as follows. Section 2 presents a review of relevant literature and discusses the hypotheses. The data and methods used to analyse the data are described in Section 3. The results are presented and discussed in Section 4 and the paper concludes in Section 5 by drawing some implications based on the findings.

2. Literature review and hypotheses

2.1. Theoretical background

According to new growth theories (Romer 1990; Aghion and Howitt 1992), technology plays a key role in the long-run economic growth. Productivity variations between countries are largely explained by differences in the countries' capability to generate technological knowledge and the ability to use knowledge generated elsewhere (Fagerberg 1994; Verspagen 1997; Lee 2013a). R&D-based generation of technologies matter most for developed countries while developing countries mostly rely on technologies produced in developed countries (Coe and Helpman 1993). In Howitt and Mayer-Foulkes's (2005) model, countries with no own R&D and technologically lagging can grow at a positive rate similar to frontier countries if they have the required absorptive capacity. In the absence of technology transfer from advanced countries to less-developed ones, the productivity and income gaps between them would increase further (Keller 2000; Griffith, Redding, and Van Reenen 2003).

International trade plays the leading role in facilitating technology transfer (Keller 2004). Grossman and Helpman (1991) discussed four channels through which technologies diffuse. First, they can diffuse following cross-country movement of intermediate inputs and capital equipment. Second, trade-related cross-border communications can facilitate learning of production processes, product design and organizational innovation. Contracting and imitation of foreign technologies make the remaining two channels. Keller (2002) also noted two basic mechanisms of technology diffusion that follow international economic activities. The first involves direct learning of foreign technologies in which less-developed-country firms access a blue print or a design developed by firms in advanced countries. The second relates to using specialized and advanced intermediate products invented in developed countries. For less-developed countries lagging behind the global technology frontier, the later channel plays the most important role if supplemented by all the corresponding important information (Coe, Helpman, and Hoffmaister 1997). However, not all countries and all firms equally exploit these alternative channels. Absorptive capacities at both micro and macro levels play important roles.

Particular to latecomers, Siyanbola et al. (2012) noted that successful technological learning and innovation are crucial for better organizational performance. Learning is the most dynamic of human capabilities (Lundvall 2011) crucial for innovation and productivity of an organization (Damijan and Kostevc 2015). Organizations with better absorptive capacity are more successful in learning external knowledge and building innovation capabilities. Heterogeneity in inter-firm productivity arises from the underlying differences in learning and innovation capabilities (Mairesse and Mohnen 2002; Mairesse, Mohnen, and Kremp 2005). Lee (2013b) indicated that technological cycle time and explicitness of knowledge also determine learning possibilities. Short cycle time and more explicit technologies are easier to learn. Therefore, the extent to which firms in less-developed countries learn from international trade-induced technology transfer is an important topic. The following section provides a brief review of empirical evidences and drives hypotheses.

2.2. Empirical evidence and hypotheses

Many empirical works have been conducted on how international trade affects firm-level performance and innovation. However, results are mixed depending on the methodologies used and different conditions at the country, industry and firm levels. Differences in methodology include using different measures of firm performance such as profit, growth, value added, labour productivity, innovation and total factor productivity (TFP). For instance, Kugler and Verhoogen (2009) indicated that using imported intermediate goods significantly raised the gross output of Columbian plants. However, they did not find such effect by using TFP as a measure of performance and controlling for plant effects. Findings depend also on whether a researcher investigates the impacts of import or export in isolation or includes the role of two-way trade. Recent studies (for instance Kugler and Verhoogen 2009; Foster-McGregor and Isaksson 2014) show the merit of analysing the roles of importing, exporting and two-way trade together as a more complete form of learning through trade. As will be seen in the following section, literature discusses the impact of variables at different levels in determining the extent to which a country benefits from trade. Among the important country-level conditions that affect the role of trade are openness to trade, institutional setup and absorptive capacity. At industry level, market structure and the type and nature of technologies are among the major factors. At firm level, firm size, linkages, ownership, quality of human resource, participation in international trade are among the major factors. Review of these literature will follow.

2.2.1. Imported inputs, capital goods and performance of firms

Literature on the relationship between importing and firm-level performance constitute those discussing the impact of all types of imported goods, including final products and those focusing only on import of intermediate and capital goods. In this section, more focus is given to the latter type of literature due to the fact that we are interested in the manufacturing firms' performance. Some evidence exists on the positive impact of import on performances of firms in both developed and developing countries. Among those evidence include Halpern, Korenand, and Szeidl (2011) in case of Hungary; Goldberg et al. (2009) and Hasan (2001) for Indian cases; Lööf and Andersson (2008) for Swedish case; Yu and Li (2014) in case of China; Aristei, Castellani, and Franco (2012) in a group of 27 Eastern European and Central Asian countries and Kasahara and Rodrigue (2008) in case of Chile. Halpern, Korenand, and Szeidl (2011) found that importing increases productivity of firms by 12% out of which about 40% was generated as a result of substitution between foreign and domestic inputs. Using data spanning over 1975–1987, Hasan (2001) showed that imported inputs and investment in domestically produced capital goods have significantly raised firm productivity in India. In addition to confirming the positive productivity effect of importing, Lööf and Andersson (2008) noted that imports from developed countries have stronger effect compared to those from underdeveloped countries. Using data over 2002–2006, Yu and Li (2014) found that imported intermediate inputs raise firm productivity in Chinese manufacturing. Similarly, Aristei, Castellani, and Franco (2012) showed positive impacts of imported inputs on both productivity and product innovation.

However, Conti, Turco, and Maggioni (2013) found that importing has no impact on TFP of firms in the Italian manufacturing. Instead, they proved 'self-selection' of more productive firms to importing inputs than less productive ones. Similarly, Kugler and Verhoogen (2008, 2009) showed that more-productive plants select into importing inputs from foreign markets where they get access to more varieties and buy higher quality inputs at a higher price. Kugler and Verhoogen (2008), particularly, investigated the quality-complementarity hypothesis (the hypothesis that input quality and plant productivity are complementary in producing quality output). They argued that the hypothesis carries an important implication regarding the role of trade in shaping industrial evolution in developing countries. In fact, the benefits earned by importing technology would vary with the type and nature of the technologies or industries. The benefits are higher in industries where technological opportunities and technology investments are highly prevalent (Hasan 2001), in sectors where technologies are more explicit and easily embodied (Jung and Lee 2010), in more concentrated sectors (Jacob and Meister 2005) and where firms produce less complex products (Yu and Li 2014).

In view of the infancy of the Ethiopian manufacturing, the above literature suggests that using imported inputs increases the opportunity for firms in learning foreign technologies. Firms in the Ethiopian manufacturing mainly belong to food processing, textile, garment and leather and products of leather. In these sectors, technologies are more traditional and explicit, and products are less complex. Therefore, the potential of learning new technologies is higher, particularly, for firms in the medium and large manufacturing sector where almost every firm relies on imported inputs but with different use intensities, as data in the current study indicate. Kasahara and Rodrigue (2008) showed that the bottom 10 percentile firms in the share of imported inputs benefitted none, while the 90 percentile importers gained 20.1% productivity. Based on this literature, it is expected that

H1: the higher the proportion of imported inputs used by a firm the greater is its productivity.

The reasons for high productivity effect of using imported inputs are related to improved access to frontier technologies, quality of inputs and firms' widened opportunities to specialize on activities of their best capability (Wagner 2012). These reasons can equally apply for firms that invest in new capital goods. However, investment in fixed capital could be counter-productive if there is over investment in demand-constrained conditions. For instance, Lee, Kim, and Lee (2010) found that the performance of Korean Chaebols was strongly smashed in 1991, owing to over investment. Nevertheless, it is more logical to expect a positive relationship between investment in capital goods and productivity either due to the fact that only more productive firms would afford to invest or new capital goods would raise productivity driven by technologies embodied in the goods (Hasan 2001; Augier, Cadot, and Dovis 2013). In Ethiopia's manufacturing sector, investment in new capital goods is the main way of introducing modern technologies. Based on this ground, we hypothesize that

H2: Firms with higher investment in new fixed capital are more productive than firms with less or no investment in new capital.

In relation to both *H1* and *H2*, it should be noted that using better quality inputs or new capital goods is not a panacea. Here input refers to raw materials while fixed capitals include machines and related equipment used in the production process. Capital goods are mostly goods that are mostly imported by firms either directly or indirectly. Manufacturing firms either buy from other importers or directly import the goods by their own. Firm-specific capabilities and market conditions determine the extent to which these goods improve performance. For example, Yasar (2013) and Augier, Cadot, and Dovis (2013) demonstrated that benefits from importing capital goods such as machineries and equipment depend on the quality of human capital of a firm.

In the Ethiopian context, the policy-induced effort to upgrade the capacity of fixed capital towards promoting better value addition on manufactured export (World Bank 2015a) implies potential correlations between exporting and investment in fixed capital. Based on this, we expected that the productivity effects of both imported inputs and capital goods are higher for exporters than non-exporters due to the fact that exporters tend to have better production capabilities. Therefore, we proposed the following auxiliary hypotheses.

H1a: The productivity effect of imported inputs is higher for exporters than non-exporters.
H2a: The productivity effect of new capital is higher for exporters than non-exporters.

2.2.2. Export and productivity

Export promotion is one of the key policy aspects in any country. Larger engagement in export is assumed to improve productivity at both country and firm levels. However, there are controversies about whether it is productivity or exporting that comes first. The seminal paper of Bernard and Jensen (2004) showed that exporting firms are better in all characteristics *ex-ante*. They found strong evidence of self-selection indicating that growth in productivity and product innovation precedes exporting. They also confirmed that exporting increases market opportunity and plant size rather than productivity. Melitz (2003) developed an analytical model which demonstrates how exporting firms exhibit higher productivity than non-exporting firms prior to exporting and how exporting increases aggregate productivity through inducing reallocation of resources from less productive to more productive entities. The major channels through which firms benefit from exporting include competitive pressure, technological or knowledge spillovers, supplier–customer relation with foreign firms, widened market, scale economies and policy incentives (Wagner 2002; Bernard and Jensen 2004).

Empirical works on the firm-level export–productivity nexus established diverse conclusions. Some concluded that exporting raises productivity of firms, whereas some others proved self-selection (Wagner 2007). Among others, Crespi, Criscuolo, and Haskel (2008) in UK; Wagner (2002) and Powell and Wagner (2014) in German; Conti, Turco, and Maggioni (2013) in Italy; Mengistae and Pattillo (2004), Van Biesebroeck (2007) and Bigsten and Söderbom (2010) in selected African countries and Srithanpong (2014) in Thailand found evidence in favour of learning by exporting. Some of the works in support of self-selection include Greenaway and Kneller (2004) in UK; Fabling and Sanderso (2012) in New Zealand and Bbaale (2011) in Uganda. Level of economic development in both exporting and export destination countries would explain parts of the observed differences in the findings. For instance, Wagner (2012) found that firms that export to highly developed countries have better opportunity to compete with or supply to technologically frontier firms which employ best capital goods and management practices. Therefore, exporting to developed country involve higher benefits than exporting to less-developed destinations. In terms of export country of origin, the impact of exporting on productivity was higher for firms originating from developing countries (Martins and Yang 2009) perhaps in relation to reasons explained in catch-up literature in terms of the importance of technological backwardness (Lee 2013a).

Kugler and Verhoogen (2008) argued that firms from developing countries strive to upgrade product qualities and processes to meet the quality requirements of export markets and compete with the growing number of exporters. To this end, firms would use more high-quality imported inputs to improve product quality and production processes. Export promotion policies such as reduced import tariff can also facilitate productivity by improving exporters' access to high-quality imported inputs (Kugler and Verhoogen 2008, 2009). In particular, export-oriented firms in Ethiopia are the prime beneficiaries of incentives in terms of access to resources and low import tariff in addition to other potential benefits African firms would generally enjoy from exporting in relation to economies of scale (Van Biesebroeck 2005) following improved market opportunity. This evidence suggests that exporting firms in Ethiopia are likely to perform better than non-exporting ones. Therefore, we can hypothesize that

H3: exporting firms are more productive than non-exporting firms.

It is important to note that productivity could also arise from export-induced import (Kugler and Verhoogen 2009) or import-induced export (Aristei, Castellani, and Franco 2012) implying the joint importance of *H1* and *H3*. Among studies that found positive productivity premium for both importing and exporting firms, Vogel and Wagner (2009) in German; Foster-McGregor and Isaksson (2014) in Africa; Andersson, Lööf, and Johansson (2008) in Swedish and Kasahara and Lapham (2012) in Chile are worth mentioning. These evidence also revealed that the productivity premiums are higher for firms engaged in both import and export due to increased international division of labour and employing high-quality inputs. Therefore, testing *H3*, *H1a* and *H2a* separately while controlling for the potential effects of other key variables would give a better picture on trade-induced learning.

3. Data and methodology

3.1. Data source

Data from the annual census of medium and large manufacturing firms over 2000–2011 periods were used to test the above hypotheses. It was gathered by the Ethiopian Central Statistical Agency (CSA), including all firms with 10 and above permanent employees. These data are appropriate for the current study as it includes most of the important variables used to measure the dynamic performance of firms. The main caveat of the data is that it lacks variables that measure in-house R&D efforts or innovation. The data for the main empirical analysis did not include all firms in the original data set as a result of dropping observations with doubtful figures and missing values on the major variables during data clearing. Besides, only firms with two and above observations were included in relation to the modelling requirement of the main econometric model. Secondary data from the World Development Indicator were also used for the purpose of deflating monetary values of some variables.

The data include both private and public-owned firms operating in 14 two-digit classified industrial sectors. These are manufacturing of foods and beverages, textile, wearing apparel, leather and products of leather, wood products, paper products, chemicals, rubber and plastic, other non-metallic minerals, basic iron and steel, fabricated metal, machinery and equipment, motor vehicles and trailers, and furniture. More than 50% of firms in all years depend on imported inputs. The intensity of their dependence on imported inputs varies from sector to sector and from firm to firm. In terms of export, only 3.5–7% of firms had participated in export market over the data periods. This information qualifies the importance of importing and exporting, which will be discussed in the empirical findings.

3.2. The empirical Models

This section presents strategies followed to estimate the productivity effects of exporting and embodied technology transfer. Productivity was measured in terms of labour productivity ($LabP$), total factor productivity (TFP) and TFP catch-up ($catch_{TFP}$). The empirical modelling follows research that were interested in identifying factors that determine firm-level productivity as reviewed in Nelson (1981). From the perspective of evolutionary theory, heterogeneities in the degrees of innovativeness and production efficiencies are attributed to the varying distributions of capital equipment of different vintages, idiosyncratic capabilities (or lack of them), mistaken-ridden learning and path-dependent adaptation (Dosi and Nelson 2010), which are assumed to be affected by international trade. Literature also emphasizes the role of in-house R&D efforts as one of the major determinants of firm-level learning and productivity. However, the absence of R&D variables in the current data set limits the scope of this study to R&D products developed elsewhere.

Therefore, this study concentrates only on the extent to which Ethiopian manufacturing firms learn through exporting and technologies embodied in imported inputs and capital. To this end, analyses were made based on estimating models of the form.

$$
\begin{aligned}
P_{it} = \gamma_0 &+ \gamma_1 P_{it-1} + \gamma_2 export_{it} + \gamma_3 NKINV_{it} + \gamma_4 MRMint_{it} + \gamma_5 \ln age_{it} \\
&+ \gamma_6 size_{it} + \gamma_7 private_{it} + \gamma_8 CI_{jt} + \gamma_9 Foreign_{it} + \gamma_{10} D_{ij} + \mu_i + \varphi_{it},
\end{aligned}
\tag{1}
$$

where P represents any of the productivity measures in natural logarithm ($\ln LabP$, $\ln TFP$ or $catch_{TFP}$) used as a dependent variable; $export$ is dummy for exporting; $NKINV$ is the ratio of new capital to total fixed capital; $MRMint$ is the proportion of imported inputs; $\ln age$ is the natural logarithm of firm age; $size$ is the natural logarithm of firm size; $private$ is dummy for private ownership; CI is concentration index; $Foreign$ is dummy for foreign ownership; γ are coefficients; D is vector of year and sector dummies; μ_i is firm-specific effect and ϕ_{it} is a random disturbance term assumed to be distributed identically and independently across firms. The subscripts i, j and t stand for firm, sector and year, respectively. Definitions of variables are given in Table A1.

Measuring productivity using labour productivity may not reflect actual differences in firm performances. The fact that firms may face different factor prices and apply other excluded inputs at different intensities, their labour productivities may differ even up on using similar production technologies. For this reason, using TFP is preferred as it does not vary with the intensity of use of observable factor inputs and their relative costs. However, problem lies with the difficulty of estimating TFP. Conceptually, TFP is the variation in output that cannot be explained by observable inputs rather is a residual or the unexplained part of a production function. If we specify a production function of Hicks-neutral technology and a Cobb–Douglass form as

$$
Y_{it} = A_{it} K_{it}^{\beta_k} L_{it}^{\beta_l} M_{it}^{\beta_m},
\tag{2}
$$

where Y_{it} represents output of firm i in period t; K_{it}, L_{it} and M_{it} are inputs of capital, labour and materials, respectively. A_{it} is the TFP or the efficiency level of firm i in period t. Different TFP estimation methods have been developed, which can broadly be classified into non-parametric, semi-parametric and fully parametric methods. Each method has its own merits and limitations as reviewed by Van Biesebroeck (2007). Semi and fully parametric methods often begin estimation by logarithmic transformation of Equation (2) to get a linear function of the form

$$
y_{it} = \beta_0 + \beta_k k_{it} + \beta_l l_{it} + \beta_m m_{it} + \varepsilon_{it},
\tag{3}
$$

where small letters represent logarithm of the variables in Equation (2) and ε_{it} denotes disturbance term.

Estimating Equation (3) using ordinary least square (OLS) causes omitted variables bias due to correlations between firms' inputs choice and unobserved firm-specific productivity shocks (Van Beveren 2010). Provided that productivity is time-invariant, adding firm-fixed effects into the estimation could solve the problem. However, this strategy is inappropriate if interest is on firm-level productivity change. Among the alternative estimation strategies developed in literature, Levinsohn and Petrin (2003) method is well known to solve the problems and hence applied in this paper. The method considers two components of the error term in Equation (3) leading to

$$y_{it} = \beta_0 + \beta_k k_{it} + \beta_l l_{it} + \beta_m m_{it} + \omega_{it} + \eta_{it}, \qquad (4)$$

where the first component of the error term (ω_t) is the transmitted productivity component: a state variable which affects a firm's choices of inputs. The second component (η_t) is uncorrelated with input choices. Thus, ignoring the correlations between inputs and the first component leads to inconsistency in estimating production function due to simultaneity problem. Assuming a Cobb–Douglas production function, Levinsohn and Petrin (2003) used firms' raw material inputs to correct for simultaneity in estimating production function.

Therefore, when TFP was used to measure performance, estimation of Equation (1) had to follow two steps where TFP was estimated in the first step using the above approach. Estimating Equation (1) on TFP catch-up is the extension of the two-step process up on computing TFP catch-up borrowing the concept from Jung and Lee (2010). In all the three versions of the equation, we analysed the effects of exporting, importing and investment simultaneously. Excluding any of these variables may result in an upward bias on productivity even when there is a simple spurious correlation (Kasahara and Rodrigue 2008; Conti, Turco, and Maggioni 2013). To test the potential associations between these variables (H1a and H2a), another TFP equation is estimated by adding the interaction of *export* dummy with *MRMint* (*Exp*imp*) and with *NKINV* (*Exp*inv*).

Equation (1) can be estimated using the traditional OLS and fixed effect methods. However, these methods suffer from dynamic panel bias due to correlation of lagged values of the dependent variables with the fixed effect in the error term (Roodman 2009). The right-hand-side variables may fail to satisfy strict exogeneity assumption required for consistency of estimators. Time-invariant firm characteristics (fixed effects) such as managerial skills may be correlated with the explanatory variables leading to endogeniety problem. Least square dummy variable (LSDV) and instrumental variable (IV) approaches would solve the problem. However, LSDV works only for balanced panel and does not address the potential endogeneity of other regressors while IV method involves difficulty of finding appropriate instrument. Arellano and Bond (1991) developed a generalized method of moment (GMM) technique that eliminates bias by transforming variables. Later, Blundell and Bond (1998) improved the estimation method noting that the validity of instruments from first differencing transformation may suffer in cases where input and output variables are persistent. They developed a system GMM that uses more moment conditions from lagged first difference of the dependent and independent variables. In this paper, we applied a one-step system GMM with heteroscedasticity consistent standard errors and using forward orthogonal deviations to transform the equations as this reduces data losses when the panel data are unbalanced (Roodman 2009). After the system GMM estimation, the Arellano and Bond tests of autocorrelation and the Hansen test for joint validity of the instruments were used as standard after GMM.

Variables ln*age*, *size*, *private*, *Foreign*, *CI* and dummies for year and sector were included to control heterogeneities among firms. Year and sector dummies were added to capture macro productivity shocks and sectoral effects, respectively. Positive significant coefficients of *export*, *NKINV* and *MRMint* suggest evidence of 'learning by exporting,' 'learning by investment' and 'learning by importing,' respectively. However, due to the potential problem of firms' self-selection into exporting, investment and importing, it is important to validate regression results using methods that could disentangle selection effects from actual productivity effects. For this purpose, we applied models of treatment effect, namely difference-in-difference (DID), matching technique and combination of the two. The first technique requires exploiting the panel nature of the data unlike the matching technique, which can best fit for cross-sectional data. The detailed estimation strategies and discussions on these alternative techniques were withheld for the sake of brevity, but available on request from the authors.

4. Results and discussion

This section discusses results of the empirical analyses corresponding to the three measures of performance, namely labour productivity (LabP), total factor productivity (TFP) and TFP catch-up. LabP and TFP catch-up were estimated using simple formula, while TFP was estimated using a semi-parametric method of Levinsohn and Petrin (2003). Arnold (2005) indicated that when TFP is estimated using this method, there should be enough variations in the data for separate identification of all input coefficients and the coefficient of intermediate input should be different from one to satisfy consistency of the measure. These conditions have been satisfied in the estimation process. Moreover, the estimated TFP appeared to have high correlation (0.817) with LabP. Therefore, results of the main estimating equations can be used for inference.

Table 1 presents the summary statistics of the main variables. Table 1 shows that the mean TFP and LabP of firms are about 6.7 and 10 log points, respectively while that of catch$_{TFP}$ is −2. The maximum TFP and LabP are 13 and 17, respectively. The mean proportion of new capital in total firms' capital asset is about 0.1 while that of imported raw material is 0.352. The mean values of market concentration, age and size of firms are 0.48, 2.36 and 3.45, respectively.

4.1. Results of regression analysis

This section discusses estimation results obtained from econometric techniques. The discussion focuses on the major variables of interest: *export*, *MRMint* and *NKINV*. One year

Table 1. Summary statistics.

Variable	Obs.	Mean	Std. Dev.	Min	Max
ln*TFP*	11211	6.694	1.015	−0.780	13.335
ln*LabP*	11211	10.257	1.521	2.220	16.779
catch$_{TFP}$	11211	−2.057	1.467	−12.362	0.000
export	11211	0.051	0.220	0.000	1.000
NKINV	10814	0.092	0.180	0.000	1.000
MRMint	11211	0.352	0.398	0.000	1.000
CI	11211	0.482	0.179	0.246	1.000
ln*age*	11211	2.361	1.067	0.000	4.605
size	11211	3.432	1.332	0.693	8.402
Foreign	10003	0.042	0.201	0.000	1.000
private	11211	0.911	0.285	0.000	1.000

lagged values of *NKINV* were included in all models expecting time lag in the effect of capital. The control variables are *CI*, ln*age*, *private*, *Foreign* and *size*. Year and sector dummies were also included (not reported). Regression results from the system GMM (SYSGMM), pooled OLS (POLS) and random effect (RE) were reported. The main analyses were based on SYSGMM while POLS and RE were included only for comparison. The autocorrelation tests (Arellano and Bond) on all the SYSGMM models indicate absence of any second-order autocorrelation. The Hansen tests also confirm the validity of all instruments included as the *p*-values exceeded any conventional values to reject the hypothesis. Instruments for orthogonal deviation equations included two years and above lagged values of dependent variables and two- to five-year lagged values of weakly exogenous independent variables.

Table 2 displays all regression results under eight columns with robust standard errors. Columns (1)–(3) display results of ln*LabP* while columns (4)–(6) are results of TFP equations estimated using SYSGMM, POLS and RE, respectively. In both ln*LabP* and ln*TFP*, estimates from the three methods are similar in their sign but slightly different in significance levels as expected. Column (7) shows SYSGMM estimation of TFP but excluding the variable *Foreign* considering its statistical insignificance in columns (4)–(6). Interestingly, the coefficients of other variables in column (7) did not show any significant difference from those in column (4) despite changes in the number of observations. The last column (8) presents result of SYSGMM on TFP catch-up (catch$_{TFP}$).

The first row of Table 2 shows one year lagged values of the dependent variables (ln*LabP*, ln*TFP* and catch$_{TFP}$). The positive and strongly significant coefficients of ln*LabP*$_{it-1}$ and ln*TFP*$_{it-1}$ indicate the persistence of productivity. The coefficient of *lage* appeared to be strongly significant in determining the *TFP* and *TFP* catch-up of firms (columns 4–8), which indicates that a 10% increase in age (or experience) of a firm leads to about 5% and 6% increases in TFP and catch$_{TFP}$, respectively. This can be taken as evidence in favour of the 'learning by doing' hypothesis of Arrow (1962).

With respect to firm size, results from labour productivity and TFP show striking differences. The negative and strongly significant effect of size on labour productivity indicates that the smaller the size of a firm, the higher is its labour productivity. The simple reason for this relationship underlies the fact that number of permanent employees was used to measure both firm *size* and labour productivity in such a way that inverse relationship happens between the two. Moreover, it is not uncommon that firms with higher labour productivity would employ less number of workers than low productivity firms. On the other hand, firm size revealed strong positive effects on both TFP and TFP catch-up, indicating higher productivity of larger firms than smaller ones.

The coefficients of *private* dummies turned negative and strongly significant in all the columns, but column (8), implying better performance of public-owned firms than their private counterparts. The positive coefficient of *Foreign* dummy on both ln*LabP* (significant) and ln*TFP* (insignificant) shows that foreign firms are more productive than domestic firms. This is expected as foreign firms are often equipped with more qualified workers, better management practices and technologies. The coefficients of concentration (*CI*) in all the columns of Table 2 show strong positive significance (below 1% level) implying greater performance of firms in more concentrate sector than firms in less-concentrated sector. Corresponding to its effect on ln*TFP* (1.931), a 10% rise in concentration leads to a 19% increase in TFP, keeping other variables constant.

Table 2. Regression results.

Dep. variable	InLabP				InTFP			catch_TFP
	(1)	(2)	(3)	(4)	(5)	(6)	(7)	(8)
$InLabP_{t-1}$/$InTFP_{t-1}$/$catch_{TFPt-1}$	0.280***	0.561***	0.319***	0.085*	0.348***	0.209***	0.095**	-0.056*
	(0.048)	(0.014)	(0.017)	(0.044)	(0.017)	(0.018)	(0.045)	(0.029)
lnage	0.037	0.005	0.044**	0.047***	0.026**	0.036***	0.054***	0.060***
	(0.024)	(0.015)	(0.021)	(0.017)	(0.011)	(0.014)	(0.016)	(0.018)
size	-0.153***	-0.079***	-0.229***	0.111***	0.098***	0.087***	0.111***	0.247***
	(0.053)	(0.014)	(0.023)	(0.034)	(0.011)	(0.016)	(0.034)	(0.032)
private	-0.397***	-0.227***	-0.344***	-0.180**	-0.100***	-0.171***	-0.168**	0.061
	(0.097)	(0.045)	(0.075)	(0.077)	(0.034)	(0.054)	(0.074)	(0.088)
Foreign	0.163**	0.150**	0.152*	0.057	0.057	0.058		-0.015
	(0.080)	(0.064)	(0.078)	(0.061)	(0.048)	(0.060)		(0.148)
MRMint	0.633***	0.278***	0.248***	0.258*	0.084**	0.049	0.254*	0.241**
	(0.202)	(0.043)	(0.054)	(0.149)	(0.034)	(0.043)	(0.149)	(0.121)
$NKINV_{t-1}$	0.044*	0.023**	0.016*	0.039**	0.011	0.008	0.038**	0.036**
	(0.025)	(0.010)	(0.009)	(0.017)	(0.007)	(0.007)	(0.017)	(0.016)
export	0.845***	0.557***	0.640***	0.452***	0.284***	0.322***	0.461***	0.356***
	(0.170)	(0.056)	(0.076)	(0.133)	(0.043)	(0.059)	(0.132)	(0.127)
CI	1.445***	0.686**	0.902***	1.931***	1.029***	1.115***	1.703***	0.923**
	(0.529)	(0.325)	(0.325)	(0.449)	(0.286)	(0.298)	(0.427)	(0.455)
_cons	8.371***	5.319***	8.343***	5.780***	4.425***	5.303***	5.241***	-3.515***
	(0.554)	(0.190)	(0.244)	(0.311)	(0.141)	(0.159)	(0.355)	(0.254)
Year & sector dummies included								
No. of obs.	7563	7563	7563	7563	7563	7563	8080	7563
No. of firms	2122	2122	2122	2122	2122	2122	2177	2122
No. of inst	680			824			825	1149
AR(1)	0.000			0.000			0.000	0.000
AR(2)	0.923			0.962			0.815	0.126
Hansen test	0.292			0.509			0.357	0.259

Notes: Robust standard errors are in parentheses; *Significance at 10% level; **Significance at 5% level; ***Significance at 1% level.

4.1.1. Imported inputs, new capital goods and performance

The first hypothesis (*H1*) proposed positive productivity effect of using more imported inputs (*MRMint*). This was supported by all regression results with varying significance levels. The coefficient of *MRMint* in labour productivity regression is higher both in terms of statistical (at less than 1% level) and economic significances (0.633) than that of TFP and TFP catch-up. Given the effect of other variables, if a firm makes a 10% increase in the proportion of imported inputs, its labour productivity would increase by 6.3%, which is far greater compared to the gains in TFP (2.6%) and TFP catch-up (2.4%). The higher impact of imported inputs on labour productivity would mainly reflect the skill upgrading effect of using imported inputs (Crinò 2011). Similarly, the positive significance (5%) of import on TFP catch-up supports Jung and Lee (2010), who stressed the crucial role of importing embodied technology for TFP catch-up of firms in latecomers. Reducing import tariff in Ethiopia was shown to benefit input importers (Bigsten, Gebreeyesus, and Söderbom 2013) perhaps due to improved access to high-quality inputs. A case study by Sonobe, Akoten, and Otsuka (2007) on the Ethiopian shoe clusters revealed that soles imported from Europe helped manufacturers produce high quality and new fashion shoes because of accessing better designs embodied in soles and adopting technologies learned from suppliers.

The second hypothesis (*H2*) implicitly assumed that productivity increases due to investment in new capital goods (*NKINV*) which embody technologies developed through R&D efforts in advanced countries. After taking one year lagged value of new capital investment (*NKINV*), the coefficients of *NKINV* turned positive and significant, confirming the hypothesis in all the three alternative measures. The coefficients indicate that if a firm increases the proportion of new capital goods by 100%, the firm would improve its performance by about 4%, *ceteris paribus*. In view of increasing competition in international market and technological advancement, investment in new capital goods implies access to 'state of the arts' technologies. Therefore, the increment in labour productivity, TFP and TFP catch-up of firms following investment in new capital goods can be associated with technologies embodied in the goods and the resulting improvement in the innovation capabilities of the firms.

4.1.2. Exporting, importing, new capital goods and performance

On the presumption that importing and investment in new capital are related to export, two auxiliary hypotheses (*H1a* and *H2a*) were proposed. Before proceeding to the estimation results, let us see a quick description of potential differences between exporters and non-exporters in terms of capital and imported input intensities using mean comparison tests (Table A3). Results of the tests demonstrated that the proportion of imported inputs in total raw materials is significantly lower for exporters than non-exporters. However, when computed relative to employment, exporters appeared to use higher imported inputs. Both capital intensity (K/L) and proportion of new capital goods were higher for exporters than non-exporters. Similarly, regression results in columns (1) and (2) of Table 3 display differences in the coefficients of imported inputs (*MRMint*) and new capital goods (*NKINV*) when estimated with and without *export*.

Direct tests of *H1a* and *H2a* correspond to results reported in columns (3) and (4) of Table 3. The coefficient of the *Exp*imp* (0.466) shows that the productivity premium from using imported inputs by exporters exceeds that of non-exporters by 46.6% confirming

Table 3. Result of *SYSGMM* on ln*TFP* (H1a and H2a).

ln*TFP*	(1)	(2)	(3)	(4)
lnTFP_{t-1}	0.126***	0.129***	0.127***	0.135***
	(0.041)	(0.045)	(0.046)	(0.044)
ln*age*	0.051***	0.049***	0.043***	0.045***
	(0.016)	(0.016)	(0.016)	(0.016)
size	0.112***	0.127***	0.147***	0.137***
	(0.035)	(0.035)	(0.035)	(0.033)
Private	−0.128	−0.164*	−0.139*	−0.142*
	(0.081)	(0.086)	(0.078)	(0.083)
CI	1.573***	1.522***	1.642***	1.490***
	(0.422)	(0.429)	(0.424)	(0.425)
export	0.425***			
	(0.132)			
MRMint	0.272**	0.241*	0.156	0.197
	(0.142)	(0.147)	(0.156)	(0.141)
$NKINV_{t-1}$	0.039***	0.030**	0.040**	0.019*
	(0.014)	(0.013)	(0.018)	(0.011)
Exp*imp			0.466*	
			(0.258)	
Exp*inv				0.142
				(0.096)
_cons	5.032***	5.050***	4.936***	4.981***
	(0.345)	(0.372)	(0.362)	(0.360)
Year & sector dummies included				
No. of obs.	8080	8080	8080	8080
No. of firms	2177	2177	2177	2177
No. of inst	885	784	761	860
AR(1)	0.000	0.000	0.000	0.000
AR(2)	0.684	0.571	0.574	0.580
Hansen test	0.782	0.246	0.115	0.641

Notes: Robust standard errors in parentheses; *Significance at 10% level; **Significance at 5% level; ***Significance at 1% level.

H1a. Compared to the coefficients of *MRMint* in columns (2) and (3), the effect of importing on the productivity of exporters is more than double of the effect on non-exporters. This can partly be caused by exporters' tendency to utilize a greater proportion of imported inputs than non-exporters. However, the mean comparison test indicates that the intensity of using imported inputs was significantly higher among non-exporters than exporters. This is evident also from the negative pair-wise correlation (Table A2) between *MRMint* and *export*. On the other hand, exporters seem to have higher import to employment ratio than non-exporters. Therefore, the greater impact of importing on the TFP of exporters is not related to the quantity, rather the higher capability of exporters in matching raw materials with labour.

Similarly, the coefficient of the *Exp*inv* (0.142), (column 4 of Table 3), shows that exporters generated 14.2% more productivity than non-exporters from investment in new capital goods. Despite the statistical insignificance of the coefficient, the economic impact appears to be far larger when compared to the coefficients of *NKINV* in column (2) and (4). This could arise for different reasons. The first reason could be due to the fact that exporters would tend to invest more on new capital goods (as shown in Table A3) than non-exporters. Therefore, a higher productivity premium from using new capital goods among exporters would partly emanate from higher quantity or quality of the goods with embodied technologies. Generally, results suggested the validity of the two auxiliary hypotheses (*H1a* and *H2a*) that embodied technology transfer is higher among exporters than non-exporters.

4.1.3. Exporting and firm performance

The third hypothesis (*H3*) is about the impact of export on the productivity and productivity catch-up of firms. Results in Table 2 display strong positive significance (less than 1% level) of the coefficients of *export* dummies in all cases but with greater magnitude on labour productivity (column 1) than on TFP (column 4) and TFP catch-up (column 8). The positive and strong significance of exports indicates that export orientation improves firm performance in terms of all the three measures. Specifically, the results showed that exporters have 132%, 57% and 43% premiums[1] over non-exporters in terms of labour productivity, TFP and TFP catch-up, respectively.

Among similar studies in Ethiopia, the finding is in line with that of Bigsten and Gebreeyesus (2009). However, the current study pushed further than the 2009 study to drive implications on sectoral productivity as indicated in Melitz's (2003) model by analysing the role of export on TFP catch-up. Accordingly, the current study shows that exporters enjoy a significantly higher TFP catch-up than non-exporters. This implies improvement in the competitiveness of exporters with reference to a frontier firm in their respective two-digit sectors. This can increase sectoral productivity due to improved competition, which can ultimately contribute to the country's aspired structural change.

4.2. Results from matching techniques

Findings from the above regressions support all the hypotheses. Despite the fact that system GMM (SYSGMM) corrects for endogeniety, results with respect to imported inputs, investment in new capital and exporting may not preclude the effect of self-selection of more productive firms into exporting, importing and investing. With respect to exporting, Wagner (2007) reviewed alternative ways of dealing with the problem, where he also noted the fact that most studies confirmed self-selection of more productive firms into export markets while exporting does not necessarily improve productivity.

Taking this into account, we checked the robustness of regression results using alternative approaches, namely propensity score matching (PSM), DID and combination of the two (PSM–DID). PSM is a useful tool if there is no baseline data and it constructs a statistical comparison group based on a model of the probability of participating in the treatment conditional on observed characteristics or the propensity score. DID estimator relies on a comparison of treatment and control groups before and after a firm engages in any of the above activities. This method purges the unobserved firm characteristics that would lead to selection bias through differencing. Combining DID and PSM would solve the potential shortcomings of the two methods provided that rich data on control and treatment areas exist (Khandker, Koolwal, and Samad 2010).

In re-assessing the 'learning by exporting' hypothesis, the treatment group is exporters while the control group constitutes non-exporters. In case of investment in new capital goods and use of imported inputs, we created dummies (denoted by *DNKINV* and *DMRMint*) from the continuous values of the two variables (assigning '1' if the values are greater than averages and '0' otherwise). Accordingly, the treatment area

Table 4. Results of matching techniques.

Technique	Variable	LabP				TFP	
		Treated	Control	ATT	t-Value	ATT(Effect)	t-Value
	DNKINV	563	513	0.238	2.456**	0.211	2.733***
PSM	*DMRMint*	846	323	0.325	3.421***	−0.033	−0.433
	export	183	119	0.644	3.756***	0.256	2.272**
DID	*export*	220	174			0.388	3.72***
PSM–DID	*export*	220	174			0.493	2.46**

Note: **Significant at 5% level; ***Significant at 1% level.

corresponding to importing inputs (investment in new capital) is high input importer (high investment in capital) while the control is low input importers (low investment in new capital).

In order to apply the PSM technique in all the three treatment effects, we generated cross-sectional data by averaging values of the outcome (productivity) and firm character-istics over years. Then matching was performed following the nearest neighbourhood technique with bootstrapped standard errors up on satisfying the balancing conditions (meaning that the distributions of the treated group and the comparator must be similar) and selecting the common support options. Table 4 presents brief results of the three alternative techniques.

Table 4 shows that the average treatment effects on the treated (ATT) in labour pro-ductivity are significantly different for firms with high investment (*DNKINV*), high import (*DMRMint*) and exporters (*export*). Their respective productivity premiums are 24%, 33% and 64%. In terms of *TFP*; however, only high investment and *exporting* have positive productivity premiums estimated to be 21% and 27%, respectively. Similar to regressions, the PSM results, generally, suggested that greater investment in capital goods, using more imported inputs and exporting improve productivity.

Regarding the impact of exporting on TFP, DID and the combination of DID and PSM were applied in addition to the PSM method. Results of DID and PSM–DID methods showed that the TFPs of exporters are higher than that of non-exporters by about 39% and 49%, respectively. These results appeared to be lower than that of regression but higher than the PSM result. Methodologically, the PSM–DID result is more robust. Details of the estimation strategies and results of the alternative techniques are not pre-sented in this paper but available up on request.

5. Conclusion

This paper examined the role of imported inputs, new capital goods and exporting on performance of firms in the Ethiopian manufacturing sector. Using more imported inputs and new capital goods were expected to improve performance of firms due to technologies embodied in the goods. Exporting was also assumed to improve perform-ance of firms. Unlike earlier studies, the paper examined the impacts of embodied tech-nology transfer along with exporting taking into account their potential interactions. Performance was measured in terms of labour productivity (LabP), Total Factor Pro-ductivity (TFP) and TFP catch-up. Firm-level data from the Ethiopian large and medium manufacturing over 2000–2011 were utilized in the analyses. The data were analysed using econometrics and matching techniques following a two-step estimation procedure.

Results from the econometric analyses indicate that imported inputs, investment in new capital goods and exporting significantly increased LabP, TFP and TFP catch-up of firms with different levels of significance. Statistically, the impact of imported inputs is stronger on LabP while that of new capital goods is higher on firms' TFP and TFP catch-up. Moreover, the positive effects of imported inputs and new capital goods on TFP turned to be higher for exporting than non-exporting firms implying exporters' greater capability to learn from embodied technologies.

The matching techniques employed to probe the potential impacts of 'self-selection' also validated the regression results with slight differences between LabP and TFP. In terms of LabP, high use of imported inputs, high investment in capital goods and exporting appeared to have strong positive effects. In case of TFP, however, only new capital goods and exporting have shown positive productivity effects. A positive significant effect of imported inputs on TFP was brought out in the regressions, but not the matching procedure. This seems to reflect a 'selection effect' rather than *ex post* productivity effect. The finding implies that firms with higher TFP tend to consume more imported inputs probably due to their better access to the inputs. However, as far as imported inputs increased LabP, a similar effect on TFP would be inevitable, at least in the long-run considering the persistence of productivity in the econometric results. Persistent increase in LabP would ultimately lead to higher TFP.

The statistically stronger effect of new capital goods on TFP and TFP catch-up in both regression and matching results indicate that investment in capital goods involve greater potential in transferring embodied technologies than imported inputs. The strong positive and far greater impact of imported inputs on LabP (than TFP and catch$_{TFP}$) implies that increasing access to more imported inputs would substantially raise labour productivity. Cutting tariffs on imported inputs is one way towards improving access to the inputs as was suggested also by Bigsten, Gebreeyesus, and Söderbom (2013). Considering the evidence that low labour productivity stood among the major constraints in the Ethiopian manufacturing (World Bank 2015a), any measure that can improve labour productivity is of strategic importance. Exploiting the country's potential in manufactured exports is also pivotal to economic transformation (World Bank 2012). To this end, increasing access to imported inputs, helping firms upgrade their capital goods, facilitating linkages with foreign suppliers and encouraging use of advanced technology to build the innovation capability of domestic firms are important as can be implied from the empirical results. Solving the problem of credit constraints, which was the second most important bottleneck of doing business in Ethiopia (World Bank 2015b), is crucial to improve the accessibility of foreign technologies. Coordinated and effective implementation of these measures can facilitate technology transfers aimed at building local innovation capabilities and accelerating structural transformation.

In general, this study provides a better view of technology transfer through international trade by dissecting the separate effects of importing, investing and exporting. It contributes to both the empirical and theoretical literature and provides directions for firm managers and policy-makers towards achieving better performance of firms and the manufacturing sector as a whole. The differential impacts of imported inputs and capital goods on the performance of exporters and non-exporters imply the potential for making better use of inputs by managers. From a policy perspective, facilitating easy access to high-quality inputs, new capital goods and implementing more pragmatic measures towards export promotion are crucial for the aspired economic transformation in Ethiopia. However, the study could not specify the type of fixed capitals and what internal capacities are crucial in building local innovation capabilities. Therefore, future research would consider using more detailed data and conducting case studies that would help identify key inputs and capitals with their respective implications on the competitiveness of firms in both domestic and foreign markets.

Note

1. Computed as 100 (exp(coefficient) − 1)%.

Acknowledgments

We are very much thankful for the invaluable comments received from two anonymous referees and the editors of the special issue, which helped us to improve the manuscript. The paper has also benefited from feedback obtained from participants at the Catch-up Seminar (which was held in 2014 at the Center for Economic Catch-up, Seoul, South Korea) and the 12th Globelics International Conference (held in Addis Ababa, Ethiopia).

Disclosure statement

No potential conflict of interest was reported by the authors.

ORCiD

Keun Lee ⓘ http://orcid.org/0000-0002-0403-6348

References

Aghion, P., and P. Howitt. 1992. "A Model of Growth through Creative Destruction." *Econometrica* 60 (2): 323–351.

Aghion, P., and X. Jaravel. 2015. "Knowledge Spillovers, Innovation and Growth." *The Economic Journal* 125: 533–573.

Andersson, M., H. Lööf, and S. Johansson. 2008. "Productivity and International Trade: Firm Level Evidence from a Small Open Economy." *Review of World Economics* 144 (4): 774–801.

Arellano, M., and S. R. Bond. 1991. "Some Tests of Specification for Panel Data: Monte Carlo Evidence and an Application to Employment Equations." *Review of Economic Studies* 58: 277–297.

Aristei, D., D. Castellani, and C. Franco. 2012. "Firms' Exporting and Importing Activities: Is There a Two-way Relationship?" *Review of World Economics* 149: 55–84.

Arnold, J. M. 2005. "Productivity Estimation at the Plant Level: A Practical Guide." Bocconi University, Milan, Italy, Unpublished preliminary note.

Arrow, K. J. 1962. "The Economic Implication of Learning by Doing." *The Review of Economic Studies* 29 (3): 155–173.

Augier, P., O. Cadot, and M. Dovis. 2013. "Imports and TFP at the Firm Level: The Role of Absorptive Capacity." *Canadian Journal of Economics* 46 (3): 956–981.

Bbaale, E. 2011. "Firm-level Productivity and Exporting in Uganda's Manufacturing Sector." *African Journal of Economic and Management Studies* 2 (2): 220–242.

Bernard, A. B., and J. B. Jensen. 2004. "Exporting and Productivity in the USA." *Oxford Review of Economic Policy* 20: 343–357.

Bernard, A. B., J. B. Jensen, S. J. Redding, and P. K. Schott. 2007. "Firms in International Trade." *Journal of Economic Perspectives* 21 (3): 105–130.

Bigsten, A., and M. Gebreeyesus. 2009. "Firm Productivity and Exports: Evidence from Ethiopian Manufacturing." *The Journal of Development Studies* 45 (10): 1594–1614.

Bigsten, A., M. Gebreeyesus, and M. Söderbom. 2013. "Tariffs and Firm Performance in Ethiopia." Paper presented on the Conference in Memory of Professor Lennart Hjalmarsson at the University of Gothenburg, December 7–8, 2012.

Bigsten, A., and M. Söderbom. 2010. "African Firms in the Global Economy." Staff paper, Department of Economics & Gothenburg Centre of Globalization and Development: University of Gothenburg.

Blundell, S., and S. Bond. 1998. "Initial Conditions and Moment Restrictions in Dynamic Panel Data Models." *Journal of Econometrics* 87 (1): 29–52.

Coe, D. T., and E. Helpman. 1993. International Diffusion of R&D. NBER working paper no. 4444.

Coe, D. T., E. Helpman, and A. W. Hoffmaister. 1997. "North-South R&D Spillovers." *The Economic Journal* 107 (440): 134–149.

Conti, G., A. L. Turco, and D. Maggioni. 2013. "Rethinking the Import-Productivity Nexus for Italian Manufacturing." *Empirica* 41: 589–617.

Crespi, G., C. Criscuolo, and J. Haskel. 2008. "Productivity, Exporting, and the Learning-by-Exporting Hypothesis: Direct Evidence from UK Firms." *The Canadian Journal of Economics* 41 (2): 619–638.

Crinò, R. 2011. "Imported Inputs and Skill Upgrading." Development Working Papers 323. Centro Studi Luca D'Agliano: University of Milano.

Damijan, J. P., and Č. Kostevc. 2015. "Learning from Trade through Innovation." *Oxford Bulletin of Economics and Statistics* 77 (3): 408–436.

Dosi, D., and R. R. Nelson. 2010. "Technical Change and Industrial Dynamics as Evolutionary Processes." In *Handbook of Innovation*, edited by B. Hall, and N. Rosenberg, 51–127. New York: Elsevier.

Fabling, R., and L. Sanderso. 2012. "Exporting and Firm Performance: Market Entry, Investment and Expansion." *Journal of International Economics* 89: 422–431.

Fagerberg, J. 1994. "Technology and International Differences in Growth Rates." *Journal of Economic Literature* 32 (3): 1147–1175.

Foster-McGregor, N., and A. Isaksson. 2014. "Importing, Exporting and Performance in Sub-Saharan African Manufacturing Firms." *Review of World Economics* 150: 309–336.

Freeman, C. 2011. "Technology, Inequality and Economic Growth." *Innovation and Development* 1 (1): 11–24.

Gelb, A., C. J. Meyer, and V. Ramachandran. 2014. "Development as Diffusion – Manufacturing Productivity and Sub-Saharan Africa's Missing Middle." Working Paper WP/2014/042, UNU-WIDER, Helsinki, Finland.

Goldberg, P., A. Khandelwal, N. Pavcnik, and P. Topalova. 2009. "Trade Liberalization and New Imported Inputs." *American Economic Review: Papers & Proceedings* 99 (2): 494–500.

Greenaway, D., and R. Kneller. 2004. "Exporting and Productivity in the United Kingdom." *Oxford Review of Economic Policy* 20 (3): 358–371.

Griffith, R., S. Redding, and J. Van Reenen. 2003. "R&D and Absorptive Capacity: Theory and Empirical Evidence." *The Scandinavian Journal of Economics* 105 (1): 99–118.

Grossman, G. M., and E. Helpman. 1991. *Innovation and Growth in the Global Economy*. Cambridge: MIT Press.

Halpern, L., M. Korenand, and A. Szeidl. 2011. "Imported Inputs and Productivity." University of California, Berkeley: Mimeo.

Hasan, R. 2001. "The Impact of Imported and Domestic Technologies on the Productivity of Firms: Panel Data Evidence from Indian Manufacturing Firms." *Journal of Development Economics* 69: 23–49.

Howitt, P., and D. Mayer-Foulkes. 2005. "R&D, Implementation, and Stagnation: A Schumpeterian Theory of Convergence Clubs." *Journal of Money, Credit and Banking* 37 (1): 147–177.

Jacob, J., and C. Meister. 2005. "Productivity Gains, Technology Spillovers and Trade: Indonesian Manufacturing, 1980–96." *Bulletin of Indonesian Economic Studies* 41 (1): 37–56.

Jung, M., and K. Lee. 2010. "Sectoral Systems of Innovation and Productivity Catch-up: Determinants of the Productivity Gap between Korean and Japanese Firms." *Industrial and Corporate Change* 19 (4): 1037–1069.

Kasahara, H., and B. Lapham. 2012. "Productivity and the Decision to Import and Export: Theory and Evidence." *Journal of International Economics* 89: 297–316.

Kasahara, H., and J. Rodrigue. 2008. "Does the Use of Imported Intermediates Increase Productivity? Plant-level Evidence." *Journal of Development Economics* 87: 106–118.

Keller, W. 2000. "Do Trade Patterns and Technology Flows Affect Productivity Growth?" *The World Bank Economic Review* 14 (1): 17–47.

Keller, W. 2002. "Trade and the Transmission of Technology." *Journal of Economic Growth* 7: 5–24.

Keller, W. 2004. "International Technology Diffusion." *Journal of Economic Literature* 42 (3): 752–782.

Khandker, S. R., G. B. Koolwal, and H. A. Samad. 2010. *Handbook on Impact Evaluation: Quantitative Methods and Practices*. Washington, DC: World Bank.

Kugler, M., and E. Verhoogen. 2008. "The Quality-Complementarity Hypothesis: Theory and Evidence from Colombia." National Bureau of Economic Research Working Paper 14418.

Kugler, M., and E. Verhoogen. 2009. "Plants and Imported Inputs: New Facts and an Interpretation." *The American Economic Review* 99 (2): 501–507.

Lee, K. 2013a. *Schumpeterian Analysis of Economic Catch-up: Knowledge, Path creation, and Middle Income Trap*. New York: Cambridge University Press.

Lee, K. 2013b. "Measuring the Elements of Knowledge Regimes and Their Links to Technological Catch-up: A Synthesis Based on the East Asian Experience." *Innovation and Development* 3 (1): 37–53.

Lee, K., J. Y. Kim, and O. Lee. 2010. "Long-term Evolution of the Firm Value and Behaviour of Business Groups: Korean Chaebols between Weak Premium, Strong Discount, and Strong Premium." *Journal of the Japanese and International Economies* 24: 412–440.

Levinsohn, J., and A. Petrin. 2003. "Estimating Production Functions using Inputs to Control for Unobservable." *Review of Economic Studies* 70 (2): 317–341.

Lööf, H., and M. Andersson. 2008. "Imports, Productivity and the Origin Markets - the Role of Knowledge-intensive Economies." Paper No. 146, Centre of Excellence for Science and Innovation Studies (CESIS), October 2008.

Lundvall, B.-Å. 2011. "Notes on Innovation Systems and Economic Development." *Innovation and Development* 1 (1): 25–38.

Mairesse, J., and P. Mohnen. 2002. "Accounting for Innovation and Measuring Innovativeness: An Illustrative Framework and an Application." *The American Economic Review* 92 (2): 226–230.

Mairesse, J., P. Mohnen, and E. Kremp. 2005. "The Importance of R&D and Innovation for Productivity: A Reexamination in Light of the French Innovation Survey." *Annales d'Économie et de Statistique* 79–80: 487–527.

Martins, P. S., and Y. Yang. 2009. "The Impact of Exporting on Firm Productivity: A Meta-analysis of the Learning-by-exporting Hypothesis." *Review of World Economics* 145: 431–445.

Melitz, M. J. 2003. "The Impact of Trade on Intra-industry Reallocations and Aggregate Industry Productivity." *Econometrica* 71 (6): 1695–1725.

Mengistae, T., and C. Pattillo. 2004. "Export Orientation and Productivity in Sub-Saharan Africa." *IMF Staff Papers* 51 (2): 327–353.

Nelson, R. R. 1981. "Research on Productivity Growth and Productivity Differences: Dead Ends and New Departures." *Journal of Economic Literature, American Economic Association* 19 (3): 1029–1064.

Paul, C. M., and M. Yasar. 2009. "Outsourcing, Productivity, and Input Composition at the Plant Level." *The Canadian Journal of Economics* 42 (2): 422–439.

Powell, D., and J. Wagner. 2014. "The Exporter Productivity Premium Along the Productivity Distribution: Evidence from Quantile Regression with Non-additive Firm Fixed Effects." *Review of World Economics* 150: 763–785.

Romer, P. M. 1990. "Endogenous Technological Change." *Journal of Political Economy* 98 (5): S71–S102.

Roodman, D. 2009. "How to do Xtabond2: An Introduction to Difference and System GMM in Stata." *The Stata Journal* 9 (1): 86–136.

Schiff, M., and Y. Wang. 2010. "North–South Technology Spillovers: The Relative Impact of Openness and Foreign R&D." *International Economic Journal* 24 (2): 197–207.

Siba, E., and M. Söderbom. 2011. *The Performance of New Firms: Evidence from Ethiopia's Manufacturing Sector*. Mimeo: University of Gothenburg.

Siyanbola, W., A. Egbetokun, B. Adebowale, and O. Olamade, eds. 2012. *Innovation Systems and Capabilities in Developing Regions: Concepts, Issues and Cases*. UK: Routledge.

Sonobe, T., J. Akoten, and K. Otsuka. 2007. "The Development of the Footwear Industry in Ethiopia: How Different is it from the East Asian Experience?" Paper presented on the Global Development Network Annual Conference, Beijing, China, January.

Srithanpong, T. 2014. "Exporting, Importing, and Firm Performance: Evidence from Thai Manufacturing." *International Journal of Economics and Finance* 6 (12): 71–82.

Subramanian, U., and M. Matthijs. 2007. "Can Sub-Saharan Africa Leap into Global Network Trade?" World Bank Policy Research Working Paper 4112.

Van Beveren, I. 2010. "Total Factor Productivity Estimation: A Practical Review." *Journal of Economic Surveys* 26 (1): 98–128.

Van Biesebroeck, J. 2005. "Exporting Raises Productivity in Sub-Saharan African Manufacturing Firms." *Journal of International Economics* 67 (2): 373–391.

Van Biesebroeck, J. 2007. "Robustness of Productivity Estimates." *The Journal of Industrial Economics* 55 (3): 529–569.

Verspagen, B. 1997. "Measuring Intersectoral Technology Spillovers: Estimates from the European and US Patent Office Databases." *Economic Systems Research* 9 (1): 47–65.

Vogel, A., and J. Wagner. 2009. "Higher Productivity in Importing German Manufacturing Firms: Self-selection, Learning from Importing, or Both?" *Review of World Economics* 145: 641–665.

Wagner, J. 2002. "The Causal Effects of Exports on Firm Size and Labour Productivity: First Evidence from a Matching Approach." *Economics Letters* 77: 287–292.

Wagner, J. 2007. "Exports and Productivity: A Survey of the Evidence from Firm-level Data." *The World Economy* 30 (1): 60–82.

Wagner, J. 2012. "International Trade and Firm Performance: A Survey of Empirical Studies Since 2006." *Review of World Economics* 148 (2): 235–267.

World Bank. 2012. *Light Manufacturing in Africa: Targeted Policies to Enhance Private Investment and Create Jobs*. Vol. 1. Washington, DC: World Bank.

World Bank. 2015a. *Overcoming Constraints in the Manufacturing Sector: 4th Ethiopia Economic Update*. Washington, DC: World Bank.

World Bank. 2015b. *Doing Business 2015: Going Beyond Efficiency*. Washington, DC: World Bank.

Yasar, M. 2013. "Imported Capital Input, Absorptive Capacity, and Firm Performance: Evidence from Firm-level Data." *Economic Inquiry* 51 (1): 88–100.

Yu, M., and J. Li. 2014. "Imported Intermediate Inputs, Firm Productivity and Product Complexity." *The Japanese Economic Review* 65 (2): 178–192.

Appendix

Table A1. Definition of variables.

Variable	Definition
TFP	Total factor productivity
LabP	Labour productivity computed as a firm's value added divided by the number of total permanent employees
$catch_{TFP}$	The difference between the TFP of a firm and the TFP of a frontier firm in a two-digit sector
age	firm age measured as the number of years since a firm started operation
size	Firm size measured as the natural logarithm of the number of permanent full time employees
Export	Dummy for exporting
MRMint	The proportion of imported raw materials to the total raw materials a firm used in each year
NKINV	The proportion of a firm's investment in new capital to the yearend book value of capital
private	Dummy for private ownership (assigned '1' if the government's share in current total paid-up capital of a firm is below 50% and '0' otherwise)
Foreign	Dummy for foreign ownership (assigned value '1' if foreigners have stock in the current total paid-up capital of a firm and '0' otherwise)
CI	Concentration Index computed as the sum of the market share of the first four largest firms in two-digit industry (called large firm dominance in Jung and Lee 2010)

Table A2. Pair-wise correlation.

	lnage	size	CI	Foreign	private	MRMint	export	NKINV
lnage	1							
size	0.331	1						
CI	−0.081	−0.110	1					
Foreign	0.037	0.112	−0.012	1				
private	−0.318	−0.414	−0.011	0.046	1			
MRMint	0.037	0.1777	−0.043	0.106	0.021	1		
export	0.111	0.314	−0.044	0.064	−0.147	−0.058	1	
NKINV	0.010	0.048	−0.024	−0.008	−0.009	0.011	0.020	1

Table A3. Mean comparison test.

	Mean_MRMint	Mean_NKINV	ln(K/L)	ln(Import/L)
Non-exporters	0.358	0.229	9.813	5.411
Exporters	0.254	0.405	10.873	6.360
Diff.	0.104	−0.176	−1.061	−0.949
t-Value	6.102	−2.154	−13.515	−15.500
Pr(T > t)	0.000	0.031	0.000	0.000

Index

For Product Safety Concerns and Information please contact our EU
representative GPSR@taylorandfrancis.com
Taylor & Francis Verlag GmbH, Kaufingerstraße 24, 80331 München, Germany